EDUCATION FLASHPOINTS

"*Education Flashpoints* provides important insight into contemporary issues in education. The critical edge to the articles will stimulate classroom discussions."

Joel Spring, Queens College and the Graduate Center of the City University of New York, USA

"This is a book of the moment that is both timely and (sadly) timeless—pointed, focused, engaging. Dr. Singer knows where he stands and makes no bones about it. He always contributes to the field of education and political discussion."

Dennis Banks, SUNY College at Oneonta, USA

Drawing on his widely read *Huffington Post* columns—rated one of the top educational blogs in the United States—Alan Singer introduces readers to contemporary issues in education in the United States. The issues are presented with a point of view and an edge intended to promote widespread classroom debate and discussion. Each section opens with a new topical summary essay followed by a series of brief essays updated and adapted from his *Huffington Post* columns. The book includes guest contributions, guiding questions, and responses to essays by teacher education students and teachers to further classroom discussion. *Education Flashpoints* is written in a conversational style that draws readers into a series of debates by presenting issues in a clear and concise manner, but also with a touch of irony and a bit of rhetorical bite. The topics examined in these essays read like the latest newspaper headlines in the battle to define public education in the United States.

Alan J. Singer is Professor of Secondary Education and Coordinator of Social Studies Education in the Department of Teaching, Literacy and Leadership, Hofstra University, USA.

EDUCATION FLASHPOINTS

Fighting for America's Schools

Alan J. Singer

Routledge
Taylor & Francis Group

NEW YORK AND LONDON

First published 2014
by Routledge
711 Third Avenue, New York, NY 10017

and by Routledge
2 Park Square, Milton Park, Abingdon, Oxon OX14 4RN

Routledge is an imprint of the Taylor & Francis Group, an informa business

Library of Congress Cataloging-in-Publication Data

Singer, Alan J.
[Works. Selections.]
Education flashpoints : fighting for America's schools / Alan J. Singer.
    pages cm
Articles previously published in the blog www.huffingtonpost.com/
    alan-singer/.
 1. Education—United States.   I. Title.
 LA210.S454 2014
 370.973—dc23
 2013045151

ISBN: 978-0-415-74384-6 (hbk)
ISBN: 978-0-415-74385-3 (pbk)
ISBN: 978-1-315-81340-0 (ebk)

Typeset in Bembo
by Apex CoVantage, LLC

DEDICATION

This book is dedicated to two of my longtime friends who died in 2013, Martin Eisenberg (1940–2013) and Steven Faulding (1948–2013). For decades, we worked together as community organizers in the East New York section of Brooklyn. I met Martin at a community center there in 1969 and Steve when we were municipal bus drivers together on the mid-night shift in the late 1970s. Martin, Steve, and I worked together, raised our children together, and shared dreams about building a better world, but our favorite past time was probably arguing. Many of those arguments are deeply embedded in this book. Martin and Steve are greatly missed.

CONTENTS

PREFACE

Resistance without Jargon

One of my favorite movie scenes is the climax of the film *The Front* (1976). Woody Allen stars as a hapless schnook, Howard Prince, whose childhood friend Alfred Miller becomes a well-known scriptwriter and a Communist. When Miller is blacklisted, he arranges for Prince to submit manuscripts to television producers under his name, hence the title of the movie, *The Front*.

Eventually Howard Prince is called to testify before a panel from the House Un-American Activities Committee (HUAC). He will be arrested for contempt of Congress if he does not answer their questions, so Prince tries to work his way around the Committee using double-talk, what he calls answering but not "replying." It does not work and Prince winds up going to jail, a hero of the left and of his girlfriend, which made it all worthwhile.

Part of the fun of Prince's verbal combat with the committee is the way he tries to use philosophical speculation to sidetrack them. When asked, "Do you know Alfred Miller?" he plays Socrates and questions what it means to really know. "When you say 'know,' can you ever really know a person? I grew up with an Alfred Miller, but do I know him? Would you say I know him? Can you know . . .? In a biblical sense, know him?"

I take a number of lessons from the movie, but I want to focus on two of them. The most obvious is the need to resist forces of oppression that are trying to strip away our most basic human rights. But another is that double-talk, what academics call jargon, is not an effective strategy for winning arguments. It can take you only so far before people tire of hearing it and either shut you off or, as in the case of Howard Prince, put you away.

This book is about contemporary controversies affecting education, schools, students, teachers, and parents in the United States today, but it is also about resistance to efforts by major global corporations and their political allies to profit off of public education, to sell so-called reform (what I call deform) to the American public in the same way they sell hope, soap, and the latest cell phones. Some of these "reformers" may sincerely believe it what they are selling, but in many cases it appears that they have little regard for the impact their proposals have on the people they are supposed to be helping. That is why any discussion of controversy must also be about resistance.

I am a big fan of Don Quixote de la Mancha from the book by Miguel Cervantes, but I hope in *Education Flashpoints* I am not just jousting with windmills. I want to make you angry. My goal is to empower you! Read the last chapter of the book if at any time you are starting to get depressed.

Pre-service and beginning teachers are entering a profession undergoing rapid transformation because of social and technological changes. They are caught up in a political maelstrom as long-standing policies and approaches are threatened by new technologies, changing job markets, pressure for increased social equality, and economic pressures. New educational leaders are grappling with conflicting models of leadership that project them as either middle managers implementing directives from above or educational leaders responsible for defining pedagogy and instruction.

My commitment is to quality education, rather than educational opportunity, for all children in the United States. Currently I am a university-based educator, but I also was a middle school and high school teacher working in predominately urban and minority communities for fourteen years. I am a writer but also an activist in campaigns to support public education from incursions by corporate profit seekers and misnamed educational reformers. My views are very political, but they are also nonpartisan, and I hold all political factions in the United States up for critical review. My online columns have drawn a range of readers, from high school students to corporate executives, and a consistent barrage of comments from readers, many of whom are teachers or teachers-to-be.

The issues discussed in *Education Flashpoints* are presented with a point of view and an edge that will hopefully promote widespread discussion and social action. React as you read, join the debates, and take sides. Each chapter opens with a topical summary essay followed by a series of brief essays updated and adapted from *Huffington Post* columns. *Education Flashpoints* also includes guest contributions and guiding questions to think about and discuss.

Education Flashpoints is based on *Huffington Post* columns and other blogs I have written since 2009 to introduce students, teachers, and the general public to contemporary issues in education in the United States and to rally the forces of opposition. In 2013, *Teach100*, a website that surveys education blogs, consistently ranked *Alan Singer (Huffington Post)* as one of the top educational blogs in the United States.

Themes and topics will be repeated throughout the book and there will be some repetition in the book, but that is because the same issues and debates keep reemerging. I decided to keep the repetitions so that each essay stands on its own.

Sometimes it will seem that there is too much focus on New York City in the book. That is for two reasons. New York is where I have lived my entire life. Its schools and streets are my home and the area I know best. But there is also a New York City focus because Michael Bloomberg, the city's mayor from 2002 to 2013, was a major player in the push for many of the so-called reforms being dissected and rejected in the book.

Education Flashpoints is written in a conversational style that draws readers into a series of debates by presenting issues in a clear and concise manner, but also with a touch of irony and a bit of rhetorical bite. The topics examined in these essays read like the latest newspaper headlines in the battle to define public education in the United States. I consistently question the values and agenda of corporate dominated "reformers" and the push for online and scripted teaching and assessment. Although I am a strong supporter of teacher unions, I do not hesitate to hold union leaders to account as well.

Because *Education Flashpoints* is directed to a general audience, as well as to teachers and people who want to be teachers, I have tried to write it with a minimum of technical jargon. Where you find jargon, cross it out. When you feel I use double-talk e-mail me at catajs@hofstra.edu and give me a piece of your mind. But if you want to team up in resistance to educational deformers, you need to contact me as well and hopefully soon. Our campaign needs as many members and allies as possible.

Acknowledgments

Many people assisted with this book, but my chief partners have been Michael Pezone (High School for Law Enforcement), Pablo Muriel (Bronx Design and Construction Academy), Jessica Cartusciello (Island Trees High School), Maureen Murphy (Hofstra University), Joel Shatzky (Kingsborough Community College-CUNY), Adeola Tella-Williams and Justin Williams (Uniondale High School), and Felicia Hirata (Baruch College-CUNY, former principal of Forest Hills High School). These Hofstra University teacher education students commented on versions of the revised manuscript: Philip Alonge, Kevin Anderson, Lauren Buckheit, Rachel Cabrera, Christine Filipkowski, Fiorella Garrido, Ashley Goguen, Shareen Hossain, Alexa Lind, Kelly Morenus, Joseph Palaia, Brittany Ruisi, Michael Schulman, Sanjay Shetty, Maxime Sinal, and Debra Willett. I also wish to thank Naomi Silverman and the staff at Routledge for their efforts.

ABOUT THE AUTHOR

Alan Singer is a former New York City middle school and high school teacher and a long-term political activist dating back to the 1960s. He, his son, and his step-daughters attended New York City public schools, as do his grandchildren, who you will meet in some of the essays.

Alan currently teaches introductory secondary school methods classes, social studies methods and curriculum classes, supervises secondary school student teachers, and leads classroom analysis seminars in which student teachers reflect on their pedagogical practices, reconsider their teaching philosophies and goals, and examine ways that teachers can develop personal connections and build classroom communities with students from diverse racial, ethnic, and class backgrounds. He is also the faculty advisor and facilitator for the Hofstra New Teachers Network, which provides support and a forum for discussion for beginning and experienced teachers, many of whom are working in urban and suburban minority school districts. Alan frequently writes about educational issues. He is the editor of *Social Science Docket*, a joint publication of the New York and New Jersey Councils for the Social Studies, and contributes regularly to the *Huffington Post*, *Daily Kos*, and *History News Network*.

INTRODUCTION

Reclaiming the Conversation on Education

This is an expanded version of an essay published on the *Huffington Post*, May 10, 2013

www.huffingtonpost.com/alan-singer/reclaiming-the-conversati_b_3252883.html

Questions to Consider

1. Is the "educational reform agenda" a movement to transform education or does it have other motives?
2. Why has the "educational reform agenda" generated so much opposition from teachers, parents, school and district administrators, and university-based teacher educators?
3. What is your "pedagogic creed" or philosophy of education?

On May 4, 2013, I attended a conference, *Reclaiming the Conversation on Education*, at Barnard College–Columbia University in New York City. It attracted educational activists opposed to part or all of the so-called "educational reform agenda" promoted by proponents of the federal Race to the Top program, the Common Core initiative, the privatization of schools, and the out-sourcing of services to for-profit companies, alternative teacher certification, a heavy investment in online instruction, and high-stakes testing.

The problem at meetings such as this one is that they tend to be "anti" meetings that do not present a clear alternative agenda defining what participants believe is the role public education should play in a democratic society. Zakiyah Ansari, a parent activist, pointed out that the opposition to public education seems to have cornered the market on all the good slogans and sound bites. They demand accountability, high standards, and that schools prepare all students for college and twenty-first century jobs. The big problem is that it is never clear how these things will be achieved except by giving private companies lots of money.

On the anti side, participants generally agreed that the looting of public education by private corporations is not reform, high-stakes testing and test prep are not teaching and learning, and education is a human right, not an entitlement. But educators need to do more. This is my attempt to "reclaim the conversation on education" and define what schools and education should be in a democratic society. I base it on an article written by American philosopher John Dewey for a magazine called *School Journal* and originally published in 1897.[1]

John Dewey (1859–1952) was one of the most important thinkers about education in United States history. He called his list of basic beliefs his "pedagogic creed." His educational philosophy, which he called progressive education, was concerned with the need to educate people for life in a democratic society. Key concepts for Dewey were experience, freedom, community, and "habits of mind." According to Dewey, students learn from the full range of their experiences in school, not just the specific thing that they are studying in class.

Students learn from what they are studying, how they are studying, who they are studying with, and how they are treated. In racially segregated or academically tracked classes, students learn that some people are better than others. In test prep academies, they learn that some people possess knowledge and others passively receive it. Through online programs they learn to crave instant stimulation and avoid deep thought and puzzling through a problem while working with others. When administrators have total control over classrooms and teachers are required to follow scripted curricula, students learn to accept authoritarianism.

For Dewey, the exercise of freedom in democratic societies depends on education. He identifies freedom with the "power to frame purposes" or to achieve individual and social goals. This kind of freedom requires a probing, critical, disciplined habit of mind. It includes intelligence, judgment, and self-control—qualities students may never acquire in classrooms where they are subject to external controls and are forced to remain silent.

In progressive schools that use a Deweyan approach, students engage in long-term thematic group projects where they learn to collectively solve problems. Classrooms become democratic communities where "things gain meaning by being used in a shared experience or joint action."[2] Dewey also believed that democratic movements for human liberation were necessary to achieve a fair distribution of political power and an "equitable system of human liberties."

Some of the teachers and pre-service teachers that I work with are concerned that a Deweyan approach to education offers students too much freedom and that children and adolescents need more structured classrooms and curricula, especially if they come from families and live in communities where structure may be missing. Both Dewey and I respond that we are not proposing unstructured classrooms and unstructured learning. We are arguing for a different type of structure, a structured environment that systematically prepares students to live, learn, and work independently and with others as part of democratic communities and societies. Dewey offers educators and the American public some pretty good slogans that I try to re-work for the twenty-first century.

Education is a process of living, not a preparation for future living. Education is the fundamental method of social progress and reform. The community's duty to education is its paramount moral duty. Education that does not build on real-life experiences tends to cramp and to deaden. Examinations are of use only so far as they test the child's fitness for social life and reveal the place in which he or she can be of most service and where he or she can receive the most help. Education must be conceived as a continuing reconstruction of experience; that the process and the goal of education are one and the same thing. The teacher is engaged, not simply in the training of individuals, but in the formation of the proper social life. Teachers must realize the dignity of their calling.

I think Dewey was telling us that our primary responsibility as educators is to help prepare human beings to be citizens in a democratic society. The process and the goal of education are one and the same thing. Citizens need to be literate, they need to be critical thinkers, they need to be respectful of others, they need to be activists, and they need to be compassionate human beings, as well as being able to earn a living and support their families.

Drawing on Dewey, these are my suggestions for positive slogans.

Educate for democracy	Educate for equality	Educate for human dignity	Educate active citizens

I used to tell my high school students, "You do not have to know this for the test. You need to know this for life."

At this point I would also like to introduce you to four other thinkers and activists who deeply shape the way I think about education and teaching—Paulo Freire, Septima Clark, Antonio Gramsci, and Herbert Kohl.

Paulo Freire (1921–1997) was born in Recife in northeastern Brazil where his ideas about education developed in response to military dictatorship, enormous social inequality, and widespread adult illiteracy. As a result, his primary pedagogical goal was to provide the world's poor and oppressed with educational experiences that make it possible for them to take control over their own lives. Freire shared Dewey's desire to stimulate students to become "agents of curiosity" in a "quest for . . . the 'why' of things,"[3] and his belief that education provides possibility and hope for the future of society. But he believed that these can only be achieved when students explicitly critique social injustice and actively organize to challenge oppression.

For Freire, education was a process of continuous group discussion that enabled people to acquire collective knowledge that they could use to change society. The role of the teacher included asking questions that helped students identify problems facing their community, working with students to discover ideas or create symbols that explain their life experiences, and encouraging analysis of prior experiences and of society as the basis for new academic understanding and social action.

In a Deweyan classroom, the teacher is an expert who is responsible for organizing experiences so that students learn content, social and academic skills, and an appreciation for democratic living. Freire was concerned that this arrangement reproduced the unequal power relationships that exist in society. In a Freirean classroom, everyone has a recognized area of expertise that includes, but is not limited to, understanding and explaining their own lives, and sharing this expertise becomes an essential element in the classroom curriculum. In these classrooms, teachers have their areas of expertise, but they are only one part of the community. The responsibility for organizing experiences and struggling for social change belongs to the entire community; as groups exercise this responsibility, they are empowered to take control over their lives. Freire believed that there is a dynamic interactive relationship between increasing academic literacy and the desire to understand and change the world around us.

Septima Clark (1898–1987) was a Freirean teacher who probably had never heard of Paulo Freire and almost certainly never would have described herself as a philosopher. Clark was a teacher and a civil rights worker in the American south during the 1950s and 1960s. In her posthumously published autobiography, *Ready from Within*,[4] she explained how she became an activist while working as a teacher in South Carolina. She sent a letter to Black colleagues asking them to protest a state policy that barred city or state employees from belonging to the National Association for the Advancement of Colored People (NAACP). Her thinking was that "if whites could belong to the Ku Klux Klan, then surely blacks could belong to the NAACP."[5]

Even though Clark sent more than seven hundred letters, only twenty-six teachers answered her. Clark later wrote, "I considered that one of the failures of my life because I think that I tried to push them into something that they weren't ready for. You always have to get the people with you. You can't just force them into things."[6]

This experience played a crucial role in shaping Clark's approach to teaching, which was based on the idea that people had to be "ready from within." She wrote: "I never once felt afraid, not on any of those marches. Bullets could have gotten me, but somehow or other they didn't. I felt very good about going, about talking to people. I knew that people had gotten to the place where they saw the type of meanness that was being shown throughout their little towns. They hadn't noticed it before, but now they were ready from within to do something about it."[7]

One of the more powerful stories in her autobiography is her account of teaching reading and writing to adults so they could qualify to vote. "To teach reading I wrote their stories on the dry cleaner's (paper) bags, stories of their country right around them, where they walked to come to school, the things that grew around them, what they could see in the skies. They told them to me, and I wrote them on dry cleaner's bags and tacked them on the wall. From the fourth grade through the sixth grade they all did that same reading. But they needed that because it wasn't any use to do graded reading when they had not had any basic words at all" (p. 106).

Septima Clark had no problem admitting that everything did not work. But she felt that her mistakes were key to her learning to be a successful teacher. "Many times there were failures. But we had to mull over those failures and work until we could get them ironed out. The only reason why I thought the Citizenship School Program was right was because when people went down to register and vote, they were able to register and vote. They received their registration certificate. Then I knew that what I did must have been right. But I didn't know it before. It was an experiment that I was trying . . . I couldn't be sure that the experiment was going to work. I don't think anybody can be sure. You just try and see if it's coming."[8]

Antonio Gramsci (1891–1937) was another very unusual person who would not allow adversity to prevent him from struggling for his goals. Gramsci lived in Italy at the beginning of the twentieth century where he was a leader of the Italian Communist Party, editor of its newspaper, and a prominent opponent of the fascist dictatorship headed by Benito Mussolini. Much of his best-known work was written while he was in imprisoned from 1926 to 1934 because of his political beliefs. In his prison notebooks Gramsci discussed two ideas that I find particularly useful for understanding the role of and potential for education in the United States: cultural hegemony and the organic intellectual.[9]

Gramsci argued that as part of cultural hegemony schools and all other institutions within a society develop in support of the dominant economic and social system and those with political power. He did not believe existing institutions such as schools could be counted on to promote progressive social change. However he did believe it was possible for radicals to promote the development of organic intellectuals, people with roots in oppressed communities and an understanding of broader political ideas, who could serve as leaders in struggles to build a more just society. The question for me has always been "How do you do it?"

Herbert Kohl (1937–), an American writer, educator, and political activist has always given me hope for the possibility of social change. Ironically, Kohl and I grew up in the same neighborhood in the Bronx, New York, and attended the same elementary, middle, and high school, although he is more than ten years older than I am.

Kohl argues that because American cultural has a stated commitment to democracy and equal opportunity, there are open spaces within institutions where teachers can raise critical ideas with students, provide them with more democratic experiences, encourage activism, and promote leadership. Kohl argues that teachers can use what he calls "creative maladjustment" to genuinely teach and support the emergence of Gramscian organic intellectuals from amongst their students.

These students will become the leaders in struggles for an equitable education and an equitable society.

From this introduction readers should realize that *Education Flashpoints* is written with a point of view and is about connecting teaching to activism for the rights of children, for education, for teachers, and for a more democratic society. Welcome to the struggle.

A popular slogan of anti-fascist forces during the Spanish Civil War of the 1930s was "venceremos." It means we will triumph. Venceremos mes amigos! We will triumph.

Notes

1. John Dewey, "My Pedagogic Creed," *School Journal* vol. 54 (January 1897), pp. 77–80, http://dewey.pragmatism.org/creed.htm.
2. John Dewey, *Democracy and Education: An Introduction to the Philosophy of Education* (New York: Macmillan, 1922), p. 19, www.gutenberg.org/files/852/852-h/852-h.htm; John Dewey, *The Problems of Men* (New York: Philosophical Library, 1946), p. 113.
3. Paulo Freire, *Pedagogy of Hope* (New York: Continuum, 1995), p. 105.
4. Septima Clark, *Ready from Within: Septima Clark and the Civil Rights Movement,* ed. Cynthia Brown (Lawrenceville, NJ: Africa World Press, 1990).
5. Ibid., p. 37.
6. Ibid., p. 37.
7. Ibid., p. 71
8. Ibid., p. 126.
9. Antonio Gramsci, *Selections from the Prison Notebooks,* edited and translated by Quinton Hoare and Geoffrey Nowell Smith (New York: International Publishers, 1971).

1

WHAT SHALL WE DO WITH THE CHILDREN?

This group of essays drawn from my Huffington Post *blog focuses on students, how they are educated, and what is happening to them in schools. I will introduce you to my twin grandchildren Sadia and Gideon whose experiences in New York City public schools helped shape my views on current events. They were both born in 2004, and in fall 2013 entered fourth grade. They are lucky to live in a community where students at the local elementary school come from an ethnically diverse mixture of middle-class, professional, and stable working-class families.*

These essays were written while Michael Bloomberg was mayor of New York City and Merryl Tisch was chancellor of the New York State Board of Regents, the governing body for New York State's public schools. Michael Bloomberg is one of the wealthiest individuals in the world. According to Forbes *magazine he was worth $31 billion in September 2013, up $4 billion from the previous March. Merryl Tisch, who is not quite as wealthy as Bloomberg and is often his political opponent, is part of the family that controls the Loews corporation and owns important downtown Manhattan real estate. Other political figures who appear in this group of essays include Joel Klein, Cathy Black, and Dennis Walcott, who served as New York City school chancellors while Michael Bloomberg was mayor. In each case Bloomberg sought and received a special waiver from the Board of Regents that governs education in New York State because they lacked the basic qualifications for the position. Joel Klein later left the Department of Education to become an executive vice-president at Rupert Murdoch's News Corp, where he runs an education division called Amplify and promotes technology-driven instruction.*

A major part of my argument in these blogs is that the school system in New York City, and schools in many parts of the United States, are controlled by the affluent and run to benefit them and their political and economic agendas. Their children and grandchildren attend private schools or are in special academic programs in public schools that serve the offspring of the elite. For example, President Barack Obama's daughters both attend a very expensive private school in Washington, DC.

In New York City during the Bloomberg years (2002–2013), school policy was aligned with real estate interests to support gentrification. In world–renowned African American communities, such as Harlem in Manhattan and Bedford-Stuyvesant in Brooklyn, real estate developers and affluent White home buyers were attracted by aging-but-elegant "brownstones" that could be renovated and transformed from multi-family rental apartments to multi-million dollar single family homes. According to a New York Times *report,[1] the 1990 federal census showed only 672 Whites living in Central Harlem. By 2000 there were 2,200 White residents and in 2008 almost 14,000, 22% of whom had moved in that year alone.*

But families have to have schools for their children to attend. The solution was to separate school from neighborhood. Affluent pioneers could purchase and fix-up homes in minority communities and displace longtime residents while their children attended themed mini-schools in other parts of the city designed to attract and educate "gifted" students who were often simply the off-spring of the city's professionals and economic elite. Other people's children in these gentrifying communities were left in failing schools or, when parents were more savvy and pushy, allowed to attend slightly better-performing charter schools and mini-schools.

Unfortunately, the issues discussed in these essays are not unique to New York City. Similar plans are being implemented in Chicago, Philadelphia, Los Angeles, and Washington, DC, all in the name of "school reform." In reality they are an effort to brand and sort children while ensuring that the economic elite have access to the housing and schools of their choice. Both Republican President Bush and Democratic President Obama said they were committed to an opportunity society. However, in a New York Times *article,[2] economist Paul Krugman detailed how social mobility in the United States has come to a virtual standstill. For example, in Atlanta, Georgia, a child born into the bottom fifth of the income distribution has only a 4% chance of ever making it into the top fifth.*

A.   What's Good for the Mayor's Kids Is Good Enough for Ours
B.   These Kids Don't Have a Shot
C.   Being Gifted Means You Get All the Gifts
D.   Why Have "Specialized" High Schools?
E.   Hempstead Freedom Walkers Challenge Long Island Segregation
F.   Pablo's Kids March on Washington
G.   People with Guns Kill People and Children
H.   The School-to-Prison Pipeline

A. What's Good for the Mayor's Kids Is Good Enough for Ours

Based on an essay published on the *Huffington Post*, December 6, 2011
www.huffingtonpost.com/alan-singer/whats-good-for-mayor-bloo_b_1128296.html

Questions to Consider

1. What is a good education and who gets to decide?
2. Should the highest-quality education be available to all children or just those from families who can afford to pay for it?

Cartoonist Al Capp added the character General Bullmoose to his "Li'l Abner" comic strip in 1953. Bullmoose epitomized the ruthless capitalist. His motto was "What's good for General Bullmoose is good for the USA!" He was supposedly based on Charles Wilson, a former head of General Motors who testified before a United States Senate subcommittee in 1952 that "What is good for the country is good for General Motors, and what's good for General Motors is good for the country."[3]

Capp, who died in 1979, was being sarcastic. If he were alive and drawing his comic strip today he might rejoice in characterizing this generation's latest Bullmoose, New York City's multi-billionaire former mayor Michael Bloomberg.

In 2011, while a guest speaker at the Massachusetts Institute for Technology, Bloomberg said that if it were up to him, he would fire half the city's teachers and double class size. He would also double teacher salaries, which would be a good idea if, as Bloomberg says, he wanted to attract and hold on to the best teachers. Bloomberg, who was involved in a prolonged legislative and public relations campaign to weaken the city's teachers union, branded 50% of New York City's teachers as ineffective, even though according to a rating system he endorsed and the union disputed, the number was less than 20%.

Bloomberg's proposal was quickly and emphatically denounced by Leonie Haimson, executive director of *Class Size Matters*. According to Haimson, the mayor ran for office on a platform calling for reducing class size, but during his tenure New York City had "the largest class sizes in 11 years." Haimson also disputed Bloomberg's call for merit pay for teachers as an experiment "we've tried and it's failed." However, she was actually less concerned with Bloomberg's proposal, which she dismissed as "idiocy," than she was with similar proposals being floated by the Gates Foundation, the right-leaning Fordham Institution, and the supposedly more liberal Center for American Progress.[4]

But maybe Mayor Mike was on to something? Maybe New York City should fire half the teachers and double class sizes in its public schools?

His proposal made me curious. What kind of education did Mayor Mike choose for his daughters, now adults, before he became mayor and was only an ordinary multi-billionaire living on the Upper East Side of Manhattan? Michael Bloomberg has two daughters, Emma, aged thirty-four in 2013, and Georgina, thirty. Both girls attended the prestigious private all-girls Spence School in New York City.

The Spence School is located on ritzy East 91 Street between 5th Avenue and Madison. According to its website,[5] for the 2011–2012 academic year, tuition was $37,500 for all grades K–12, about the tuition cost of an expensive private university. By comparison, the tuition cost at the elite public Stuyvesant High School is zero. I do not know if either Bloomberg daughter took or passed the test for admittance to selective New York City public high schools, although Emma was supposed to be a top student and later attended Princeton University.

Because Spence alumnae are routinely accepted by Harvard, Princeton, and Columbia universities, the school can afford to be very selective. It received 707 applications in the 2008–2009 academic year, and accepted 129 students or only 18% of the applicants.

Of course it does not hurt to be rich or well known when applying for a spot for your children. Among the celebrities whose children attend or have attended Spence are Sigourney Weaver, Kevin Kline, Gabriel Byrne, Revlon's Ronald O. Perelman, Walter Cronkite, and Katie Couric.

In addition to its high tuition charge, the school has a "voluntary" annual fund, which because it is tax deductible, allows the wealthy to "contribute" even more money to the school while claiming a deduction on their local, state, and federal income taxes. According to Spence's website, "the Annual Fund helps pay for everything from faculty salaries and professional development opportunities to new curriculum initiatives, from financial assistance programs to technology maintenance and upgrades, from the electricity needed to keep the lights on to supplies and books. It helps Spence attract and retain a talented and committed faculty and provides support for extracurricular activities clubs, sports, arts initiatives and other programs."[6]

The Spence School had an endowment of over $25 million and very valuable property holdings, partly because of multimillion-dollar gifts from wealthy notables such as Bloomberg and Fiona Biggs Druckenmiller, a philanthropist who attended the school as a child.

If you can afford the tuition and the voluntary donation, there are many good reasons to have your daughters attend Spence. Its mission statement explains the school is a "diverse community of enthusiastic, scholastically motivated girls . . . taught by a devoted and passionate faculty."[7] In a world where public school students are forced to take an array of standardized assessments and test prep classes, a program enthusiastically supported by Bloomberg for everyone else's children, Spence "students are encouraged to dig deep and ask questions, understanding that learning is a lifelong process, beyond an exam or diploma. Day-to-day, they aspire to their school motto 'Not for school, but for life we learn.'"[8]

To facilitate this kind of learning, the average class size at Spence is limited to approximately sixteen to eighteen students and only fourteen students per class in the high school. Visiting artists, lecturers, and scholars have included Pulitzer-Prize-winning author Jhumpa Lahiri, playwright J. T. Rogers, Metropolitan Museum curator Joan Mertens, artist Barnaby Furnas, novelist Sue Monk Kidd, choreographer Doug Varone, and Tony-Award-winning director Julie Taymor.

At Spence, the extras are not considered extra. It has six science labs, six art studios and an art history room, two music rooms, a computer lab, a photography darkroom, two gymnasiums and a fitness room, two performance spaces, two dance studios, and two libraries. Spence also offers both international and domestic study programs to upper school (high school) students.

I kind of like what I read about Spence. I would like this kind of education for my grandchildren who attend public schools. And what is good for General Bullmoose, I mean Michael Bloomberg, should be good for all the children of New York City and the nation.

Post-It Note: In November 2013, New York City elected a new mayor, Bill de Blasio, whose own children attend public schools, albeit designer schools for children from professional families. Hopefully with a new mayor things will change.

B. These Kids Don't Have a Shot

Based on an essay published on the *Huffington Post*, November 17, 2011
www.huffingtonpost.com/alan-singer/nyc-education_b_1088476.html

Questions to Consider

1. Are students from poor and minority families being warehoused rather than educated?
2. Do race, ethnicity, and economic class continue to play a defining role in educational and life opportunities in the United States today?
3. Do students attending schools like those described in this essay have a real shot at a decent education and life?

There are three types of schools in New York City: Bloomberg schools, Gates schools, and orphans. The Bloomberg schools are the specialized small academies and charters that the Bloomberg administration set up to attract and keep middle-class families in the city. Student populations are often predominately White and Asian, although higher-performing Black and Hispanic students from more stable home environments are generally welcomed. Gates schools are the foundation-supported schools that get extra resources from their benefactors, especially from the Bill and Melinda Gates Foundation. The Bloomberg and Gates schools get all the cookies.

The orphan schools are everybody else. Students and teachers in these schools sink or swim on their own. On November 8, 2011, Merryl Tisch, chancellor of the New York State Board of Regents, denounced the Bloomberg administration's policy of closing troubled schools and replacing them with equally unsatisfactory, poorly performing new ones. An angry Tisch charged that Bloomberg "closed a lot of the large schools and they've warehoused thousands of kids. When I say warehouse, I mean warehouse." She added, "These kids don't have a shot."[9]

Schools are either orphan schools because they are large schools, such as John Adams and Richmond Hill in Queens or Lehman in the Bronx, that the Bloomberg administration wanted to phase out as part of its small-school initiative or small schools that predated the Bloomberg and Gates reforms, so no one gets political credit for them. University Heights High School in the Bronx was a typical orphan school. It was relocated from the Bronx Community College campus to a building in the South Bronx when a Gates school was moved out of the space into a new facility. The students and families, who had opted for the school because of its relationship to the college, were furious, but no one in the Department of Education (DOE) or the Bloomberg administration was interested in hearing from them—because they were just orphans.

Now another orphan school is under attack because of Bloomberg and neglect by the DOE—Law, Government and Community Service High School in Cambria Heights, Queens. I worked with this school for almost twenty years as a member of its advisory board, placing student teachers there as part of the Hofstra University teacher education program and field-testing the state "Great Irish Famine" curriculum and the "New York and Slavery" curriculum in its classrooms. After two consecutive D grades on its school report card, it was slated to be either reorganized or closed unless parents, students, teachers, local politicians, and community residents could launch a campaign pressuring the DOE to back off and actually support the school. It was an especially difficult struggle because the Bloomberg administration was suspected by teachers of desiring the site to use for a new Bloomberg mini-middle school, a small, separate program that would move into at least part of the building.

I am not suggesting that Law, Government and Community Service High School was an idyllic school. But on the other hand, the problems there were not new and New York City had ample opportunity to address them. It was the city and the Bloomberg administration that failed the students and community, not the school or the teachers. Clara Hemphill, author of *New York City's Best Public High Schools: A Parents' Guide*, visited the campus in 2003 and noted continuing safety issues. She was struck by the inhospitable and prison-like conditions, especially the long lines of students forced to pass through passing metal detectors each morning and made late for classes. She reported that curricular innovations the city had promised when it had created the school had been abandoned.

The DOE claimed that despite the best efforts of the community and the DOE to support the Law, Government and Community Service High School, the school continues to struggle to meet basic requirements for student success. The DOE support, which I believe was largely fictional, is supposed to have included "supporting school leadership, providing resources to increase the rigor of student work, offering supports to strengthen classroom instruction, ensuring the school is organized to focus on student achievement, working to improve the learning environment and culture of the school, and fostering community relationships and partnerships." "Unfortunately," the DOE reported, "our best efforts have not turned around the school."[10]

I would like to see a detailed accounting of all the support provided by the DOE and to learn what its best efforts entail. The school had three principals in four years. The last two were brand-new principals. I do not understand how this represents the "best" the DOE could do.

The DOE claimed it was offering parents and community residents a series of options. These options included reorganizing the school and shutting it down. However, in March 2013, a rubber-stamp DOE Panel for Educational Policy ignored protests by parents, teachers, and students at a raucous public meeting and voted to phase out Law, Government and Community Service High School.

As New York State School Chancellor Merryl Tisch made clear, "these kids don't have a shot."

Post-It Note: At the same time University Heights High School was evicted from the Bronx Community College campus, other cities and states were discovering the value of connecting ordinary high school students with colleges. North Carolina has a total of seventy early-college high schools that target at-risk students. In Raeford, North Carolina, high school seniors were taking classes at Sandhills Community College. The program was designed to attract students whose parents did not have college degrees and allowed the students to earn up to two years of college credit tuition for free. The Gates Foundation helps fund two hundred similar high school-college partnerships in the United States. The Gates Foundation found that high schools affiliated with college campuses had higher daily attendance rates than ordinary high schools, higher student proficiency on math and reading tests, higher graduation rates, and 40% of their graduates earned at least a year of college credit.

C. Being Gifted Means You Get All the Gifts

Based on an essay published on the *Huffington Post*, January 11, 2010
www.huffingtonpost.com/alan-singer/being-gifted-means-you-ge_b_417660.html

Questions to Consider

1. What does it mean to be "gifted"?
2. Why are so many children identified as "gifted" White and Asian or from professional and more affluent families?
3. Should children identified as "gifted" be sent to separate programs or schools?

At their fifth birthday party my grandchildren, Sadia and Gideon, got all the gifts. It would be one thing if children were only inundated with gifts on their birthdays, and if all children got to share in this ritual. But what if some children are gifted every day, while other children never get a fair share of the goodies? I think justifying a fundamentally unequal distribution of resources is the primary purpose of most school "gifted programs."

Labeling the children of upper-middle-class professional parents as gifted allows society to segregate them in their own classes, while sentencing other supposedly less-gifted children to remedial instruction in test prep academies. This helps to keep down the cost of educating, or mis-educating, the other children who need more help, not less, to achieve, but who do not receive it. It also helps secure the support of talented go-getters—the parents of the chosen—for the politicians themselves and for a system based on social inequality.

New York City operates a series of programs for supposedly "gifted and talented" children starting when they are five years old. One of the programs, the city-funded Hunter College Elementary School on the Upper East Side in Manhattan, averages over 1,800 applications a year for fifty kindergarten seats. In 2009, two hundred children with the highest test scores were invited to an on-site interview where three-fourths of them were weeded out.

There are a series of questions that need to be asked about these programs. They include:

- Who gets selected?
- How do children qualify as gifted?
- Why are there only a limited number of places in gifted programs?
- Are these programs justified?

What a surprise, the successful children are overwhelmingly from White, professional families, in a city where the vast majority of children are non-White and are from working-class and poor families. Of course not all of the children in gifted classes are White. To justify the system, some non-White, working-class youth with exceptional ability always pass the tests. The classes, while overwhelmingly segregated, are not completely so. In theory, everyone has the same chance to pass the tests. But the life experiences of young children are so different, especially if they are Black and Latino and poor, that most children never have a fair chance on these tests.

As of October 2009, New York City had an astounding 1,027,775 children attending its public schools: 39% were Hispanic, 30% were Black, 15% were Asian, 14% were White, and 2% were Other. But its eight elite high schools served a totally different population. For the 2008–2009 freshman class, only 6% of the Blacks and 7% of the Hispanics who took the test were offered admission. More than two-thirds of Stuyvesant High School's 3,247 students were Asian. At Brooklyn Technical High School, 365 of the 4,669 students, or 8%, were Hispanic. At the Bronx High School of Science, there were 114 Blacks, 4% of the 2,809 student body.

How Do Children Qualify as Gifted?

The simple answer is that some children pass the test; however, that is not the complete answer. The reality is that seats in programs that provide real educations are rationed in American society. During the past two decades, the number of Black and Hispanic students attending elite schools in New York City declined as the number of Asian students in these programs dramatically increased. Black and Hispanic students who would have been accepted based on their test scores in the past were closed out because of an artificial cap on the number of seats available. Students who used to be defined as gifted, students who can do the academic work required in these programs, were closed out because of demographic shifts and the rationing of education—for no other reason.

According to the *New York Times*, during the 2005–2006 school year, Black students made up 4.8% of the Bronx Science student body, down from 11.8% in 1994–1995. At Brooklyn Technical High School, the proportion of Black students dropped from 37.3% to 14.9% during the same time period. At Stuyvesant, the number of Blacks declined from 4.4% to 2.2% of the student body. Hispanic enrollment also declined at the three schools, as did White enrollment at Stuyvesant and Bronx Science, although it rose at Brooklyn Tech. Meanwhile, the Asian population at Bronx Science rose from 40.8% to 60.6%.

Why Are There Only a Limited Number of Places in Gifted Programs?

There are many factors. One is elitism that is presented as meritocracy. If people understood that education was being rationed and most of their children, especially if they are non-White, were being sacrificed, they would rebel. But if their children are just not good enough, there is no one to blame. Another factor is that the schools are designed to replicate the society. Children must learn to fit into a hierarchical society where jobs and resources are distributed unequally. Finally, better schools that respond to the needs of diverse learners would be more expensive.

Are These Programs Justified?

When I was fourteen, I passed the admission test for the prestigious Bronx High School of Science. There were nine hundred students in my class. About one hundred were the children of professionals and the school was run to help them get into elite private universities. The rest of us were working-class kids who were going to attend the free municipal colleges. We passed the test for this elite high school and were punished for three or four years by tons of meaningless homework and alienation from our friends in our home communities. I always check the newspapers and Internet for news of the "geniuses" I went to high school with. We are over sixty years old, should be at the peak of our careers, and as far as I can tell, no one has won a Nobel Prize or justified the claims made about our specialness.

I would like to see the elite public schools serving private interests closed. I would have been better off attending a regular school with a diverse student population. It would have better prepared me for the diverse world that we all live in. In the suburbs, where schools by and large function, top academic students are not isolated from everybody else and they seem to perform adequately in high school and college.

The challenge is to educate everybody's children and to educate them in such a way that they learn to work with and respect people who are different from themselves. It is time to suspend class-based educational opportunity. It is time that the same children stop receiving all the gifts.

D. Why Have "Specialized" High Schools?

Based on essays published on the *Huffington Post*, October 4 and 30, 2012

www.huffingtonpost.com/alan-singer/clueless-nyc-mayor-defend_b_1930940.html

www.huffingtonpost.com/alan-singer/new-york-specialized-schools_b_2030498.html

Questions to Consider

1. Should "gifted" children attend separate "special" schools?
2. If there are "specialized" schools for "gifted" students, should admission be competitive?
3. Who benefits when a school system sorts out students into separate schools based on performance on high-stakes tests?

On Saturday, October 27, 2012, more than fifteen thousand New York City middle school students took a difficult ninety-five question test hoping for admission to one of the city's elite public high schools. Thousands more took the test later in November. Meanwhile, Civil Rights groups sued New York City and its Department of Education, charging that the entire admission process was biased against poorer predominately Black and Latino students because it is based on a one-shot test.

The NAACP Legal Defense Fund argued that "racial disparities result in large part from admissions policies that rely too heavily or even exclusively on standardized tests, even though the three leading organizations in the area of educational test measurement," the American Psychological Association, the American Educational Research Association, and the National Council on Measurement in Education, "have concluded that a high-stakes decision with a major impact on a student's educational opportunities, such as admission to a specialized or gifted/

talented program, should not turn on the results of a single test. There is also a marked failure to provide African Americans and Latinos with opportunities to learn the material or otherwise prepare to meet the admissions standards used to determine whether students will be placed in these specialized programs."[11]

Daily News columnist Juan Gonzalez[12] called the specialized high school admission test "a tool for more affluent New Yorkers to buy their children's way to the front of the line, and for school officials to justify excluding a scandalous number of African-American and Hispanic kids from the city's best high schools."

According to Gonzalez, in 1999 Black students comprised 24% of the student body at Brooklyn Tech but during Bloomberg's terms as mayor the percentage has plummeted to 10%. Stuyvesant's student body, which was nearly 13% Black in 1979 is now 1.2%.

The New York City Specialized High School Test is given each fall. Middle school students select up to eight high schools they would like to attend and learn the results the following February. The schools include the prestigious Stuyvesant High School, the Bronx High School of Science, and Brooklyn Technical High School, as well as newer schools such as Brooklyn Latin School, High School of American Studies at Lehman College, High School for Math, Science and Engineering at City College, Queens High School for the Sciences at York College, and Staten Island Technical High School.

New York City Mayor Michael R. Bloomberg defended the select schools, the admission process, and the legitimacy of the admission tests claiming the schools were "designed for the best and the brightest" and that he saw no need to change the admissions policy or state law. The mayor declared, "I think that Stuyvesant and these other schools are as fair as fair can be. . . . There's nothing subjective about this. You pass the test, you get the highest score, you get into the school no matter what your ethnicity, no matter what your economic background is. That's been the tradition in these schools since they were founded, and it's going to continue to be."[13]

Apparently the mayor was unaware of the way the admission process for the Specialized High Schools actually works. There is no passing grade. Instead, New York City rations seats in these schools. It admits only the top scorers and the "passing" score varies from year to year. Students with the highest test scores get their choice of schools with many qualified students closed out. For example, in 2004, a score of 567 earned a student admission to Stuyvesant High School. The minimum score for Bronx Science was 522 and it was 493 for Brooklyn Tech. However in 2006, a student could be admitted to Stuyvesant with a 558 and Bronx Science with a 510. Because of these fluctuations and the rationing of seats, qualified students capable of doing the work can miss the cut off and can be denied admission.

The controversy over admission to New York City's elite high schools was not new. In May 1971, *New York Times* education columnist Fred Hechinger reported that efforts were being made to eliminate a "discovery" program that allowed for greater Black and Hispanic enrollment and School Chancellor Harvey Scribner had ordered a study to investigate charges that the entire admission process was discriminatory.[14] To prevent changes, the state legislature passed a law in 1972 to effectively prevent efforts to racially diversify the city's select high schools continuing the single high-stakes test as the only way to gain admission.

In 2005, the *New York Times* reported that the admissions test had not been changed in thirty years and city officials acknowledged they had never conducted studies to gauge the validity of the test.[15] Other select schools around the country, including the Boston Latin School and the Thomas Jefferson High School for Science and Technology in Fairfax, Virginia, evaluate student applications based on test scores, grades, essays, and teacher recommendations.

Part of the problem with the admission process is that it favors students from more affluent families who can pay for expensive test prep classes. Based on online advertising, New York Academics offers one-on-one instruction at fees ranging from $100 to $120 per hour.

The Kaplan company offers individual SHSAT Premier Tutoring starting at $2,599 and classes at $849. The Princeton Review also has multiple levels of preparation. Its Premier Level costs $6,300, its Master Level costs $3,879, and its low-cost online offering is a bargain at only $1,500. The Kuei Luck Enrichment Center in Fresh Meadows, Queens, targets Chinese-American students and offers tutoring for only $2,200. The problem would be eliminated if there actually was a passing score and every qualified student was assigned to a specialized high school.

Post-It Note: Similar special programs exist in Virginia, Massachusetts, and North Carolina, so the issue of defining "gifted" and whether they should be segregated into separate schools is a national concern. Southern states greatly expanded "gifted education" when they were forced to desegregate racially segregated public schools. Today several southern states sponsor public high schools for students who are considered advanced in math and science including Alabama, Arkansas, Georgia, Kentucky, Louisiana, Mississippi, North Carolina, South Carolina, Tennessee, Texas, and Virginia and provide stipends for tuition and expenses. The student population at the Mississippi School for Mathematics and Science is three-quarters White (61%) and Asian (15%), while the overall student population of the state of Mississippi is 44% White with very few Asians.

E. Hempstead Freedom Walkers Challenge Long Island Segregation

Based on an essay published on the *Huffington Post*, June 17, 2011
    www.huffingtonpost.com/alan-singer/hempstead-freedom-walkers_b_878930.html

Questions to Consider

1. Does deep learning require real life applications?
2. Should students be involved in civic action projects?

Forty strong, the eighth-graders marched out of the middle school cafeteria singing: "Ain't gonna let nobody turn me around, turn me around, turn me around, turn me around, ain't gonna let nobody turn me around, turn me around, turn me around, turn me around, gonna keep on walking, keep on talking, marching to the freedom land."

The temperature on Thursday, June 9, 2011, was in the mid-nineties, but it could not weaken their spirits. They were the Freedom Walkers, wearing T-shirts of their own design demanding an end to racial apartheid on Long Island. They were marching from overwhelmingly Black and Latino Hempstead to neighboring overwhelmingly White Garden City where they planned to have a picnic in a local park. I was glad to be with them and part of their campaign.

It was a one-mile walk to the Hempstead-Garden City border and another mile to Grove Street Park. Each time they came to a "stop" sign they chanted: "The sign says stop but we're not stopping." They gathered at a sign demarking the border between Hempstead and Garden City and sang "Ain't gonna let nobody turn me around" again.

In Hempstead the Freedom Walkers passed older wood-frame homes. Some were in poor condition. Many had "for sale" signs in the front yard. The people they saw were Black and Hispanic. At Meadow Street they entered Garden City. Suddenly there were well-kept Tudor brick homes and tree-lined boulevards. The only non-White people they saw were gardeners and nannies. Behind the homes on the south side of Meadow Street was a wood fence separating Garden City and Hempstead. It is a frail fence but it is symbolically important. It represents many of the racial and ethnic divisions that continue to exist on Long Island.

The sign at the entrance to Grove Street Park says "town residents and guests only." However, the Garden City Recreation Department graciously gave the students permission to enter the park and have a picnic. When the Freedom Walkers gathered at the entrance to the park, I spoke with the group: "Why can't all the people of Long Island share their parks? If people can play in parks together, maybe we can go to school together. If we can go to school together, maybe we can live together. If we can live together, maybe the world will change."

The eighth-grade students at ABGS Middle School in Hempstead, New York, have been studying about the African American Civil Rights Movement of the 1950s and 1960s. They learned that the Supreme Court decision in Brown v. Board of Education meant that schools could not be kept segregated based on race. They learned how Rosa Parks and Martin Luther King, Jr. challenged racial segregation laws in the south. They learned that 2011 is the fiftieth anniversary of the Freedom Riders, who traveled through the South in racially mixed teams to integrate public transit in the United States. Many of the Freedom Riders were attacked and seriously injured, but they maintained their commitment to nonviolent civil disobedience and ultimately succeeded.

But these eighth-graders also know that the towns and neighborhoods on Long Island continue to be racially and ethnically segregated even after all of these struggles. Along with their teachers Dawn Sumner and Claire LaMothe, and with the support of the social studies education program in the Hofstra University School of Education, Health and Human Services, they organized the Freedom Walk to honor the 1961 Freedom Riders and to make a statement that racial integration and equality should still be valued by our society today.

Many local battles of the Civil Rights era took place in Hempstead, so Dawn Sumner and Claire LaMothe had students learn about these struggles. Students discovered that in August 1963 the Hempstead School Board voted unanimously to approve a motion requesting that the Hempstead school district merge with neighboring Garden City schools to "end racial imbalances." At the time, Garden City schools were nearly 100% White while Hempstead schools were 89% "Negro." The merger never took place and almost fifty years later the school districts remain racially segregated.

According to the New York State District Report Card, Garden City schools today are 95% White, 1% Black or African American, and 4% Other. Hempstead has changed demographically over the decades. The student population is now 46% Black or African American and 53% Latino or Hispanic. However, there are almost no White children in the district.

The Freedom Walkers march from Hempstead to Garden City was favorably covered in *Newsday*, a local newspaper specializing in Long Island news stories. Some residents of Garden City and local teachers have questioned the legitimacy of the Freedom Walkers campaign as misleading and as educationally inappropriate. I welcome their questions but strongly support what Dawn, Claire, and their students did and we plan to march again next year. In Nassau County each small town has exclusive use of its own parks, but it does not have to be that way. I live in Brooklyn, a borough of New York City with a very diverse population of over two-and-a-half million people. In Brooklyn the parks are for everyone and everyone uses the parks.

It is also important that we were not calling the people of Garden City racist because they live in a nice community. Just like during the Civil Rights era of the 1950s and 1960s, the Freedom Walkers were challenging a system that divides people and which we believe must change, but recognize that people of goodwill live in many communities and come in all colors and ethnicities.

Post-It Note: Many teachers are afraid to involve students in projects that can be interpreted as political in nature. This project and the one described next occur outside the political arena. No candidates or political parties are endorsed or even discussed. They are civic action projects designed to promote active, aware citizenship in a democratic society and fall under the guidelines of most state and national social studies standards.

F. Pablo's Kids March on Washington

Based on an essay published on the *Huffington Post*, October 3, 2010
   www.huffingtonpost.com/alan-singer/pablos-kids-march-on-wash_b_748643.
html

Questions to Consider

1. Should citizenship education require real life experience?
2. Is Pablo engaging students as active citizens in his role as their teacher or is he using them to promote his own political agenda?

   Glenn Beck was not there for this rally; it was for the wrong side. Comedians Jon Stewart and Stephen Colbert would not be in Washington until October 30. Apparently Barack Obama was too busy to make an appearance—he spent the weekend at the presidential vacation house in Camp David where he often goes to play golf.

   Fox News used the rally as an excuse to tout the Tea Party movement, accusing liberals of trying to tap into Tea Party anger. Beck warned that dangerous radicals might be attending. The *New York Times*, supposed bastion of the "liberal" media, gave the demonstration a quarter of a page of coverage on the bottom of page 18.

   The bus provided by the United Federation of Teachers was late in arriving, the five-hour ride to Washington stretched to six, subways there were overcrowded, and port-a-potties on the National Mall were foul smelling. But nothing could take away from the excitement twenty-seven students from University Heights High School in the South Bronx felt as they stormed the nation's capital. The students were members of the school's political action club and were accompanied by faculty advisor Pablo Muriel along with other teachers, school personnel, and community residents. Along with tens of thousands of union members and civil rights and peace activists, these students traveled to Washington to demand social justice for all Americans, full employment, school funding, and an end to wars in Iraq and Afghanistan.

   The UHHS students felt immense pride standing around the reflecting pool at the Lincoln Memorial where Martin Luther King, Jr. spoke about his dream and millions of Americans demanded that government act to meet the needs of people. They live and attend school in the poorest congressional district in the United States. They had heard about rallies and the capital, but they had never been there. Now they had a chance to be part of history.

   Tyrek Greene, a twelfth-grader at University Heights High School, said he went to Washington because he wanted to know what it is to participate in a cause. He believes that decent jobs for all Americans should be a right. He wants students in the public schools to get the same quality education as students who attend elite private schools. Stephen Martinez, also a twelfth-grader, wanted to practice his first amendment right and hoped to participate in something that would make a significant change in American society. Torrick Dixon, an eleventh-grader, was thinking about future jobs when he and his classmates graduated from college. He wants to have a career so when he has a family he can support them "the best way I can."

Christina Gomez, a twelfth-grader, saw the rally in Washington as an amazing opportunity to learn about people from different places and how they approach the problems we are facing today in the United States and all around the world. She wants to end the trillion dollar wars in Iraq and Afghanistan that have been going on for years and she does not want her country fighting wars for oil. For Universal Berrios, an eleventh-grader, the priority is decent jobs for all Americans. When people have jobs, it changes their behavior. Taylor Cabrera, a twelfth-grader, is an activist who went to Washington to educate himself and his peers so they can be part of democracy in action. For Tykeem Seawell, a twelfth-grader, education is the most important thing because education empowers people. He believes that when you educate the masses everything else will fall into place.

Pablo Muriel was glad his students attended the rally. He is a strong advocate of experiential learning. He believes it was important for students to see what political activism actually looks like and to meet people trying to promote progressive change. "Students need to have a sense that they can be real participants in democracy. They are not just pawns to be manipulated by people in power."

On the bus on the way back from Washington some UHHS students expressed surprise that people were not angrier than they came across as at the rally. Most of the speeches were about hope for the future. They saw lots of people wearing pro-Obama T-shirts.

I think that many participants were deeply frustrated with President Obama's first two years in office. They were unhappy with the poor state of the economy and high unemployment, with compromises on health care reform, with continued anti-immigrant hostility in the nation, and with Obama's continuation of the wars in Iraq and Afghanistan. However, they were not yet prepared to challenge the Obama record, partly because they feared other mainstream political options would be worse. They were also not yet ready to step outside the Democrat and Republican parties and seek other alternatives.

The rally, called "One Nation Working Together," was sponsored by three hundred groups including the NAACP, the AFL-CIO, the National Council of La Raza, the National Gay and Lesbian Task Force, the United Methodist Church, the United Church of Christ, the National Baptist Convention, and several Jewish organizations. Major supporters from New York City included 1199 SEIU, a health care union local that chartered five hundred buses to carry twenty-five thousand union members to the rally, and the United Federation of Teachers.

Jon Stewart of "The Daily Show" was promoting his October 30, 2010 rally as the "Rally to Restore Sanity" and to challenge negativism and extremism from both the left and right. I am a big fan of Mr. Stewart and regularly watch his show on Comedy Central, but in this case he was downright wrong. October 2 was the march of reasoned opposition. This was the march of thoughtful criticism. This was the march of positive activism. Too bad Stewart missed it. He would have liked meeting Pablo and the kids from the Bronx.

G. People with Guns Kill People and Children

Based on an essay published on the *Huffington Post*, December 15, 2012
    www.huffingtonpost.com/alan-singer/gun-violence_b_2303760.html

Questions to Consider

1.   How should adults discuss terrible things with children?
2.   Why is the United States plagued by an epidemic of gun violence?
3.   Where do you stand on stricter limitations on gun ownership?

During the 2012 presidential election debate at Hofstra University, a member of the audience asked President Barack Obama, "What has your administration done or planned to do to limit the availability of assault weapons?" Both President Obama and Republican challenger Mitt Romney started by stating their belief in the Second Amendment and the right of Americans to "bear arms." They also argued that the country has to enforce existing guns laws and that if "our schools are working" there would be less gun violence. Romney expressed his belief that "if we do a better job in education, we'll give people the hope and opportunity they deserve and perhaps less violence from that." In addition, he argued "We need moms and dads, helping to raise kids. . . . Tell our kids that before they have babies, they ought to think about getting married to someone, that's a great idea . . . If there's a two-parent family, the prospect of living in poverty goes down dramatically." The implication here was that the failings by schools and teachers as well as of parents in single-parent families was behind gun violence, not the lack of gun control laws.

The debate took place three months after twelve people were shot to death and fifty more were wounded in a movie theater in Aurora, Colorado. According to its municipal website,[16] Aurora, which is part of the greater Denver metropolitan area, is the eighth-safest city in the United States. The accused killer used a semi-automatic military-style rifle, a 12-gauge shotgun, and a semiautomatic pistol, all acquired legally because of the absence of effective gun control. Not only was he from an "intact" two-parent family, but he was highly educated and had recently dropped out of a doctoral program.

Colorado was also the site of the Columbine High School shootings, the fourth most deadly in United States history, in 2009. The two teenage perpetrators, who committed suicide at the site, also had legally acquired semiautomatic weapons. Both of the shooters were from "intact" two-parent families and they attended one of the few public high schools in Colorado to receive a "distinguished" rating from the website GreatSchools.org.

I attended an elite public high school during the 1960s where I felt pretty much like a misplaced piece of furniture. I had passed the stiff admissions test, but the school was set up for the privileged few, and the rest of us received little support or attention.

At school, I had a group of friends who could fairly be described as weird. Where possible, we sat in the back of rooms and tried to remain anonymous. During our free time we read and discussed science-fiction and fantasy novels. Our particular favorite was Doc Savage and we imagined joining his band of superheroes.

For three alienating years, we listened to dark and heavy music such as the Doors, the Animals, and the Stones; experimented with alcohol and hallucinogenic drugs; and dreamed of having girlfriends. At one point we organized our own mythic religion, which we called Zo'olium, and we discussed building a rocket ship in shop class and blowing up the school. We did not want to hurt anybody, but we did want to do away with a hated place that we experienced as a prison.

My friends and I were pretty serious about some of our fantasies. After graduation, two of us spent the summer searching for Bigfoot in the Pacific Northwest, and the following year three of us traipsed through the Andes and along the Amazon River in South America. Our parents were deeply worried about our behaviors, our sullen demeanors, and our use of drugs, but there was little they could do to change things. Mostly our parents just hung on to tenuous relationships, hoping we would grow up before we hurt ourselves or ruined our lives.

I have lost track of most of the guys from Zo'olium, but from what I have heard, they have generally done all right with their lives. A couple of them are engineers, one is a restaurateur, one is an astronomer, one is a postal worker and part-time author, and I am a teacher.

I think about my friends and our high school experiences whenever I hear about another new case of school or teenage violence. I suspect that many other adults have also been rethinking their pasts as a result of the shooting deaths at places like Aurora and Columbine High School in Littleton, Colorado, and at Sandy Hook Elementary School in Newtown, Connecticut. What I have tried to figure out is what was different then, and why we did not take the same destructive path.

Many commentators have called for increased vigilance by school authorities to target suspect youth before they have a chance to injure themselves or others. Sometimes this profiling would be coupled with psychological support services, but usually it just means keeping an eye on teenagers that people find "too different" because of their appearance, music, or ideas. Some have suggested that the solution to this type of violence is increased school security. They want teachers and principals to have the power to search and suspend students, metal detectors installed at entrances, and police officers assigned to buildings.

These proposals share three things in common: They are premised on the idea that alienated young people are somehow different from the rest of us and do not deserve our concern; they violate fundamental democratic rights that are cherished in our society such as freedom of speech, the right to due process, and the right to privacy; and they generally ignore why those two young men at Columbine High School were able to kill and injure so many other people and then to kill themselves.

As I think back on the past and my friends, what emerges most clearly is that our culture has changed. Today, we live in a culture that glorifies violence in sports and the movies, and where the evening news celebrates the death of others through hygienic strategic bombings. It is a society that promotes the need for instant gratification and uses youthful alienation to sell products, where those who do not fit in are ignored, where schools still rank and sort out young people and brand them as failures. And we live in a country where unhappy people have easy access to plans to make bombs on the Internet and can purchase weapons of immense destructive capacity.

Although I do not absolve them of responsibility for their actions, there is more to blame for what happened in Aurora and Columbine than those young men. I can only think of two solutions that would help prevent future violent explosions like this one. As a former high school teacher, I am convinced that if these young men had had a place where they felt they belonged, where people cared about them, they might not have committed those violent acts against others.

But even more crucially, if our country had strict gun control laws, maybe no one would have died in the incidents at Aurora, Columbine, and Newtown, Connecticut. When I was in high school, we were weird and we were alienated, but we did not have guns.

Post-It Note: I wrote this blog after trying to explain what happened at Sandy Hook Elementary School in Newtown, Connecticut, to my eight-year-old grandchildren. In the end I really did not know what to say so I just gave them a chance to speak. They did not really know what to say either. Deaths in Colorado, Connecticut, and Washington, DC, have stimulated a national debate on the sources of violence and violence prevention, especially in schools.

H. The School-to-Prison Pipeline

Based on an essay published on the *Huffington Post*, January 24, 2012
    www.huffingtonpost.com/alan-singer/school-to-prison-pipeline_b_1219950.html

Questions to Consider

1. Do school disciplinary policies prepare and channel many students into prison?
2. Do school disciplinary policies discriminate based on race and ethnicity?

According to *Rethinking Schools*, a magazine written for teachers by teachers, "zero tolerance" disciplinary policies in schools are responsible for transforming minor transgressions of school rules, which could be handled as educational opportunities, into disciplinary matters where students are subject to suspension and often even into legal issues involving the police and courts. The editors of *Rethinking Schools* blame federal No Child Left Behind and Race to the Top programs that focus what takes place in schools on social control and test scores rather than on meeting student needs; accelerating the trend toward increasing severe punishment.

Punishment in school and in American society often has a racial dimension. The United States imprisons a larger percentage of its Black population than South Africa did at the height of Apartheid. In Washington, DC, three-fourths of African American men are arrested at some point in their lives. Since 1970, the United States prison population has grown from about three-hundred thousand people to over two million, even while crime rates have dropped. More than seven million children have a family member who has passed through the prison system.

The connection between prisons and schools dates back to the Reagan and Clinton administrations. The term "zero tolerance" came into popular usage during the Reagan presidency when Congress passed the Drug-Free Schools and Communities Act. During the Clinton years, the Safe and Gun-Free Schools Act mandated expulsion for any student, no matter how young, who brought a gun to school. Public fear of school violence was ignited by the Columbine shootings in 1999. Although the perpetrators were White and the incident had nothing to do with race, Black and Latino students in inner-city schools increasingly became the target of the anti-crime, anti-violence programs.

State policies, not the students, are often the actual criminals. According to a 2011 study, "Breaking Schools' Rules,"[17] in Texas, with a school population of 4.7 million students, there were 1.6 student suspensions during the 2009–2010 school year. Fifty-four percent of the students in Texas were suspended or expelled at least once while in secondary school. Overwhelmingly, 97% of the suspensions were for minor infractions that could have been treated as educational rather than disciplinary problems.

The "school-to-prison pipeline," with schools seemingly designed to prepare students for incarceration, is alive and well in New York City. According to a 2007 New York Civil Liberties Report, *Criminalizing the Classroom: The Over-Policing of New York City Schools*,[18] in 1996 the Giuliani administration transferred control over the school safety program away from school officials to the police department. The NYPD school safety division has over five thousand officers making it the fifth-largest police force in the country. Semi-skilled, low-paid school safety officers now decide when student behavior is criminal and warrants police intervention rather than teachers, guidance counselors, or school administrators. Principals or teachers who question these decisions and intervene are themselves subject to arrest.

Metal detectors at school entrances make many New York City schools feel more like prisons than places where young people want to be and contribute to the sense that these are not places where people are respected or treated with dignity and fairness. Approximately 100,000 New York City school children pass through a gauntlet of metal detectors every day. Their bags are searched and they are subject to pat downs as if going to school is suspected criminal behavior. Although we live an era of severe financial restraints, since 2002 the city's budget for police and security equipment in schools has increased by 65% to more than $221 million.[19]

In September 2011, the *New York Post* reported that metal detector scanning was being done at 88 Department of Education buildings housing more than 150 schools.[20] This does not include mobile scanning units, similar to those deployed at airports, that circulate between schools where they arrive unannounced for inspections. At an unannounced scanning at Murray Bergtraum High School in Manhattan in December 2010, police confiscated a reported five hundred cell phones, but no dangerous weapons.

Students in schools with large Black and Latino populations are subject to the most searches. *Post* reporters observed that at the Martin Luther King Jr. complex near Lincoln Center where the student population of the High School for Law, Advocacy and Community Justice is 93% Black and Latino, students had to remove belts and jewelry and wait on a twenty minute long line to enter the building. During this operation, their cell phones and open drink containers were confiscated. Meanwhile, students next door at the selective Fiorello H. LaGuardia High School of Music & Art and Performing Art, a much more middle-class school with a larger White (48%) and Asian (20%) student population, were allowed to simply swipe an ID card to enter the building.

A major focus of the *Rethinking Schools* theme issue was discussion of a book by Michelle Alexander, *The New Jim Crow: Mass Incarceration in the Age of Color Blindness*.[21] In an interview with a *Rethinking Schools* editor, Alexander, a legal scholar and civil rights activist who is also African American, explained that the explosion in the prison population and increasingly harsh punishment in schools has had a devastating impact on Black children and the Black community. Families are separated, lives are uncertain, older siblings are stopped and frisked by police, and children experience harassment starting at a young age and become resentful of authority figures whether they are teachers or police officers.[22]

Alexander believes school discipline policies were shaped by the war on drugs and the "get tough" movement. She charges that zero tolerance language in school disciplinary codes was taken from a Drug Enforcement Administration manual. She feels that students, parents, and teachers need to resist these policies and promote programs that will actually improve the quality of education and community life. "We're foolish if we think we're going to end mass incarceration unless we are willing to deal with the reality that huge percentages of poor people are going to remain jobless, locked out of the mainstream economy, unless and until they have a quality education that prepares them well for the new economy."[23]

Courts, including the United States Supreme Court, have ruled on student rights on a number of occasions. The best-known case is *Tinker v. Des Moines* (1969). In this case the United States Supreme Court decided that students do not "shed their constitutional rights to freedom of speech or expression at the schoolhouse gate." However in *Ginsberg v. New York* (1968) the Supreme Court recognized that states must exercise greater authority over children than over adults, partly because they are responsible for ensuring an environment that is safe and conducive to learning.

In *Safford Unified School District v. Redding* (2009), Associate Justice Clarence Thomas argued: "For nearly 25 years this Court has understood that maintaining order in the classroom has never been easy, but in more recent years, school disorder has often taken particularly ugly forms: drug use and violent crime in the schools have become major social problems. . . . For this reason, school officials retain broad authority to protect students and preserve order and a proper educational environment under the Fourth Amendment. This authority requires that school officials be able to engage in the close supervision of school children, as well as enforce rules against conduct that would be perfectly permissible if undertaken by an adult."

In testimony before the New York City Council Committees on Education and Civil Rights regarding the impact of suspensions on students' education rights, Donna Lieberman of the New York Civil Liberties Union argued that as part of their "zero tolerance" policy toward student "misbehavior," "school and police personnel meted out harsh punishment in situations that should have been resolved through counseling, conflict mediation, and similar supportive methods." In effect, these policies "push students out of school and into the criminal justice system."[24]

School officials are ratcheting up the level of infraction so that instead of treating a minor violation of school policies, such as a dress code infraction, as a guidance issue, administrators suspend students for insubordination because they failed to obey an authority figure. Insubordination, "defying or disobeying the lawful authority of school personnel or school safety agents," is considered a Level 3 infraction on the same level as the destruction of school property, fighting, or "engaging in gang related behavior." Students accused of insubordination can be given detention and excluded from extracurricular activities, recess, or communal lunchtime. They are also subject to a principal's suspension from school for up to five days.[25]

If these trends continue government and school officials won't have to worry any longer about the school-to-prison pipeline because the schools, especially those for Black, Latino, and poor students, will have effectively been transformed into prisons.

Notes

1. Sam Roberts, "No Longer Majority Black, Harlem Is in Transition," *New York Times* (January 6, 2010), p. A16.
2. Paul Krugman, "Stranded By Sprawl," *New York Times* (July 29, 2013), p. A17.
3. http://deniskitchen.com/Merchant2/merchant.mv?Screen=CTGY&Category_Code=bios.gen.bullmoose.

4. Mary Ann Giordano and Anna Phillips, "Mayor Hits Nerve in Remarks on Class Sizes and Teachers," *New York Times* (December 3, 2011), p. A19.

5. Spence School, www.spenceschool.org/.

6. www.spenceschool.org/support_spence/annual_fund/index.aspx.

7. www.spenceschool.org/about_spence/index.aspx.

8. Ibid.

9. Ben Chapman, "New York State Board of Regents Chancellor Merryl Tisch Blasts Mayor Bloomberg's School Reforms," *New York Daily News* (November 9, 2011), www.nydailynews.com/new-york/education/new-york-state-board-regents-chancellor-merryl-tisch-blasts-mayor-bloomberg-school-reforms-article-1.974918.

10. Rich Bockman, "City Plans to Close Three Struggling Boro Schools," www.timesledger.com/stories/2013/2/phaseoutschools_all_2013_01_10_q.html.

11. www.naacpldf.org/case-issue/new-york-city-specialized-high-school-complaint.

12. Juan Gonzalez, "New York City Specialized High Schools Admission Test a Tool for Affluent Residents to Buy Their Children's Way into Elite Public Schools," *New York Daily News* (September 27, 2012), www.nydailynews.com/new-york/education/new-york-city-specialized-high-schools-admission-test-tool-affluent-residents-buy-children-elite-public-schools-article-1.1170080.

13. Al Baker, "Charges of Bias in Admission Test Policy at Eight Elite Public High Schools," *New York Times* (September 28, 2012), www.nytimes.com/2012/09/28/nyregion/specialized-high-school-admissions-test-is-racially-discriminatory-complaint-says.html?_r&_r=1&http://select.nytimes.com/gst/abstract.html?res=FB0815F8355F127A93C1AB178ED85F458785F9.

14. Fred Hechinger, "Education; High School: Challenge To the Concept Of the Elite," *New York Times* (May 23, 1971), http://select.nytimes.com/gst/abstract.html?res=FB0815F8355F127A93C1AB178ED85F458785F9.

15. David Herszenhorn, "Admission Test's Scoring Quirk Throws Balance Into Question," *New York Times* (November 12, 2005), www.nytimes.com/2005/11/12/nyregion/12exam.html?pagewanted = print.

16. http://www.auroragov.org/cs/groups/public/documents/document/006989.pdf.

17. Council of State Governments Justice Center, http://csgjusticecenter.org/youth/.

18. www.nyclu.org/publications/report-criminalizing-classroom-2007.

19. www.nyclu.org/schooltoprison/lookatsafety.

20. Susan Edelman, Schools at 'Scan Still,'" *New York Post* (September 25, 2011), http://nypost.com/2011/09/25/schools-at-scan-still/.

21. Michelle Alexander, *The New Jim Crow: Mass Incarceration in the Age of Color Blindness* (2010), New York: New Press, 2012.

22. Jody Sokolower, "Schools and the New Jim Crow: An Interview with Michelle Alexander," *Rethinking Schools,* www.rethinkingschools.org/restrict.asp?path=archive/26_02/26_02_sokolower.shtml.

23. Ibid.

24. Donna Lieberman, "The Impact of School Suspensions, and a Demand for Passage of the Student Safety Act," www.nyclu.org/content/impact-of-school-suspensions-and-demand-passage-of-student-safety-act.

25. NYCLU, *Education Interrupted,* www.scribd.com/doc/47686951/Suspension-Report-FINAL-Spreads.

2
DEFENDING TEACHERS

This group of essays focuses on an ongoing debate over defining the job of teacher and what I see as real possibilities for improving teaching and student performance. In recent years there have sharp disagreements about how to best prepare new teachers (see Chapter 3), support working teachers, and evaluate the performance of teachers, as well as about what to do with teachers repeatedly deemed unsatisfactory. One of my concerns is that the goal of the so-called education reformers is to de-professionalize teaching. They present their plans to the public as a way to improve student performance and save districts money on salaries, benefits, and pensions. But it seems that standing behind every "reformer" is a venture capitalist hoping to make money by selling scripted learning, high-stakes assessments, and classroom and school administrative programs, along with the needed computer hardware and software.

Very powerful and wealthy individuals and groups seem determined to transform teaching into a temporary job that people leave before even learning how to do it. Transient teachers would be dependent on scripted learning and technology and would lack judgment about how to meet the needs of diverse students and how to resist unfair demands and inappropriate working conditions.

According to a report in the New York Times,[1] *longevity for teachers at traditional public schools in the United States is fourteen years. Based on my own history as a teacher and teacher educator, it takes extended experience, at least three to five years of hard work, to master the skills needed to be an effective teacher. By the way, it also takes five years to qualify as a master plumber.*

However, Teach for America, which places many of its recruits in charter schools, only assigns them for two years and provides little, if any, training. Wendy Kopp, the founder of Teach for America, justifies this with the argument that "the strongest schools develop their teachers tremendously so they become great in the classroom even in their first and second years." At the thirteen YES Prep schools in Houston, Texas, teachers average two-and-a-half years experience. At Achievement First, a charter operator with 25 schools in

Connecticut, Rhode Island, and Brooklyn, New York, the average teacher has a little more than two years of classroom experience. At KIPP, one of the largest charter operators with 141 schools in twenty states, the average teacher is in the classroom for about four years. Meanwhile, scientific studies of teachers and teaching repeatedly show that higher-than-average teacher turnover such as this diminishes student achievement.

In a number of my Huffington Post blog essays I described the "bizarro" world of former New York City Mayor Michael Bloomberg, a world where nothing was quite the way it was made out to be. I got the phrase from an old "Jerry Seinfeld" episode. I also compared the New York City Department of Education (DOE) to the Court of the Queen of Hearts in Lewis Carroll's Alice in Wonderland. For most of Bloomberg's tenure as mayor, the DOE was ruled not by a crazed queen but by an autocratic king, Joel Klein, who later moved on to a much higher paying position as a lawyer defending media mogul Rupert Murdoch and as his point man in efforts to sell technology to public schools across the United States.

A. Why Tenure for Teachers Is Important
B. Tomahawks and Teachers
C. Teach for America—It's All About "Me"!
D. Measure for Mis-Measure with Teacher Assessments
E. Testing Teachers by Testing Kids Is an Awful Idea
F. Fire Half of the Teachers!
G. Who Is Charlotte Danielson and Why Does She Decide How Teachers Are Evaluated?

A. Why Tenure for Teachers Is Important

Based on an essay published on the *Huffington Post*, February 24, 2010
   www.huffingtonpost.com/alan-singer/why-tenure-for-teachers-i_b_461540.
html

Questions to Consider

1. Where do you stand on tenure for teachers?
2. How do politicians manipulate school reports to further their own agendas?
3. Should political considerations influence educational policy?

When the New York City teachers union's contract was up for renegotiation in 2010, Mayor Michael "Bizarro" Bloomberg and School Chancellor Joel "King" Klein used the city's financial woes to hold back on salary increases and undermine traditional practices. Bizarro Bloomberg wanted to lay off teachers without regard to seniority and King Klein wanted to chip away at tenure by making it more difficult to secure and easier to lose.

Many Americans are unsympathetic to teacher tenure. Anti-union politicians have dubbed it lifetime protection for incompetents. In my over forty years as an educator and as a parent of three children who attended public schools, I have met my share of incompetent teachers—but we might not all agree on who they are.

I have also met my share of incompetent lawyers, clerical workers, bank personnel, and elected officials, especially mayors. Based on my own experience as a public school teacher, I am a strong advocate of tenure. While it protects the less than satisfactory by requiring that due process be followed before they can be removed, it also protects exceptionally good teachers from being undermined and removed by anxious administrators, covering their own rear ends, and blustering politicians.

I was a secondary school social studies teacher for fourteen years. I like to think I was a good teacher, but I also know I was often a very bad boy. In 1982, I transferred to a new high school. The administrative assistant principal, who later became a friend, approached me and said, "We heard you were very good but also a pain in the ass." I nodded my head in agreement and said, "It's a package deal."

As a teacher, I took seriously the idea that teachers were supposed to respect students and to prepare them to be active citizens in a democratic society. I organized student clubs that testified at public hearings against budget cuts in education and in favor of condom availability in schools. Club members organized debates on reproductive freedom and informational meetings on the Sandinista in Nicaragua, the meaning of Islam, equal rights for gays, and the importance of the census. They met with public officials and participated in protest marches to defend Roe v. Wade, to oppose apartheid in South Africa and war in Southwest Asia, and to end racial violence. They also wrote op-ed pieces for newspapers and appeared on radio and television programs.

These were all controversial issues, but I did not believe it was my responsibility to shy away from controversy. I am very proud that one club member later organized a union of livery cab drivers, another became a lawyer and activist in the local South Asian community, a third helped organize students at a local public university to oppose budget cuts and tuition increases, and a fourth became a United Nations weapons inspector helping to prevent genocide in conflict regions around the world.

Sometimes my actions brought me into conflict with colleagues and administrators. I was accused of trying to indoctrinate students and defending students who were brought up on disciplinary charges by teachers when I felt the teachers had provoked the incidents; as a result my classes were visited and lesson plans were checked by administrators more frequently than was required under the union contract.

What protected me was better-than-average scores on standardized tests by my students, the fact that I worked in very difficult schools by choice, the school and departmental administrators who respected what I did, and tenure, which made it virtually impossible to remove a teacher without documented evidence of malfeasance or incompetence.

But all of this is changing. When a school in New York City is reorganized and subdivided by Bizarro Bloomberg and King Klein, senior teachers are cut loose by new principals because they are considered too expensive to keep and because the new principals, fresh out the Bloomberg/Klein Mis-Leadership Academy, fear people who know how to teach will not simply follow arbitrary directives issued from above.

If anybody doubts that teachers, students, and parents need to worry about what will happen if tenure is canceled, let me cite two very recent examples of political considerations determining educational decisions.

In the early 2000s, I was a curriculum consultant to the Paul Robeson High School Social Studies Department for three years. I found it to be a well-run school serving students from a very poor section of Brooklyn. In 2010, students at Robeson were amongst the most vocal and best organized in the battle against the closing of large comprehensive high schools. I was proud of the way they handled themselves and I am sure their parents and teachers were proud as well. But not Bizarro Bloomberg and King Klein. They were pissed off that anyone would defy them, and decided that they needed to frighten potential dissenters into silence. The school's long-term principal, a decent man who related well with teachers, students, and parents, was removed from his position and reassigned to Staten Island, a four-hour round-trip from his home.

Bizarro Bloomberg and King Klein considered Bronx Aerospace, one of the mini-schools placed in what used to be a large comprehensive high school, to be one of the jewels of the small school movement. Its principal was a graduate of the Bloomberg/Klein Mis-Leadership Academy and it was continually graded A on its academic report cards. Because of affiliation with and funding by the Air Force, the school attracted academically strong students and had one of the highest graduation rates for any New York City high school.

But despite the high grade for the school, student grades were not that high. In 2006, only twenty-seven out of fifty-six of the school's graduating seniors, 48%, earned New York State Regents diplomas, compared to 74% at comparable schools in New York State. Furthermore, 0% of the students earned diplomas with advanced distinction, compared to 32% statewide. Even more disturbing, 0% of the graduates stated that they planned to attend four-year colleges.

It turned out that the Air Force was not so happy with Bronx Aerospace. According to an article in the *New York Daily News*,[2] it placed the school on probation because of rule violations and over $60,000 in unaccountable funds. The Air Force finally had enough and ended its affiliation with the school in June 2009.[3] But in the world of Bizarro Bloomberg and King Klein, Bronx Aerospace still earned an A.

For Bizarro Bloomberg and King Klein the problem was always the teachers, and it could only be solved if they got rid of tenure.

B. Tomahawks and Teachers

Based on an essay published on the *Huffington Post*, April 1, 2011
www.huffingtonpost.com/alan-singer/tomahawks-and-teachers_b_843526.html

Questions to Consider

1. Why do schools always seem to be cut disproportionately during economic downturns?
2. Do you agree or disagree with the idea of measuring the cost of military intervention based on its impact on schools and teachers? Explain.

In his address to the nation on March 28, 2011, President Barack Obama justified the bombing of Libya as a defense of vital national interests in the region and as part of the traditional role of the United States as the world's primary defender of global security and advocate for human freedom. He also assured the American people that the military actions would be temporary and that the United States would turn over military operations to its allies in NATO.

Whatever you may think of the bombing of Libya and of Obama's promise that these United States military actions would be temporary, what was definitely missing from the speech was any discussion of the economic and social costs of the new war. Given the costs of prolonged military ventures in Iraq and Afghanistan that were also supposed to be temporary, but each turned out to be over a decade long, the American people had a right to be suspicious.

This was especially the case given the slumping national economy, persistent unemployment, and threatened new rounds of teacher layoffs across the nation. On March 15, 2011, more than 30,000 pink slips were mailed to teachers in California, including 2,800 in the Bay Area, according to the California Teachers Association.[4] Detroit, Michigan, planned to close 70 of its 142 schools. In Providence, Rhode Island, layoff notices were sent to every single teacher. New York City projected over 4,500 teacher layoffs at the end of the school year.

Between March 19 and March 28, 2011, alone the United States spent approximately $550 on military operations in Libya. By the time President Obama had delivered his speech to the nation, United States warships had fired nearly 200 Tomahawk land attack cruise missiles at Libya, which cost almost $1.5 million each. United States aircraft had dropped 455 precision-guided bombs. Those weapons vary in price, but according to an Air Force fact sheet, cost roughly $22,000 each. The government's cost assessment did not include the $30 million lost when an F-15E Strike Eagle fighter crashed in Libya.

In New York State, the average starting salary for a new teacher was $37,321 a year and the overall average salary for teachers was $57,354. That means that each Tomahawk missile dropped on Libya cost the equivalent of the annual salary of forty new New York State teachers or twenty-six experienced teachers. The two hundred Tomahawk missiles were worth 8,000 new teachers or 5,200 experienced teachers. In states like North Dakota, where teacher salaries are much lower, those Tomahawks would have bought at least a third more teachers.

The wars in Iraq and Afghanistan lasted much longer and were much more expensive than anticipated. In March 2003 Vice-President Dick Cheney estimated United States involvement in Iraq would last two years and cost approximately $100 billion or 27,000 new New York State teachers. As of February 2010, the official estimate was that the war in Iraq had cost $700 billion or 190,000 new New York State teachers; however, Nobel Prize-winning economist Joseph Stiglitz put the real total cost of the war in Iraq alone at $3 trillion or the equivalent of 810,000 new New York State teachers. Using Stiglitz' estimates, the combined cost of Iraq and Afghanistan approached $5 trillion, or well over a million new New York State teachers.

Before presidents try to sell us a new war, they should at least tell us the cost, especially when firing one lowly Tomahawk missile could mean laying off forty teachers.

Post-It Note: The missiles in Libya helped to bring down the government and launch a period of chaos there and in much of the Middle East, including Egypt and Syria. President Obama later called for United States military action in Syria but there was very limited public support for this idea.

C. Teach for America—It's All About "Me"!

Based on an essay published on the *Huffington Post*, July 16, 2010
      www.huffingtonpost.com/alan-singer/teach-for-america---its-a_b_646948.html

Questions to Consider

1. Who is getting Teach for America jobs?
2. Will inner-city minority students benefit from having temporary teachers from affluent families and elite colleges?

3. Why do Teach for America recruits leave teaching before learning how?
4. Why would the United States adopt a program of placing temporary teachers in poorly performing schools?

Coaches like to say there is no "I" in team. But there is definitely an "I" in Teach for America and also a "ME."

An article in the *New York Times* made it clear just how much this program is about "me," just how little it actually provides for kids, and that it is a colossal waste of money.[5]

Teach for America (TFA) is really a relatively well-paid temporary missionary program that sends the children of the wealthy into the inner cities for resume building and career enhancement. It pays much better than the Peace Corps or church work, you get to stay in this country, and you do not have to move back into your parent's house after college. A Yale University graduate, getting paid $45,000 a year for a two-year stint in San Antonio schools, explained it well: "I feel very fortunate. I know a lot of people at Yale who didn't have a job or plan when they graduated."[6]

Ironically, because of the economic recession, it is harder to get into TFA than into a number of the more prestigious law and business schools. College graduates are really desperate for jobs. At Harvard and Yale, 18% of the senior classes of 2010 applied for TFA positions but few were actually accepted. Nationwide, applications were up 32% over 2009, and fewer than 10% of the applicants were accepted.

In New York State, where there was no teacher shortage, the governing body for education in the state endorsed TFA and other programs as alternative routes to certification and empowered the organization to issue advanced degrees. The seventeen regents on the governing board, all affluent and most committed to private schooling, were probably looking for temporary work for their own children and their children's friends in a very tight economy.

In 2010, TFA had an annual operating budget of $185 million, two-thirds of it from private donors and about $60 million from tax dollars. Why the United States ran a jobs program for the wealthy and well connected while terminating extended unemployment benefits for the working class is unclear.

In exchange for the private and public support, TFA provides 0.2% of American teachers. The TFA missionaries are trained and paid by the local districts, and leave in droves when their contracts expire. In New York City, an estimated 85% are gone within four years. According to a 2008 Harvard doctoral thesis,[7] few of the TFA missionaries remain "teachers" anywhere in the United States beyond five or six years.

What is this all about? Rather than improving education in the United States, TFA is part of the campaign to de-professional teaching and the concerted campaign to "charterize" and privatize public education. As far as I can tell, wealthy donors are really investors waiting to cash in when the educational system switches to privately operated, publicly financed schools. Think Halliburton and the United States military.

One thing is certain: TFA is not about children or America. For the young missionaries who sign up to visit inner city America, it is all about "me."

D. Measure for Mis-Measure with Teacher Assessments

Based on an essay published on the *Huffington Post*, March 17, 2012

www.huffingtonpost.com/alan-singer/measure-for-missmeasure-w_b_1320790.html

Questions to Consider

1. How is good teaching measured?
2. Do value-added measures measure anything of value?
3. Is it possible to balance a passion for teaching with a full life?

When Michael Bloomberg was elected mayor of New York City in 2001, the unemployment rate was about 5%. By 2012 it was 9%. That certainly qualifies as poor performance in office. Value decline rather than "value-added." Let's fire him.

When Andrew Cuomo was first elected to statewide office as attorney general in 2006, the unemployment rate was 4.5%. In 2012 it was 8%. That certainly qualifies as poor performance in office. Value decline rather than "value-added." Let's fire him also.

Maybe you think I am being unfair. After all, how can we hold the mayor and governor accountable and assess their performance in office based on a decline in a statistical measure such as unemployment when they are hardly responsible for the national and global economic situation during the last decade. Yet that is exactly what they want to do with classroom teachers.

I am not sure if William Shakespeare was anticipating the current wave of computer-driven data analysis when he wrote *Measure for Measure* in 1603. In this play, Shakespeare tackles the complex meaning of mercy, justice, and truth, and the way they are impacted by both pride and humility. It certainly seems like he was describing Cuomo and Bloomberg, or maybe some other arrogant and autocratic officials, and their attack on teachers when he wrote: "Some rise by sin, and some by virtue fall."

Four things stand out for me in much of the news coverage of the public release of ratings for eighteen thousand New York City elementary and middle school teachers:

1. The unreliability of the ratings.
2. The complexity of the rubric.
3. The arbitrariness of the scoring.
4. The quick exit from the classroom by many of the highest-ranked teachers.

1. If you are going to make a big fuss about a new ratings system, it should at least be based on reliable data. However, according to the *New York Times*,[8] the ratings had a "high margin of error" and were based on tests the state Department of Education considered in need of major revision. Michael Winerip, education columnist for the *New York Times*,[9] described one of the highest-achieving schools where four of the best fifth-grade teachers each received an unsatisfactory rating because students performed poorly on standardized assessments. Actually their students did not perform poorly at all, just below computerized expectations. This school did extensive test preparation in the fourth grade to prepare students for acceptance into selective middle schools. In the fifth grade, instruction was much more project oriented. As a result, 97% of the fourth-graders reached proficiency on the tests, but in the fifth grade, where real teaching took place, only 89% reached proficiency. Winerip estimated that the difference between the 89% and 97% proficiency ratings was the result of only three children in a class of thirty "scoring a 2 out of 4 instead of a 3 out of 4."[10]

2. If something is too hard for an ordinary person to understand and there is no way to explain it to them, that may be because it does not make sense. Because the Bloomberg administration acknowledged it was unfair to directly compare teachers who work in different schools and communities and with different student populations, the Department of Education created an elaborate formula that was supposed to take into account student race, economic class, ethnicity, parental income, language ability, and special needs, but did not ask whether they ate breakfast the morning of the test, had a fight with a sibling or parent, spent the night in the hospital emergency room, or just had a bad hair day. Maybe there are just too many factors to take into account to evaluate teachers on a single test score.

3. A big problem with rating teachers according to the average is that people who fall below average may still be very good teachers and there may be reasonable explanations for the "below average" performance of their students on standardized tests. Seventy-three teachers were rated below average although their students performed at or above the 84th percentile citywide on the standardized tests because they teach in schools where other teachers did even better. In the meantime, some teachers in poorly performing schools received above average ratings because their students performed less poorly than the school average.

4. If you ever saw the movie *Freedom Writers* (2007), a young woman pours her heart into teaching, changes the lives of her students, and then quits to work at a college. A similar scenario plays out in the book *Small Victories* (1990); only the all-star teacher lasts a little longer. She was Jessica Siegel, a single woman in her thirties with no children, who did amazing things as an English teacher at Seward Park High School in Manhattan, but who left the public school system to become a professor of journalism at a local college. The reality is

that all-stars often turn out to be shooting stars. They burn brightly and then flame out because no one can sustain the intensity and pace that they set. The *New York Times* highlighted three of the highest-ranking teachers on the city's list.[11] Walter Galiano became an assistant principal. Natalie Guandique left the special education classroom to return to graduate school. Alison Epstein transferred to a gifted and talented class in another school. Three classroom all-stars, three shooting stars, each one of them had already moved on.

When I was a high school teacher, I had a reputation for successfully reaching angry, unhappy, or disruptive students. They would often be placed in my classroom by guidance counselors or the assistant principal to protect other teachers and spare other students from their outbursts. This benefited my colleagues and all of the students, and I did not mind. But if I agreed to this now I would probably be lowering my rating. If Bloomberg gets his way and merit pay bonuses are issued to teachers based on student performance, I would lose the bonus because of sound educational practice. In the future the incentive will be for teachers and administrators to jack-up their scores, and their salaries, by passing along their problem students to unsuspecting or naïve colleagues. Every child's education will suffer.

Post-It Note: At the end of Measure for Measure, *Duke Vincentio reveals his identity; Angelo the autocratic administrator confesses his misdeeds; the duke proposes to Isabella; Claudio, Isabella's brother, is pardoned; and everyone is forced to be honest. Maybe we can skip the play and find a way to force public officials to be honest about the politicization of education and its negative impact on schools, teachers, and children.*

E. Testing Teachers by Testing Kids Is an Awful Idea

Based on an essay published on the *Huffington Post*, May 26, 2011
www.huffingtonpost.com/alan-singer/3tk-testing-teachers-by-t_b_867378.html

Questions to Consider

1.   Should schools test teachers by testing their students?
2.   Why are school districts buying into this plan?
3.   Do you think the proposed movie is well cast?

In May 2011, the *New York Times* reported that the New York City Department of Education (DOE) was developing sixteen new standardized tests whose main purpose would be to grade teachers rather than the students who were actually taking the tests: "Elementary school students would most likely take at least one or two additional tests every year, beginning in the third grade. High school students could take up to eight additional tests a year."[12] The tests would be used to satisfy requirements that allowed New York State to secure $700 million in federal Race to the Top money. Under a new state law, 40% of a teacher's performance would be based on student performance on standardized tests or other "rigorous, comparable" measures.

Most New York State districts did not create their own standardized tests because it was too expensive and it would eat up a lot of the Race to the Top money. However, the New York City DOE initially planned to spend one-quarter of its $256 million share of the federal money, approximately $64 million, creating new tests. Testing teachers by testing kids (3TK) is an awful idea for many reasons:

1.   3TK is part of a national campaign to blame teachers and teacher unions for student performance rather than improve schools and address the underlying causes of poor performance—poverty, displacement, lack of language skills, and stresses on families. 3TK is a cheap solution to major social problems that will not work.

2.   When teachers know their jobs depend on student test scores, all they will do is prep kids for tests. It is a matter of survival. School becomes oppressive and boring. Reading and writing are chores, not pleasures. Whether the learning sticks and travels with students to the next grade or is transferable to other topics is not their problem. That will have to be addressed by the teacher in the next grade who also has to worry about getting fired.

3.   The validity of tests themselves has been challenged. In a study published by the National Education Policy Center in May 2011,[13] Professor Bruce Baker of Rutgers University analyzed claims made for the reliability of testing students as a way of evaluating teachers. The bottom line, according to Baker: "We technocrats have started to fall for our own contorted logic—that the available metric is the true measure—and the quality of all else can only be evaluated against that measure." He accused academics and school administrators of succumbing to political fashions because it is not clear that the tests actually provide us with any type of reliable information about student learning.

4.   The real beneficiaries of the 3TK testing craze will be educational publishing and computer companies. They will sell school systems the full package of textbooks, classroom displays, individualized instructional programs, and standardized assessments that are seamlessly integrated together, but only measure each other and not what students understand about the world.

3TK is a disaster waiting to hit a classroom near you. In the early 1980s I taught at Charles E. Hughes High School in Manhattan where students were mostly performing poorly. One semester a drug dealer set up business during the change of periods in a stairwell near my room. Students told me about it and every period I went into the stairwell to disrupt sales until he finally moved to a new location. But if 3TK had been in place, he could have simply disrupted my classroom on testing days, student scores would have plummeted, I would have been fired, and he would have been free to pursue his business interests.

Based on my experience as a high school teacher, I can just image how the movie version of 3Tk will play out.

Scene one is a press conference. A sinister Mayor Bloomgarden played by Danny DeVito announces his new program to test teachers by testing their students and using the test result to hire and fire. Bloomgarden tells reporters "This is the final answer. This plan will save our city's schools." A timid young female reporter played by Amy Adams raises her hand and quietly asks the mayor to explain exactly how the plan will work. Bloomgarden's tall, mean-looking press secretary played by Glenn Close steps to the microphone and announces that there will no questions at this time. At that point Bloomgarden and his press secretary stomp off the stage.

In scene two, the young reporter is sobbing. The camera zooms in on a letter she is reading. It is a dismissal notice.

In scene three, two new teacher candidates report to the principal's office in the Bernie Madoff High School for Entrepreneurship and Criminal Behavior. Mr. Gosling is played by Ryan Gosling and Mr. Jackson is played by Samuel L. Jackson. They are second-career recruits who always really wanted to be math teachers in dysfunctional inner-city high schools. Principal Kutcher is played by Ashton Kutcher. He is very friendly but lacks gravitas and does not appear to know which end is up.

Bernie Madoff High School for Entrepreneurship and Criminal Behavior is actually run by an ethnically diverse triad of tough-looking drug dealers played by Jaden Smith, Justin Bieber, and David Archuleta. After they are hired, Jackson and Gosling team up and vow to clean up the school. They instantly become great teachers despite having no training and without knowing very much math. Two of their protégés, teenage girls played by Raven-Symoné and Naya Rivera, will be accepted by Harvard if they can just pass the next citywide, standardized math test.

The drug triad learns that the math test is really being used to evaluate teachers and not students. They decide to "convince" students to fail the test to get rid of the teachers who are plaguing them and cutting into their profits. The girls played by Raven and Naya resist their pressure but on the day of the test they disappear. The other students, who all love Jackson and Gosling, panic and fail the test on purpose. As a result, the school is rated "D" and Jackson and Gosling are removed as unsatisfactory.

In the final scene the drug triad is meeting to divide up the profits. The character played by Jaden Smith says, "Gosling and Jackson had to go. They did not understand the school's mission statement. After all, this is the high school for entrepreneurship and criminal behavior. Nothing personal. This was just business."

Anybody who wonders how 3TK will work out should remember the immortal words of Forrest Gump, "Stupid is as stupid does."

F.   Fire Half of the Teachers!

Based on an essay published on the *Huffington Post*, March 5, 2010

www.huffingtonpost.com/alan-singer/fire-half-of-them_b_486720.html

Questions to Consider

1.   Why would President Obama support a plan to fire half of the teachers in a school?
2.   Do you think politicians who send their own children to elite and expensive private schools are equipped to make decisions for public schools?

In a March 2010 speech to the United States Chamber of Commerce, President Barack Obama demanded that states identify schools with graduation rates of 60% or less. To qualify for federal School Turnaround Grants, school districts would have to take drastic actions. Among the options would be firing the principal and at least half of the staff of a troubled school.

New York City Mayor Michael Bloomberg must have been jumping up and down with glee. He had already pledged to improve Gotham City schools by getting rid of the incompetent teachers who were undermining the education of our children. It is a laudable goal, but the problem is that he did not seem to be able to find that many. According to the *New York Times*,[14] in 2009 the city's Department of Education fired only three out of fifty-five thousand tenured teachers.

Even when you add to the three tenured teachers who were fired the ten teachers who were charged and left voluntarily, the nine who were retrained and reinstated, the one who was deported for immigration violations, and the fifty cases that were still pending, that only brought the total to seventy-three possibly incompetent tenured teachers out of a total of fifty-five thousand, which is about 0.1%.

And it is not as if the mayor was not trying. Of the fifty-five thousand tenured teachers in the school system, only 1.8% received an unsatisfactory rating by their principals in 2008. This was after Bloomberg threatened to remove school principals if their schools performed poorly on state assessments and promised them substantial bonuses for improved test scores.

Bloomberg was quick to place the blame for his own incompetence elsewhere. He argued that state laws that enforced due process were interfering with his ability to summarily remove teachers he and Klein did not like.

Due process, a fundamental right guaranteed by the United States Constitution, might be slow, but blaming it in this case was a pretty lame excuse. Bloomberg had been mayor for more than eight years. If there were a large number of incompetent teachers in the city's schools they should have been discovered and removed a long time before.

In almost sixty years as a student, teacher, and teacher educator, I have seen more than my share of incompetent teachers. But I suspect Bloomberg, President

"Fire Half of Them," and I do not use the same criteria to identify incompetent teachers. I have a friend who always asks when evaluating a public school teacher, "Would I want that person to teach my child?"

I think this is probably the best measure to use, although Bloomberg and Obama would have difficulty applying it since they never sent their own children to public schools. As a teacher educator, former teacher, and student, and as a parent and grandparent, I value teachers who respect students as people. That means listening to them when they speak and being interested in their lives and identities. It also means making demands on them to learn and to act appropriately in different situations and with different groups of people.

The best teachers are good communicators and have a deep love of learning that they share with their students. They are also willing to stand up to school administrators and government officials like Bloomberg and Obama who advocate the latest gimmick "solutions" that will never work in practice.

In my experience, "teachers" who constantly prep students for standardized tests rank at the bottom on the scale of good teaching. Would you want that person to teach your child? I am sure Bloomberg and President "Fire Half of Them," if they were honest, would say "No way!"

G. Who Is Charlotte Danielson and Why Does She Decide How Teachers Are Evaluated?

Based on an essay published on the *Huffington Post*, June 10, 2013
www.huffingtonpost.com/alan-singer/who-is-charlotte-danielso_b_3415034.html

Questions to Consider

1. What is the Danielson Framework for Teaching?
2. Why is the Danielson Framework the subject of controversy?
3. Do you think rubrics such as the Danielson Framework are useful tools for teachers?

A *New York Times* editorial endorsed a state-imposed teacher evaluation system for New York City as "an important and necessary step toward carrying out the rigorous new Common Core education reforms."[15] The system is based on the Danielson Framework for Teaching developed by Charlotte Danielson and marketed by the Danielson Group of Princeton, New Jersey.

Michael Mulgrew, the president of the city's teachers union, and Mayor Michael Bloomberg, also announced that they were generally pleased with the plan. According to the mayor, "Good teachers will become better ones and ineffective teachers can be removed from the classroom." He applauded State Commissioner John King for "putting our students first and creating a system that will allow our schools to continue improving."

Unfortunately, nobody, not the *Times*, the New York State Education Department, the New York City Department of Education, nor the teachers union demonstrated any positive correlation between teacher assessments based on the Danielson rubrics, good teaching, and the implementation of new higher academic standards for students under Common Core.

A case demonstrating the relationship should have been made, if it actually exists. A format based on the Danielson rubrics was already being used to evaluate teachers in at least thirty-three struggling schools in New York City and by one of its supervising agencies. Kentucky has been using an adapted version of the Danielson Framework for Teaching to evaluate teachers since 2011 and according to the New Jersey Department of Education, 60% of nearly five hundred school districts in the state were using teacher evaluation models developed by the Danielson Group. The South Orange/Maplewood and Cherry Hill, New Jersey, schools have used the Danielson model for several years.

According to the *Times* editorial, the "new evaluation system could make it easier to fire markedly poor performers" and help "the great majority of teachers become better at their jobs."[16] But as far as I can tell, the new evaluation system is mostly a weapon to harass teachers and force them to follow dubious scripted lessons.

Ironically, in a pretty comprehensive search on the Internet, I had difficulty discovering independent sources describing who Charlotte Danielson really is and what her qualifications are for developing a teacher evaluation system. According to the website of the Danielson Group,[17] "the Group consists of consultants of the highest caliber, talent, and experience in educational practice, leadership, and research." It provides "a wide array of professional development and consulting services to clients across the United States and abroad" and is "the only organization approved by Charlotte Danielson to provide training and consultation around the Framework for Teaching."

The group's services come at a cost, which is not a surprise, although you have to apply for their services to get an actual price quote. Individuals who participated in a three-day workshop at the King of Prussia campus of Arcadia University in Pennsylvania paid $599 each. A companion four-week online class cost $1,809 per person. According to a comparison chart prepared by the Alaska Department of Education,[18] the "Danielson Group uses 'bundled' pricing that is inclusive of the consultant's daily rate, hotel and airfare. The current fee structure is $4,000 per consultant/per day when three or more consecutive days of training are scheduled. One and two-day rates are $4,500/per consultant/per day. We will also schedule keynote presentations for large groups when feasible. A keynote presentations is for informational/overview purposes and does not constitute training in the Framework for Teaching."

Charlotte Danielson is supposed to be "an internationally-recognized expert in the area of teacher effectiveness, specializing in the design of teacher evaluation systems that, while ensuring teacher quality, also promote professional learning" who "advises State Education Departments and National Ministries and Departments of Education, both in the United States and overseas."[19] Her online biography claims that she has "taught at all levels, from kindergarten through college, and has worked as an administrator, a curriculum director, and a staff developer" and has degrees from Cornell, Oxford, and Rutgers,[20] but I could find no formal academic resume online. Her undergraduate degree from Cornell seems to have been in history with a specialization in Chinese history, and she studied philosophy, politics and economics at Oxford and educational administration and supervision at Rutgers. While working as an economist in Washington, DC, Danielson obtained her teaching credentials and began work in her neighborhood elementary school, but it is not clear in what capacity or for how long. She developed her ideas for teacher evaluation while working at the Educational Testing Service and since 1996 has published a series of books and articles with the Association for Supervision and Curriculum Development. I have seen photographs and video broadcasts online, but I am still not convinced that she really exists as more than a front for the Danielson Group to sell its teacher evaluation product.

The United Federation of Teachers and the online news journal *Gotham Schools* both asked a person purporting to be Charlotte Danielson to evaluate the initial Danielson rubrics being used in New York City schools. In a phone interview reported on in *Gotham Schools*,[21] Danielson was supposedly in Chile selling her frameworks to the Chilean government: "Danielson was hesitant to insert herself into an union-district battle, but did confirm that she disapproved of the checklist shown to her." The checklist "was inappropriate because of the way it was filled out. It indicated that the observer had already begun evaluating a teacher while in the classroom observation. She said that's a fundamental no-no."

The bottom line is that 40% of a teacher's evaluation will be based on student test scores on standardized and local exams and 60% on in-class observations. I am most concerned with the legitimacy of the proposed system of observations based on snap-shots, fifteen-minute visits to partial lessons that are conducted by supervisors with potentially limited or no classroom experience in the subject being observed, followed by the submission of a multiple-choice rubric that will be evaluated online by an algorithm that decides whether the lesson was satisfactory or not.

Imagine an experienced surgeon in the middle of a delicate six-hour procedure, where the surgeon responds to a series of unexpected emergencies, being evaluated by a computer based on data gathered from a fifteen-minute snap-shot visit by a general practitioner who has never performed an operation.

Imagine evaluating a baseball player who goes three for four with a couple of home runs and five or six runs batted in based on the one time during the game when he struck out badly.

Imagine a driver with a clean record for thirty years who has his or her license suspended because a car they owned was photographed going through a red light, when perhaps there was an emergency, perhaps he or she was not even driving the car, or perhaps there was a mechanical glitch with the light, camera, or computer.

Now imagine a teacher who adjusts instruction because of important questions introduced by students, who is told the lesson is unsatisfactory because it did not follow the prescribed scripted lesson plan, and because during the fifteen minutes the observer was in the room they failed to see what they were looking for. But what might have actually happened before they arrived or after they left?

When I was a new high school teacher in the 1970s, I was observed six times a year by my department chair, an experienced teacher and supervisor with expertise in my content area. We met before each lesson to strengthen the lesson plan and in a post-observation conference to analyze what had happened and what could have been done better. Based on the conferences and the observations we put together a plan to strengthen my teaching; changes the supervisor expected to see implemented in future lessons. The conferences, the lesson, and the plan were then written into a multi-page observation report that we both signed. These meetings and observations were especially important in my development as a teacher and I follow the same format when I observe student teachers today.

As I became more experienced the number of formal observations decreased. I still remember a post-observation conference at a different school and with a different supervisor who had become both a mentor and a friend. After one lesson he virtually waxed poetic at what he had seen, but then suggested three alternative scenarios I could have pursed. Finally I said I appreciated his support and insight, but if I had done those other things, I would not have been able to do the things he really liked. He paused, said I was right, and said to just forget his suggestions.

But under the new system, principals will drop in for a few minutes and punch in some numbers. Teachers then will be rated, mysteriously or miraculously, based upon a computer algorithm using twenty-two different dimensions of teaching. Astounding!

And this assumes principals know what they are doing, have the independence to actually give teachers a strong rating, and are not out to get the good teacher who is also a union representative or just a general pain in the ass like I was.

But that is a big assumption. Teachers in the field reported to me that from the start the New York City Department of Education was trying to undermine the possibility of a fair and effective teacher evaluation system. Within hours after an arbitrator mandated use of the Danielson teacher evaluation system, New York City school administrators received a 240-page booklet explaining how to implement the rubrics in the following fall. Teachers received six hours of professional development so they knew what to expect, not so they knew how to be successful. Teachers were being told that while there was no official lesson plan design, they better follow the recommended one if they expect to pass the evaluations.

Administrators were instructed how to race in and out of rooms and punch codes into an iPad with evaluations actually completed in cyberspace by an algorithm. Teachers would fail when supervisors did not see things that took place before or after they entered the room, if lesson plans did not touch on all twenty-two dimensions of the Danielson rubric, or when teachers adjusted their lessons to take into account student responses.

Teachers expected to be evaluated harshly. In December 2012 the *New York Daily News* reported that the Danielson rubric, while still unofficial, was already being used to give teachers unsatisfactory ratings.[22]

To add to this, there also appeared to be an informal quota system for granting tenure. Teachers recommended for tenure by building administrators were being denied by central administration, which suggests how low the opinions of building-based administrators were valued.

Post-It Note: There are useful educational goals established by the Common Core standards. But unless the standards are separated from the high-stakes testing of students and the evaluation of teachers and schools they will become an albatross around the neck of education and a legitimate target for outrage from right-wing state governments, frustrated parents, and furious teachers, and they will never be achieved.

Notes

1. Motoko Rich, "At Charter Schools, Short Careers by Choice," *New York Times* (August 27, 2013), www.nytimes.com/2013/08/27/education/at-charter-schools-short-careers-by-choice.html.
2. Erin Einhorn, "Air Force May Ground Bronx H.S.," *New York Daily News* (May 13, 2008), www.nydailynews.com/new-york/education/air-force-ground-bronx-h-s-article-1.327399.
3. http://insideschools.org/high/browse/school/535.
4. Jill Tucker, "California Teacher Pink Slips Snag Veterans," *San Francisco Chronicle* (March 16, 2011), www.sfgate.com/education/article/California-teacher-pink-slips-snag-veterans-2389209.php; Rehema Ellis, Victor Limjoco, and Alex Johnson, "Teacher Layoffs Raise Class-Size Tensions," *Education Nation* on NBCNews.com, www.nbcnews.com/id/41739184/ns/today-education_nation/#.Ut72lxb0Bz8.
5. Michael Winewrip, "A Chosen Few Are Teaching for America," *New York Times* (July 12, 2010), www.nytimes.com/2010/07/12/education/12winerip.html?adxnnl=1&ref=teach_for_america&adxnnlx=1279310540-S78oAf3mfF4gYQHH9wNePA.
6. Ibid.
7. Cited in ibid.
8. Sharon Otterman and Robert Gebeloff, "In Teacher Ratings, Good Test Scores Are Sometimes Not Good Enough," *New York Times* (February 26, 2012), www.nytimes.com/2012/02/26/nyregion/in-new-york-teacher-ratings-good-test-scores-arent-always-good-enough.html.
9. Michael Winerip, "Hard-Working Teachers, Sabotaged When Student Test Scores Slip," *New York Times* (March 5, 2012), www.nytimes.com/2012/03/05/nyregion/in-brooklyn-hard-working-teachers-sabotaged-when-student-test-scores-slip.html?_r=1&ref=nyregion.
10. Ibid.
11. Winnie Hu and Robert Gebeloff, "After Release of Ratings, a Focus on 'Top' Teachers," *New York Times* (February 27, 2012), www.nytimes.com/2012/02/27/education/after-release-of-ratings-a-focus-on-top-teachers.html?_r=1&scp=1&sq=top%20teachers&st=cse.
12. Sharon Otterman, Test for Pupils, but the Grades Go to Teachers, *New York Times* (May 24, 2011), www.nytimes.com/2011/05/24/education/24tests.html?_r=1&scp=1&sq=testing%20teacher&st=cse.

13. Bruce Baker, *Passing Muster Fails Muster? (An Evaluation of Evaluating Systems)*, http:// nepc.colorado.edu/thinktank/passing-muster-fails-muster.

14. Jennifer Medina, "Progress Slow in City Goal to Fire Bad Teachers," *New York Times* (February 24, 2010), www.nytimes.com/2010/02/24/education/24teachers.html?pagewanted=all.

15. Editorial Board, "Better Teachers for New York City," *New York Times* (June 6, 2013), www. nytimes.com/2013/06/06/opinion/better-teachers-for-new-york-city.html?src=rechp.

16. Ibid.

17. www.danielsongroup.org.

18. education.alaska.gov/ . . . teacher_eval_model_comparison_chart.docx.

19. www.msetonline.org/keynote-speakers.html.

20. www.iobservation.com/danielson-collection/Biography/.

21. Geoff Decker, "What Charlotte Danielson Saw When the UFT Came Calling," http:// ny.chalkbeat.org/2011/11/07/what-charlotte-danielson-saw-when-the-uft-came-calling/.

22. "*NY Daily News:* Some Schools Already Using Danielson Rubric to 'Rate Teachers,'" http://perdidostreetschool.blogspot.com/2012/12/ny-daily-news-some-schools-already.html.

3

TEACHER EDUCATION

I confess that I work at a school of education. But I was also a high school teacher for fourteen years before I became a teacher educator, which is probably fourteen years more teaching experience than most people in educational leadership positions in school districts, state education departments, and the federal government's Department of Education have.

I also have another confession to make. I am not a big fan of many teacher education programs. Not because they teach too much educational theory as charged in a 2013 report by a group called the National Council on Teacher Quality, but because they often do not effectively connect theory to practice, which of course is the hardest thing to do in any field of study. Too often schools of education put the cart before the horse, discussing underlying explanations before teacher education students have an idea of how classrooms can be organized, how and why students respond to different educational approaches, and what is important to know and why.

My experiences as an undergraduate pre-service teacher at the City College of New York in the 1960s left much to be desired. After a series of disagreements between us in class, my first education professor said I should never become a teacher and recommended that I drop out of the program. The history of education professor lectured about things that those who remained awake considered irrelevant. Once I approached him and asked why we needed to know these things to become effective teachers. His response was that if teachers did not know this history, who would? It was the last time that I spoke with him. After that I did my assignments and just waited for the semester to be over. The educational psychology professor in the secondary education program was enamored with B. F. Skinner and Konrad Lorenz, so he spent all of his time discussing experiments with pigeons and geese rather than discussing how children learn. The social studies methods teacher was especially disappointing. His specialty was operating outdated audiovisual equipment, so we had workshops on each machine. At the end of his class, I swore I would never use an overhead projector in class, even if it meant permanent unemployment.

It was only after I became a teacher and began to think more seriously about the issues confronting schools, debates about what should be taught, and how students most effectively learn, that the material presented in my undergraduate program had any meaning to me and I began to read and think more about it.

All of this makes schools of education convenient scapegoats for the problems facing education in the United States. In fact, as a teacher educator I have met many highly skilled, thoughtful teacher educators who are experienced in their fields, deeply concerned with the quality of teaching, and advocates for improving schools as well as conditions in American society.

The first essay in this chapter was part of a series of essays published on the Huffington Post *on "Reclaiming the Conversation on Education." It turns a critical eye on the people and corporations behind attacks on teacher education. A number of essays in this chapter were written in response to articles from the* New York Times. Times *educational coverage is frequently so biased that I sometimes refer to the newspaper as the* New York Crimes. *At one point I was so angry with what I saw as a conflict in interest between* Times *coverage and its business projects that I threatened to cancel my subscription. The next-to-last essay in this chapter highlights a group of college students challenging new teacher certification requirements that they and I believe make teacher education worse rather than better. The last essay is a follow-up to the student campaign that focuses on problems with the evaluation system being marketed by Pearson, the private, for-profit, education and publishing company, and efforts by teacher educators to set-up an alternative assessment as a check against Pearson.*

A. Are Schools of Education Why Children Don't Learn?
B. We Need to Make Eye Contact
C. Arizonafication of Teacher Education
D. Anger in the Heartland over Unfair Teacher Tests
E. Problems with Pearson's Student Teacher Evaluation System

A. Are Schools of Education Why Children Don't Learn?

Based on an essay published on the *Huffington Post*, July 10, 2013
    www.huffingtonpost.com/alan-singer/are-schools-of-education-_b_3563103.
html

Questions to Consider

1. How should schools of education prepare future teachers?
2. How should schools of education be evaluated?
3. Should schools of education be held responsible for the poor performance of American children on high-stakes standardized tests?

    They think they found the solution to fix American schools and it is really very simple: get rid of schools of education because they fail to adequately train teachers. According to a scalding report recently issued by a private group that calls itself the National Council on Teacher Quality (NCTQ): "The field of teacher preparation has rejected any notion that its role is to train the next generation of teachers."[1] The problem, teacher educators try to "expunge the prejudices of teacher candidates, particularly those related to race, class, language and culture" and refuse to "arm the novice teacher with practical tools to succeed."[2] Teacher educators have "thrown their own field into disarray and done a great disservice to the teaching profession,"[3] so get rid of schools of education and then American children will miraculously learn.

    If someone claimed that schools of education in the United States were responsible for racial inequality, persistently high levels of unemployment, income disparity, segregated schools, single-parent families, gridlock in Congress, and globalization that ships jobs overseas, you would be very leery about buying their solutions.

    If they also claimed that college professors who teach teachers could somehow inoculate their pupils so that for the next thirty years they would only do the best job possible, you would think they were out of their minds.

    Unbelievably, and suspiciously, influential people are rushing to embrace the NCTQ findings. The NCTQ website claims that "24 state school chiefs, over 100 district superintendents, the Council of the Great City Schools and 77 advocacy organizations across 42 states and the District of Columbia have endorsed the Review."[4]

    United States Secretary of Education Arne Duncan announced that the "NCTQ deserves praise for working to give consumers—both teacher candidates and districts—better information to use in selecting the most effective teacher preparation programs."[5] Consumers? Not parents, not children?

    Michelle Rhee, who has been in constant battles with teachers and teachers unions as chancellor of Washington, DC, schools and as CEO of a group called

StudentsFirst, enthusiastically praised the report: "Its groundbreaking scope and approach, provides exactly the kind of information that teachers, districts, and policymakers need to guide better decision-making. Creating high quality traditional prep programs are key to consistently putting effective teachers in front of kids."[6]

The study claims to have rigorously examined curricula, syllabi, and admissions standards and used a four-star rating system similar to ones used by a lot of movie reviewers. Less than 10% of the 608 teacher education programs evaluated in the study earned three or more stars. Only four programs were four-star blockbuster hits: Lipscomb University, Vanderbilt University, Furman University, and Ohio State University. Lipscomb is a private Christian college in Nashville, Tennessee, where Vanderbilt University is also located. Furman University is in Greenville, South Carolina. Hofstra University, where I teach, was not one of the schools of education evaluated.

The location of the four-star teacher education programs is somewhat surprising and for me makes the entire report suspect. In 2011, Tennessee students ranked second to last on the ACT and, in the National Assessment of Educational Progress, Tennessee scored in the bottom 20% of the states, with below national average scores in every area tested. South Carolina's scores were essentially the same.

Schools in Tennessee and South Carolina do poorly by almost every objective measure, which makes one wonder how their schools of education are so fantastic. In 2009, they ranked fortieth (South Carolina) and forty-first (Tennessee) in percentage of population twenty-five years old with a high school diploma. On *Education Week's 2013 Quality Counts* report card,[7] both states earned grades of C+ overall, but only D in K-12 student achievement.

I will not defend every school of education and every professor that works there, but I know we are not the "problem" with education in the United States.

As a former high school teacher and as a teacher educator, I believe schools of education are being attacked because we present a message critics of schools do not want to hear. For me, the best teachers not only master the tools of the trade, but learn to be classroom decision-makers who understand how to adjust lessons to connect to students, which means they have to be concerned with race, class, language, and culture. They become curriculum creators who master the content of their subject area over time and design lessons and activities that appeal to the interests of the students that they are teaching. They also become student advocates who build classroom learning communities based on mutual respect and fight for and defend their students against unfair practices and inadequate funding. Decision-makers, creators, and advocates are exactly the kinds of teachers that we need and exactly the kinds of teachers that corporate interests with the processed, scripted, tech-driven programs they are selling to school districts hate and want to eliminate.

The NCTQ posted a list of the advisory committee for its study on teacher education and its major funders. The lists confirmed my belief that major corporations want to get rid of schools of education so they can remove impediments to their control over and profiting from education in the United States. They include:

- Sir Michael Barber, chief education advisor to Pearson in the UK.
- Frederick M. Hess, resident scholar and director of education policy studies at the right-wing American Enterprise Institute.
- Colorado State Senator Michael Johnston, a Democrat and an educational advisor to Barack Obama, who became an expert on education during the two years he spent in Mississippi as part of Teach for America, and of course, Wendy Kopp, founder and chair of the board of Teach For America.
- Representing Rupert Murdoch and Fox News is Joel I. Klein, CEO of the Educational Division and executive vice president of News Corporation.
- Representing the anti-teachers union movement are Jim Larson, director of special projects at Educators 4 Excellence, and Celine Coggins, founder and CEO of Teach Plus.
- Charter school companies are represented by Mike Feinberg, co-founder of the Knowledge Is Power Program (KIPP), and Michael A. Goldstein, founder and CEO of the Media and Technology Charter High School in Boston.
- Also on the board of advisors are Eric Hanushek, a senior fellow at the Hoover Institute, and Stefanie Sanford, chief of Global Policy and Advocacy for the College Board who previously spent ten years at the Bill and Melinda Gates Foundation.

NCTQ and its highly critical study of teacher education programs was funded by the usual suspects, the Bill and Melinda Gates Foundation, the Eli and Edythe Broad Foundation, Carnegie Corporation of New York, the Michael and Susan Dell Foundation, the Joyce Foundation which equates school reform with charter schools, and the Teaching Commission, founded by former IBM chairman and CEO Louis V. Gerstner, Jr.

But there are also a few surprises representing right-wing pro-entrepreneurial groups among NCTQ's funders. They include the Lynde and Harry Bradley Foundation, which is committed to preserving and defending the tradition of free representative government and private enterprise; the Laura and John Arnold Foundation, which supports rigorous and comprehensive entrepreneurial problem-solving approaches; the Searle Freedom Trust which defends individual freedom and economic liberty; and the Ewing Marion Kauffman Foundation, whose mission is to promote the powerful economic impact of entrepreneurship and that runs its own charter school in Kansas City.

Excuse me. Which of these people and groups can actually be trusted to evaluate teachers and schools or to place the needs of American children first?

B. We Need to Make Eye Contact

Based on an essay published on the *Huffington Post*, April 22, 2010
www.huffingtonpost.com/alan-singer/we-need-to-make-eye-conta_b_
546974.html

Questions to Consider

1. What should someone know before becoming a teacher?
2. What would genuine educational reform look like?
3. Why do teachers and politicians seem to disagree on what constitutes good teaching?

Change is not automatically good. When the weather changes from sunny to rainy we do not usually celebrate. Reform suggests improvement. But people do not always agree on what will make things better. Change for the sake of change certainly does not mean reform. Neither does change that makes things worse.

In April 2010, the New York State Board of Regents, the governing body that makes educational decisions in the state, unanimously enacted changes in teacher certification. I wish I could say that these changes were reforms, there certainly is a need for reform. However, my feeling is that the changes are foolish, at best window dressing, but potentially destructive.

The regents decided to allow, as a pilot program, Teach for America and the New York City Teaching Fellows to grant master's degrees in education, circumventing university-based teacher education programs. Their justification was that the universities were too focused on abstract notions, such as the role of schools in a democracy, and concerns that schools perpetuate social inequality. The change was designed to enhance the state's application for federal Race to the Top money.

According to the New York State Learning Standards,[8] teachers are supposed to encourage their students to utilize higher-order thinking in all grade-levels. But apparently, the regents consider teachers themselves to be too stupid to think very hard.

The Commissioner of the New York State Department of Education wanted practical instruction for teachers such as telling them to make eye contact with students, to call on students by name, and to wait for fuller answers when they ask questions. I have nothing against this advice, but is the commissioner really prepared to give a master's degree to someone based on these three things? Are you awarded a master's degree for making eye contact? That certainly will bring schools, teaching, and students into the twenty-first century.

But shouldn't teachers also know something about their subject and how to teach it to students on different academic and grade levels? Perhaps teachers should also know something about planning lessons and units, how schools are organized, debates in education, adolescent behavior, how child learn, how to promote reading, and ways to reach students with special needs.

If these recommendations were not made by a state education commissioner they would have been dismissed as a joke. That they were made by a state education commissioner is very scary. That the Obama-Duncan, state, and local "edu-deform" regimes are promoting these changes as significant reforms is outright frightening.

Big ideas and small-scale practices need to be integrated so that teachers can become thinkers, curriculum creators, concerned counselors, and school leaders, rather than just people who follow scripts and hand out punishments and rewards. That type of training takes time and hard work and it merits a master's degree. In the real world, it takes about three to five years of practice with a lot of support to become an effective teacher. But Teach for America and the New York City Teaching Fellows have such high turnover rates that virtually everyone quits before they learn what they are supposed to do.

The regents' plan and the federal Race to the Bottom grants are all really about de-professionalizing teaching in inner-city schools so they can hire low-paid temporary workers with little training who will follow scripts and be too afraid to question what is going on. If these were real reforms we would see teachers being hired this way in elite schools and suburban communities, but those parents would never stand for it.

City, state, and federal governments are promoting these deform plans because they do not want to address, probably have no idea how to address, the real problems confronting education in the United States. They also want to distract public attention from their gross mismanagement of the economy. It is easier to blame teachers and teacher education programs than it is to promote genuine reform.

Declining revenues are forcing states and localities to drastically cut school budgets. In 2010 California proposed laying-off twenty-two thousand teachers and Illinois seventeen thousand. New York City warned that fifteen thousand teachers might be let go. Meanwhile families were in distress because official national unemployment remained about 10%, with pockets of unemployment in some communities well over 20%. Was this the time to propagate new paths to teacher certification? Are there going to be that many new jobs?

The technocrats, both Democrats and Republicans, who govern the United States think they can solve major social problems with minor adjustments and a few twists of the dial because they are so smart. These guys have become so blinded by their own arrogance that they have grown stupid.

My grandchild asked me not to use the word "stupid" because it is banned as mean in their kindergarten classroom. Some of my colleagues and former students who are now teachers have also asked me why I get so sarcastic in some of my posts. I guess I am feeling a little desperate about what is happening in our schools and country. I hope with my sarcasm I can make "eye contact" with the arrogant and take them down a peg. Jon Stewart of "The Daily Show" has become my hero. We need more people to shout out, "The emperor has no clothes."

C. Arizonafication of Teacher Education

Based on essays published on the *Huffington Post*, July 6 and 12, 2011
www.huffingtonpost.com/alan-singer/cancel-my-subscription-to_b_887029.
html
www.huffingtonpost.com/alan-singer/arizonafication-of-teache_b_893219.
html

Questions to Consider

1. Should Arizona schools be models for schools in other states?
2. Do you want your children to have teachers with online certification from suspect schools that are based in other parts of the country?

In July 2011, the *New York Times* "Knowledge Network" announced a joint enterprise with Rio Salado College,[9] an online community college that is part of the Maricopa Community College system, which is based in the Phoenix, Arizona, area and not one of the leading educational institutions in the United States, to provide an alternative path to teacher certification. Rio Salado also offered initial certificates for entry-level positions in substance-abuse counseling, as flight attendants, and in customer service at banks and insurance agencies.

Rio Salado, while a public community college, was not part of the Arizona state university system, and was accredited by the Higher Learning Commission of the North Central Association of Colleges and Schools, which accredits many of the major proprietary, or for-profit, edu-businesses in the United States. The Higher Learning Commission was in the process of conducting an internal "investigation" of its member institutions, including the University of Phoenix, the nation's largest private "university," which was charged by the federal government General Accounting Office with unscrupulously recruiting people eligible for federal financial aid who had no hope of achieving any type of credentials or jobs.

The Goldwater Institute, a Phoenix, Arizona-based conservative public policy research organization, has been especially critical of the Maricopa Community Colleges.[10] It called Maricopa, which receives local property tax dollars and pays bloated administrative salaries with 460 employees making over $100,000 per year in 2010, a "dropout factory" with only 16.9% of the community college district's full-time students graduating after three years, although Rio Salado, at 45%, has the best graduation rate in the system.[11]

I hope I am not so entrenched in tradition that I dismiss all alternatives. My problem is not tradition, but the state of education in Arizona and the potential Arizonafication of education in the United States. What follows is a brief list describing the state of education in Arizona. School boards around the country and state education departments must decide if this is the quality of education they want to offer people in their communities and whether a teacher certification program based in Arizona is going to provide the quality of teachers that they want working in their schools and teaching their children.

1. An analysis by the Arizona Education Network published by the Arizona Department of Education "shows a significant decrease in the number of excelling schools in Arizona. In 2008–2009 there were 321 traditional schools and 74 charter schools excelling in the state. In 2009–2010 the number of excelling school dropped to 221 traditional and 51 charter. While changes to the AIMS test may explain part of the difference, it is likely that three years of significant cuts to school funding, including the elimination of many gifted programs, is now affecting our best schools."[12]
2. According to an editorial in the *East Valley Tribune*:[13] "Arizona lawmakers, struggling like so many of their counterparts across the nation to make ends meet, got some sobering words this week from executives, who said the state is not producing the caliber of high school and college graduates we need to turn the economy around. But it didn't stop legislators from endorsing a budget proposal that savages state aid to public schools, cuts contributions to community colleges by more than half and forces universities to dig even deeper in the face of record enrollment."
3. According to the National Assessment of Educational Progress,[14] Arizona fourth- and eighth-graders perform below the national average in math.
4. Only two states scored below Arizona on a 2009 national science assessment given to a sample of students.[15]
5. A 2005/2006 EPE Research "Report Card on American Education: Ranking State K–12 Performance, Progress, and Reform" reported that Arizona ranked fiftieth in the United States in per student spending adjusted to regional cost differences.[16]
6. The American Legislative Exchange Council, a conservative think tank committed to free markets and limited government, ranked education in Arizona forty-fifth out of fifty-one states and the District of Columbia.[17]
7. According to the United States Census Bureau,[18] Arizona ranked thirty-ninth out of fifty-one in the number of residents who have at least a high school diploma.

Shame on Arizona and shame on the *New York Times* for partnering with the Maricopa Community Colleges to offer online teacher certification.

Post-It Note: A member of the Maricopa County Community College District Governing Board responded to this blog.[19] He wrote: "It appears Mr. Singer is long on criticism and very short on detail. . . . This is a new certification program so there's no data on its success yet. It's a program that breaks tradition with typical teacher preparation colleges. I hope Mr. Singer is not so entrenched in his traditions that he dismisses all alternatives." On July 31, 2012, the New York Times Corporation closed down its Knowledge Network.

D. Anger in the Heartland over Unfair Teacher Tests

Based on an essay published on the *Huffington Post*, October 7, 2013
www.huffingtonpost.com/alan-singer/anger-in-the-heartland-ov_b_4044596.
html

Questions to Consider

1. Why are these teacher education students so angry?
2. Are they being treated fairly?
3. Will proposed reforms improve teacher education and teacher performance?

Cortland, New York, is dairy country. The town and the State University of New York campus in Cortland are surrounded by dairy farms. Many of the students at the college come from the local area. This is where they grew up and this is where they want to stay. Many plan to become teachers in the local schools. But there is anger brewing in this heartland community over unfair new teacher tests.

On October 1 and 2, I visited SUNY-Cortland and nearby SUNY-Oneonta where I was invited to discuss corporate influence over education policy in the United States, the new teacher certifications, and the implications of Common Core standards for classroom practice. At both campuses I spoke with packed crowds and as is usually the case, I think I learned more from them than they learned from me.

At SUNY-Cortland the opposition to unfair teaching tests was more pronounced and better organized. Students are outraged at the attitude of the governor toward public school students and teachers. Instead of providing money and support to struggling schools and school districts, as is his constitutional responsibility, he outrageously called for the "death-penalty" for poorly performing schools.

Prospective teachers are also deeply upset by the governor's call to raise the undergraduate grade point average needed by students for admission into teacher education programs at the State University. They worked hard for their grades and to become teachers, but some started out in other majors where they did not perform as well and feel they are being unjustly penalized. They also demanded to know what evidence there is that a higher grade point average actually makes you a better teacher. One student in the audience claimed Governor Cuomo would fail the Common Core exams because he expressed opinions without providing supporting evidence. Another shouted out, "Show me the Carfax."

Two of the pre-service teachers, Melissa Howard and Ryan Aldrich, both undergraduates at SUNY-Cortland, organized an online petition protesting against a new portfolio submission for teacher certification that requires a teaching video. It is scheduled to go into effect in May 2014.

They protested against both the cost of the test and additional expenses and other mandated tests that they estimate at $500 per student. They also protested against the plan itself, which is being implemented and evaluated by the private testing mega-giant Pearson.

Howard and Aldrich charged that the guidelines for the video are unclear, the wording is vague, and the requirements contradict best practice in the educational literature. They do not understand how a company like Pearson with a history of testing irregularities was put in charge of teacher certification in New York State.

The petition included a series of questions about issues they find the most troubling:

> Who is evaluating our work?
> Are the people evaluating our work qualified enough to do so? How long are scorers taking to evaluate our work?
> We have seen that they have two hours—is that really enough time?
> Are we ever going to receive feedback about our assessment from Pearson?
> Are we responsible for maintaining the confidentiality of our students in videos even after we have completed student teaching?

Howard and Aldrich demanded the suspension of edTPA as a certification requirement until it has gone through multiple levels of pilot testing. Along with other SUNY-Cortland students they sent letters to members of the State Assembly Education Committee hoping they would be willing to discuss the matter.

The anger in the heartland is more than justified. An examination of the guidelines for new teacher certification exams published on the New York State Teacher Certification Examinations website raises even more questions about the validity of the tests.[20]

The sample reading passage from the ALST (Academic Literacy Skills Test),[21] a test supposedly designed to assess the "academic literacy" of prospective teachers, is about Gertrude Stein, who operated a salon for artists in Paris during the 1920s. The passage has nothing to do with teaching, the evaluation of students, or the knowledge teachers are expected to possess. Even worse, like other Pearson-developed tests the questions people are expected to answer are ambiguous and the choices are confusing.

One questions asks readers:

The sentence below appears in Paragraph 2:

> It was that her way of thinking and seeing, her curiosity about the collision of old and new, was perfectly tuned for a moment when Europe was, cataclysmically, struggling with that collision.

Which phrase is closest in meaning to the word "cataclysmically" as it is used in the sentence above?

a.   with furious upheaval
b.   with unrelenting violence
c.   with reckless abandon
d.   with shocking suddenness

The question calls for the opinion of the reader, not the identification of a fact, and all of these choices are potentially correct. However for Pearson, there is only one right choice. The only acceptable answer is "A."

According to the test guide,[22] "This item requires examinees to interpret words and phrases as they are used in a text. As it is used in this sentence, the word cataclysmically refers to the cultural upheaval resulting from the clash between a traditional way of life and the new sensibilities that found expression in the work of modernist writers and artists."

Meanwhile, according to the New York State teacher certification website, the edTPA content test and video guidelines are still in draft form and were last updated on August 6, 2013. The site includes the warning: "The materials posted here are revised drafts. The information in these documents is expected to change, and any changes will fully supersede the information contained in this draft. Subsequent revised versions will be posted here as they become available."[23]

According to the latest "draft" posted at the American Association of Colleges for Teacher Education (AACTE) edTPA Resource Library website,[24] in one to three unedited video segments totaling twenty minutes, student teachers must demonstrate classroom "respect and rapport." Candidates are told "As you go through your footage, you will want to find clips that not only feature respectful interactions between your students and you but also among your students." Candidates must also "demonstrate a positive learning environment that supports and challenges students;" "show active engagement of students in their own understanding of the concepts, skills, and/or processes related to the learning objectives;" demonstrate how they are "deepening student understanding;" and provide a "subject-specific pedagogical focus."

As the students at Cortland said, while it may be possible to do these things in three video clips totaling twenty minutes if they had some idea what these things actually looked like in real classroom practice, they are going into the test blind.

Post-It Note: According to the edTPA website, members of the Teacher Performance Assessment Consortium include Colorado, Connecticut, Delaware, the District of Columbia, Georgia, Hawaii, Idaho, Illinois, Iowa, Indiana, Maryland, Massachusetts, Minnesota, New York, North Carolina, Ohio, Oklahoma, Oregon, South Carolina, Tennessee, Virginia, Washington, Wisconsin, and Wyoming.

E. Problems with Pearson's Student Teacher Evaluation System

Based on an essay published on the *Huffington Post*, October 14, 2013
    www.huffingtonpost.com/alan-singer/problems-with-pearsons-te_b_4093772.
html

Questions to Consider

1. Why are student teaching assessments with little established validity being promoted by Pearson and its non-profit partners?
2. Why did faculty at the State University of New York challenge Pearson's edTPA assessment of student teachers?
3. What do you think of the idea of Pearson-issued "merit badges" for teachers?

During the spring of 2013, four of my secondary education social studies students participated in a field test of the Pearson edTPA (Teacher Performance Assessment). They created elaborate online portfolios demonstrating planning, instruction, and assessment and including video segments from three lessons and sample student work. I cannot provide specific details about the assessment for student teachers because in order for my students and Hofstra University to participate in the field test I was required to sign a confidentiality agreement. However, information about edTPA is available online from the American Association of Colleges for Teacher Education.[25]

Three months later the Hofstra School of Education received from Pearson numbered ratings on each portion of the submission for each of the students. However, the evaluations did not include any comments on their strengths and weaknesses and there was no notice about what is considered a passing grade. The Pearson website simply says passing grades will be determined in the future for each cohort by individual states.

Hofstra University administrators recently received access to closed online edTPA material with sample teaching videos in different subject areas, but these were also unevaluated so again I could only guess at how they were rated.

University faculty who are supposed to prepare new teachers can only guess why the students who participated in the field test received the scores they received and how to help students improve in the future. Thirty-three states are listed as participating in edTPA, but only six of them have approved the performance assessment. They include New York, Tennessee, Georgia, Wisconsin, Minnesota, and Washington. I have no idea what education departments in these states will decide constitutes an acceptable score for certification or if they will ever agree, but the new tests are scheduled to go into operation in May 2014 anyway.

The edTPA website has answers to the commonly asked question, "What are the expected pass rates for edTPA?" But try to make sense out of the answer!

"Following additional analysis of the field test, a recommended passing standard that uses a professionally acceptable and credible standard-setting approach will be provided as a guide for states. As is the case with current licensing exams, each state adopting edTPA can elect to set its own passing score to determine who is permitted to practice in that state. This state-level process will determine the ultimate percentages of teacher candidates who pass the assessment."[26]

This response is especially curious because the national edTPA project is based on the Performance Assessment for California Teachers (PACT). In the 2009–2010 school year, one-third of California's applicants to teacher certification participated in PACT and 94% of them passed all sections on the first try. According to Linda Darling-Hammond, a professor at Stanford University who worked with Pearson to design the edTPA, the national test, the high pass rate on the PACT was expected.[27]

But three questions occur right away:

1. If everybody passes, what do these tests actually test?
2. Is the same thing going to happen in all states that use the Pearson edTPA?
3. Is it fair that states use different passing scores when this is supposed to establish a national standard for teacher certification?

What a mess!

Currently the edTPA system is only being used to evaluate student teachers applying for state teaching certification. However, once it is up and running, and even if the bugs are never worked out, the system could potentially be used to evaluate working teachers as well. An even bigger mess awaits.

In the meantime, other problems with Pearson's edTPA keep popping up.

I received an email from a faculty member at Hobart and William Smith Colleges in Geneva, New York, that the director of Teacher Certification and Placement applied to the New York State Education Department for edTPA scholarships for twenty-four students who received federal Pell grants. Millie Savidge, coordinator, Office of Research and Information Systems, Higher Education of the State Education Department, replied to the request and informed the school that Pearson was responsible for distributing the vouchers.

On October 3, 2013, Eileen Cahill, director of Client Program Management Evaluation Systems Assessment and Instruction at Pearson informed Hobart and William Smith Colleges by email that the vouchers were in the process of being emailed to deans of education at the New York institutions and would be distributed by end of day October 4.

On October 7, 2103, Hobart and William Smith Colleges received an email from ESTestVoucher saying that New York State had "authorized Evaluations Systems to issue test fee e-vouchers for New York State Teacher Certification

Examinations (NYSTCE) for students in your Teacher Education programs. The e-vouchers were allocated proportionally to institutions based on the number of undergraduate Pell recipients reported by your institution."

Hobart and William Smith Colleges, which had twenty-four eligible students, received two vouchers for written exams and one voucher for the $300 edTPA!

Faculty at the State University of New York were so outraged by the lack of direction from Pearson on the edTPA assessments and possible bias that they organized an edTPA Alternative Scoring Consortium. According to Julie Gorlewski of SUNY-New Paltz they wanted to create their own alternative to the Pearson scoring set-up. In an email, Professor Gorlewski wrote "The worry is that edTPA will feed into an existing cycle in which the public school teaching population does not share cultural characteristics of the students it serves. A scoring consortium consisting of a partnership of public and private institutions reflecting a range of selectivity has the potential to address this critical issue. . . . We would develop a scoring process that reflects our own goals and desires for new teacher graduates (not an easy, but hopefully a joyful task). Then, we would ask 5–10 students at each institution to submit their work for this alternative scoring process (simultaneous to submitting their work to Pearson for "official" scoring of their edTPA portfolio)."

One last new Pearson tidbit borders on the ridiculous. Faced with intense opposition to its testing programs for students and teachers, Pearson has decided to issue merit badges to teachers who participate in its online "My Education Community" for teachers. Teachers "can earn badges by adding to discussions, commenting on articles, completing polls, contributing case studies, sharing resources, etc. Some of our badges have levels—bronze, silver, gold and platinum—so the more you engage the higher your level of achievement. Once you earn a badge it is yours to keep." Just like in the Boy Scouts, teachers can earn badges in instructional technology, course design, and syllabi. Apple badges are awarded for "great comments" that help other members. However my favorite is the "Future Hero" badge that I guess is for future heroes.

I frequently write about problems with Pearson testing programs. As former New York Yankee great Yogi Berra probably would have said, "It's like déjà vu all over again."

Notes

1. NCTQ, *Training Our Future Teachers: Classroom Management,* p. 6, www.nctq.org/dmsStage/Future_Teachers_Classroom_Management_NCTQ_Report.
2. Ibid., p. 93.
3. Ibid.
4. www.nctq.org/teacherPrep/ourApproach/support/endorsements.jsp.
5. Joy Resmovits, "Teacher Preparation Program Rankings Make U.S. News Debut," *Huffington Post* (June 18, 2013), www.huffingtonpost.com/2013/06/18/teacher-preparation-program-rankings_n_3456389.html?ncid=edlinkusaolp00000003&ir=Education.

6. Ibid.

7. www.edweek.org/ew/qc/2013/state_report_cards.html.

8. www.p12.nysed.gov/ciai/standards.html.

9. www.riosalado.edu/web/selfStudy/Rio%20SaladoCollege%20Self-Study%202012/
Resource%20Room%20Documents/Self-Study%20Criterion%205/RSC_NYT
ConsortialAgreementApplicationExec.Summary_5-2011.pdf

10. http://goldwaterinstitute.org/article/cancel-my-subscription-new-york-times.

11. http://goldwaterinstitute.org/article/arizonas-community-colleges-produce-
dropouts-not-graduates.

12. www.arizonaeducationnetwork.com/2011/06/az-achievement-profiles-show-top-
schools-suffering-from-budget-cuts/.

13. Editorial, "Our View: A Bleak Assessment of Education in Arizona," *East Valley Tribune*
(April 5, 2011), www.eastvalleytribune.com/opinion/article_a7071f04–5cc2–11e0–
9f49–001cc4c03286.html.

14. http://nces.ed.gov/nationsreportcard/mathematics/stateassessment.asp.

15. Michelle Reese, "Arizona Students Near Bottom in National Science Assessment,"
East Valley Tribune (January 25, 2011), www.eastvalleytribune.com/local/education/
article_350f7cc6–28af-11e0–89da-001cc4c002e0.html.

16. http://blog.bestandworststates.com/2009/01/29/state-rankings-on-education-
spending.aspx.

17. www.alec.org/docs/Report_Card_13.pdf.

18. www.census.gov/compendia/statab/cats/education/educational_attainment.html.

19. His comment was July 6, 2011. It is at www.huffingtonpost.com/alan-singer/cancel-
my-subscription-to_b_887029.html.

20. www.nystce.nesinc.com.

21. www.nystce.nesinc.com/STUDYGUIDE/NY_SG_SRI_202.htm.

22. Ibid.

23. www.nystce.nesinc.com.

24. www.nystce.nesinc.com/NY_annProgramUpdate.asp#TPA; http://edtpa.aacte.org/
news-area/2013–14-handbooks-are-now-available-in-the-resource-library.html.

25. http://edtpa.aacte.org.

26. http://edtpa.aacte.org/faq.

27. Jackie Mader, "Do New Exams Produce Better Teachers? States Act While Educators Debate," *Hechinger Report* (May 16, 2013), http://hechingerreport.org/content/
do-new-exams-produce-better-teachers-states-act-while-educators-debate_12057/.

4

TEACHERS UNIONS

In September 2012, unionized Chicago, Illinois, public school teachers went on strike for two weeks, closing one of the largest school systems in the United States. The strike took on national significance because Chicago Mayor Rahm Emanuel was a former chief of staff for President Barack Obama and a strong supporter of the president's Race to the Top program. The final settlement was a compromise that appeared to provide victories for both sides. The school day was lengthened; teachers agreed that they would be evaluated, at least partially, based on student scores on standardized tests; laid-off teachers with high performance ratings would have priority for available openings in new schools; and teachers received annual raises.

I like to see labor unions as a force for progressive change and greater economic and political democracy, but I have no illusions that this is always true. In the past and today, there are many cases where union leadership and unions have been autocratic, corrupt, restrictive, and limited. In a capitalist society such as the United States, especially in a hostile political environment, there is tremendous pressure on unions to collaborate with corporate interests and policies rather than to challenge them. But on balance, I want a country and a job where there is union representation. Labor unions are vital to national political and economic health in the United States.

I believe labor unions are essential to democracy. Collective organization of working people balances the power of capital and the wealthy. Labor unions help ensure government policies that benefit all people. Without labor unions there would have been no New Deal during the 1930s or Great Society during the 1960s. Labor unions were prominent in struggles for civil rights, women's rights, and social security. Without labor unions would be no such thing as weekends, vacations, or health benefits.

Globalization has undermined the labor movement in the United States since the 1960s as corporations abandoned communities in the United States in an effort to maximize profits. This has weakened the labor movement, especially in the private sector, and has left public sector workers isolated and vulnerable to political attack.

In 1983, 20% of the American workforce was unionized. It is now about 11%. But in the private sector only 6% of workers are unionized compared to about one-third of the public sector workforce. Private sector non-union workers increasingly identify as taxpayers, or as Whites, rather than as members of the working class, and resent other workers, especially Black and Latino workers, who are members of public sector unions and have union benefits.

In these posts I offer strong views on the need to reorganize and redirect the American Federation of Teachers and the National Educational Association if these unions are to survive as a meaningful force for and ally of public education. I believe teachers and their unions have the potential to be agents for progressive educational and social change, but I am not sure that they will. It means taking risks that their organizations so far do not appear willing to take.

A. Redefining and Rebuilding the Teachers Unions
B. Why I Am Pro-Union and Pro-Teacher
C. Chicago Teachers Strike for Us All
D. The "People's Budget" Movement

A. Redefining and Rebuilding the Teachers Unions

Based on an essay published on the *Huffington Post*, October 19, 2013.
www.huffingtonpost.com/alan-singer/teachers-unions_b_4132918.html

Questions to Consider

1. What is your position on the role of labor unions?
2. How should teachers unions respond to proposed reforms?
3. Should teachers unions be willing to challenge powerful politicians and companies even if it means violating the law?

While I am a strong supporter of the right of workers in both the public and private sectors to organize labor unions, I am not an uncritical supporter. I am pro-public education, pro-teacher, pro-student, and pro-union, but while their interests often overlap, they do not always, and when they do not I favor the students. Sometimes union leadership or its official position is wrong and needs to be challenged. In the 2013 New York City mayoral primary, the teachers union local, the United Federation of Teachers (UFT), endorsed a candidate primarily because he appeared most likely to give teachers a retroactive pay raise. Other candidates were more hesitant because the teachers' last contract expired in 2008 and the cost to the city of a retroactive pay raise for teachers and other municipal workers could be in the billions of dollars.

While teachers and municipal workers deserve a raise, there certainly were more pressing educational issues facing students and parents—and I argue facing teachers as well. They include school closings, charter schools, teacher assessments, and poor performance on new standardized tests, especially by Black and Latino students. My own experience with the leadership of the UFT during the past four decades is that while they consistently promote better education for students, especially when they are negotiating new contracts for teachers and want parental support, they inevitably drop all other demands in exchange for a pay raise, or in this case, for retroactive pay.

The two national teachers unions should definitely have more influence on education in the United States, but they share some of the responsibility for their own futility. Part of the problem is their schizophrenic nature as both bread-and-butter unions and as professional organizations that advocate for just and effective educational policies.

The American Federation of Teachers (AFT) has over 1.5 million members, including pre-K through twelfth-grade teachers; paraprofessionals and other school-related personnel; higher-education faculty and professional staff; federal, state, and local government employees; and nurses and other healthcare professionals. In addition, the AFT represents nearly 250,000 retiree members. The National Educational Association (NEA) is even larger. It has 3.2 million members including a half million teachers and other school personnel, 200,000 higher education employees, and almost 300,000 retirees. However, it is generally more involved in lobbying than in traditional union activities and does not actually represent that many teachers who have union recognition.

At the July 2013 AFT "TEACH Conference" in Washington, DC, national union President Randi Weingarten argued that the teachers union was a force for both progressive and education change. Among other actions, she spoke about how "the AFT and community partners from 12 cities throughout the country have organized a series of town hall community conversations aimed at developing 'bottom-up' solutions for struggling schools. In several cities, we're working together to fix, not close, struggling schools and to wrap services around those schools—because we know this helps kids and ensures that neighborhoods are not hollowed out." Among specific examples, she cited "Philadelphia, where, with our community partners, we are fighting draconian cuts that starve the schools to the point that they can no longer function."[1]

Unfortunately, given the AFT's history, it will have to go a long way to establish its credibility as a trusted partner with parent and other educational activist groups. In Chicago, teachers went out on strike in September 2012 with a list of demands that included smaller class sizes, an elected school board, support for children exposed to violence and poverty, and more social workers, counselors, audio/visual and hearing technicians, and school nurses. But in the end, the union settled for a three-year contract that included pay increases and a new evaluation system. A year later, the Chicago public school system, faced with a $1 billion deficit, closed fifty schools forcing thousands of students to travel to different schools in unfamiliar and sometimes unwelcoming neighborhoods. It was the largest school closing in United States history.

Karen Lewis, president of the Chicago Teachers Union called the school closings "a day of mourning for the children of Chicago. Their education has been hijacked by an unrepresentative, unelected corporate school board, acting at the behest of a mayor who has no vision for improving the education of our children."[2] However, this time the teachers' union did not go on strike, it would have been a violation of their contract, although it did join parent groups that organized a series of protests.

Both the AFT and the NEA will also have difficulty convincing anyone that they are serious about educational reform or workers rights when both organizations take millions of dollars from the Bill and Melinda Gates Foundation to champion the Gates school agenda. Between 2009 and 2013, the AFT accepted $11.3 million and the NEA over $7 million to promote Common Core standards and teacher assessments.

The AFT even describes the Gates Foundation as its partner. Meanwhile, Microsoft Corporation, founded by Bill Gates, is a notorious anti-union employer that outsources high-tech jobs overseas and calls its American workers contractors rather than employees so that they can be denied union collective bargaining rights.

One grievance that I have with the UFT and the AFT is that as unions they are fundamentally undemocratic. Most of the UFT Executive Board and union officers are elected at-large. This means that all members of the union, including retirees, vote for each position. In the 2013 union election, more than half of the votes cast for union officers came from retirees, which meant that the union leadership effectively represents them rather than working teachers. Since representation at the AFT national convention where national union elections take place is proportional and New York City is the largest local by far, union officials elected by New York City retirees control this national teachers' union. The role played by retirees tends to keep entrenched leadership in power and contributes to more conservative union policies.

This leadership's commitment to the sanctity of union contracts at all costs and its unwillingness to challenge even unfair labor laws is a major reason for its weaknesses. It has become risk-adverse. In New York State, the teachers' union has what is known as agency shop status. The state government designates the union as the official bargaining agent for all teachers whether they chose to be union members or not and as the administrator of benefit programs. In a process called check-off it also requires school districts to deduct membership dues or service fees from union members and non-members. The teachers union essentially becomes an agency of the state and union leaders its employees. Because the union loses these rights if its members go on strike in violation of state law and potentially a lot of money, there is tremendous pressure on union leadership to uphold the contract rather than to aggressively defend public education. The unions are so constrained by their unwillingness to strike that their largest function has become defending teachers who feel they were treated unfairly by supervisors, even when other teachers and union members in the building know the real problem is that the aggrieved teacher is not competent.

In places like New York City, where teachers had been without a new contract since 2008, the union leadership was afraid that any job actions, including a strike, would cost its members established benefits. However, when municipalities or school districts know you will not strike as in New York City, or will only strike for limited wage and hour demands as in Chicago, they have all the leverage and non-union allies have no reason to trust that unions will follow through on promises to support broader educational issues.

Whatever its benefit or lack of benefit for union members and their students, this system worked well for union leaders. The Unity Caucus, a political party within the union, has controlled most union offices since the early 1960s. National AFT President Randi Weingarten earns over $400,000 a year with an expense account that brings her remuneration to almost $500,000. The New York City local president earns about $250,000 a year with an even more generous expense account. National Education Association President Dennis Van Roekel earns over $360,000. In 2011, his salary, stipends, and other paid expenses were $460,060.

There are other options to just obeying anti-strike anti-union laws. In the 1940s, during World War II, coal miners defied the federal government and went on strike because their families were mired in poverty and due to speed-up in the mines that led to unsafe working conditions. In the 1960s the New York City local of the AFT went on strike twice in violation of the law and remained out even after union officials were sent to jail. In the 1970s I did some work with the United Electrical, Radio and Machine Workers Union (UE), a radical union that considered its contract at best a temporary truce between workers and employers; a tool to defend their rights, but nothing more. For example, in the union's national contract with General Electric, union locals retain the right to strike over grievances. More recently, in 2005, Transit Workers Local 100 closed the New York City subway and bus systems for five days in a strike that was illegal under the provisions of the Public Employees Fair Employment Act, also known as the Taylor law. There are penalties to breaking this and similar laws, but unless you are willing to break them, you are not really a labor union and cannot influence local, state, and national educational policy.

The kind of action I am calling for by teachers and their unions means developing a level of what used to be called working-class consciousness. In the post-Occupy Wall Street era it means supporting the 99%, even if the 1% offer you a sweetheart deal if you are willing to ally with them against other working people. It means recognizing the necessary relationship of teachers to the public and to parents. It means that we rise together or we do not rise at all. It means that the teachers unions can compromise on their own wages and hours, but not on their commitment to students and their families. In Chicago it would have meant keeping community schools from being closed for budgetary reasons was more important than a small wage increase.

Going on strike in defiance of the law is not easy and should not be done without carefully laying the groundwork for union and community support as was done in Chicago before the 2012 teachers strike, which was led by an insurgent caucus within the union. It is a multi-year endeavor that includes organizing the membership and preparing teachers for potential lost wages; supporting political candidates in elections, including third party candidates, who will be sympathetic to unions; and punishing the major parties when they do not deliver. It means lobbying for pro-union legislation, negotiating with an attitude, and providing financial and political support for allied parent and community groups. It means working with parents and community groups to define a good education and to make sure it is available to all children.

Before going on strike the union has to build a network of school-based leaders and insist that new teachers and minority group members are encouraged to play leadership roles. A dynamic union must insist on collective decision-making. It must be a union where officers do not get paid more than members and where local leadership is required to do the same job as everyone else. To convince parents, especially minority parents, and community groups that the teachers unions are serious, it means that the unions can no longer automatically defend incompetents and teachers who are disrespectful of the students and families in the communities where they work.

If teachers and their unions can do these things, I believe they can help revive the labor movement in the United States and transform education.

Post-It Note: A lead article in the September 26, 2103, issue of New York Teacher,[3] *a UFT publication, demanded to know, "Where is the curriculum?" It protested that teachers would be evaluated on new Common Core aligned tests but that teachers had not yet received Common Core aligned lessons and teaching material. What was missing in the article was any protest against scripted lessons, packaged material, and high-stakes assessments prepared and sold to the schools by for-profit companies. It appeared that the union had surrendered in the struggle by teachers to be curriculum creators and classroom decision-makers and in the struggle by teachers and parents against the high-stakes testing regime.*

B. Why I am Pro-Union and Pro-Teacher

Based on an essay published on the *Huffington Post*, April 16, 2010.

www.huffingtonpost.com/alan-singer/why-i-am-pro-union-and-pr_b_540403.html

Questions to Consider

1. Why are labor unions necessary in the United States today?
2. Should government protect the right of workers to organize labor unions?
3. How should teachers unions respond to the so-called educational "reform" movement?

I strongly support labor unions. Obama, Duncan, Bloomberg, and Klein, the educational czars in the United States and New York City, do not. But I have always worked for a living, and they are either members of the privileged rich or identify with them. Whatever his origins, Obama paid taxes on over $5 million in earnings in 2009.

In 1975, New York City laid off thirteen thousand teachers, including me; five thousand of us were laid off permanently. Without enough teachers, the Board of Education and mayor cut back the school day, eliminated electives, and put sixty students into high school classrooms designed for thirty-two. Students were hanging out of the windows and no learning took place. It was only the teachers union that forced city officials to reduce class size and transform the schools from warehouses into places where students learn.

When I was finally rehired three years later, the Board of Education tried to deny me pension credit from my previous service, claiming that I was only a temporary employee when I was let go in 1975. It was the teachers union that forced them to credit me with time put in. When principals and other administrators played favorites with teaching, buildings, and room assignments, it was always the union chapter that insisted that we all be treated equitably.

In 2010, the nation has been rocked by a methane gas explosion at the Upper Big Branch coal mine in Montcoal, West Virginia, about thirty miles from Charleston, West Virginia, the state capital. There were twenty-nine reported deaths at a coal mine and company, Massey Energy, that had repeatedly been cited by the federal Mine Safety and Health Administration for violations. It had a total of 1,342 violations between 2005 and 2010.

What the mainstream media ignored in its coverage of the Upper Big Branch mine disaster was that it was a non-union mine. The United Mine Workers of America virtually collapsed after 1978, its active membership declining from over 120,000 members to 14,152 in 2010.[4] Without union representation, workers were afraid to report unsafe conditions because they would be fired. Without union representation to pressure coal companies, politicians, and federal regulators, the American coal industry is in a race to the bottom as it enforces third-world labor standards, economic realities, and safety conditions on its workers.

That brings me back to the nation's schools. Barack Obama and Arne Duncan are pushing "reforms" that will emasculate, if not destroy, teachers unions. Race to the Top grants are predicated on ending union protection for teachers. Anti-union cities and states like Tennessee, Delaware, Florida, Georgia, and Washington, DC, are lauded as models for change.

The interests of unionized teachers and their students are not always identical. But they live together for six hours and twenty minutes a day, five days a week, 180 days a year. They develop bonds that connect them. While parents get stressed out by the pressures of life, teachers generally remain the best advocates for our children.

Just as in the coal mines, the destruction of teachers unions would silence the very voices that need to be heard. Without effective unions, teachers, who are in contact with students every day and who have the most experience motivating them and helping them learn, will be ignored by the pencil pushers and budget cutters who control the schools. Just as in the coal mines, Race to the Top will become a race to the bottom and our children will get hurt.

C. Chicago Teachers Strike for Us All

Based on an essay published on the *Huffington Post*, September 13, 2012
www.huffingtonpost.com/alan-singer/chicago-teachers-strike-f_b_1877178.html

Questions to Consider

1. Why was the Chicago teachers strike of national significance?
2. Did the Chicago teachers union strike for the children of Chicago?
3. Do teachers unions deserve public support?

First I want to clarify what I mean by "us all." I believe the Chicago teachers strike was an important stand in the battle to improve, even save, public education in the United States. The strike had the potential to benefit teachers, students, and parents, not only in Chicago but across the entire country, as well as both unionized workers and non-unionized workers. I hoped the strike would go down in history along with other labor actions, such as those in Homestead, Lawrence, Paterson, Ludlow, and Flint, that ultimately built the union movement in the United States and transformed life for what used to be known as the working class but what politicians today euphemistically refer to as the middle class. That is why I strongly supported this strike and why I wore a red T-shirt to work in support of the teachers and public education.

Of course everybody cannot be included in the "all." Conservatives as always were quick to take an anti-union stance. In 2012, Republican presidential candidate Mitt Romney quickly denounced the teachers union for having interests in conflict with those of the children. So did Chester Finn, head of the right-leaning Fordham Institute, who charged that teachers unions continued to strongly resist change.

The mayor of Chicago was clearly not part of the "all." He seemed determined to break the strike and the Chicago teachers union. Others who opposed the strike were the self-proclaimed educational reformers and their corporate and financial allies whose real goal was to break up the public school system in Chicago and the rest of the country in order to privatize and profit from its demise.

The Obama administration, because it had depended on union support for manpower and money, distanced itself from the dispute. Also because in many ways this was a strike against Obama administration policies, particularly its Race to the Top program that was trying to impose an evaluation system that many teachers and school-based administrators found unwieldy, unfair, and inaccurate. The mayor of Chicago, Rahm Emanuel, was formerly Obama's chief of staff and Secretary of Education Arne Duncan, who was charged with implementing Race to the Top and the new teacher assessments, formerly headed the Chicago school system.

I recommended that President Obama take a look at the Chicago Teachers Union website because it may be the only place he could learn the teachers' side of the story, which I saw as the real story.[5] The Chicago Teachers Union demands would benefit both parents and teachers while establishing fair play for workers. They were concerned that a new evaluation system mandated by Race to the Top "could result in 6,000 teachers (or nearly 30 percent of our members) being discharged within one or two years."[6] Chicago teachers, as well as teachers and school-based administrators, were "concerned that too much of the new evaluations will be based on students' standardized test scores. This is no way to measure the effectiveness of an educator. Further there are too many factors beyond our control which impact how well some students perform on standardized tests such as poverty, exposure to violence, homelessness, hunger and other social issues beyond our control."

The union made clear that it did not unilaterally oppose school reform. "We stand in solidarity with parents, clergy and community-based organizations who are advocating for smaller class sizes, a better school day and an elected school board. Class size matters. It matters to parents . . . Our children are exposed to unprecedented levels of neighborhood violence and other social issues, so the fight for wraparound services is critically important to all of us. Our members will continue to support this ground swell of parent activism and grassroots engagement on these issues. And we hope the Board will not shut these voices out."[7]

Among other things, the chronology supplied at the website made it clear that the strike could have been avoided if Chicago school officials and the mayor seriously addressed teacher concerns. In June 2012, an independent fact-finding commission found that Chicago wanted teachers to work 20% longer without a corresponding increase in pay. The fact-finding commission also recommended "a general wage increase of 2.25 percent for School Year 2012—essentially a cost of living increase" and "an additional increase of 12.6 percent to compensate teachers for working a longer school day and year representing a combined first-year increase of 14.85 percent."[8] Although the teachers' contract expired at the end of June, negotiations between the Chicago school administration and the teachers union were stalled all summer. Finally, in compliance with Illinois state law, the union filed a ten-day notice with the Illinois Education Labor Relations Board of its intent to strike on August 29, 2012. The reason parents were caught by surprise is that while the union acted responsibly, the city administration did not take the strike threat seriously and prepare for contingencies.

The Chicago Teachers Union President Karen Lewis made a clarion call that resonates with me and should resonate with anyone who supports public education and genuine school reform. At a rally in Chicago she declared, "This fight is for the very soul of public education, not just only Chicago but everywhere. We did not start this fight, but enough is enough."[9]

To that I say, "Amen"!

D. The "People's Budget" Movement

Based on an essay published on the *Huffington Post*, May 9, 2011.
www.huffingtonpost.com/alan-singer/nyc-teachers-take-on-the-_b_859091.html

Questions to Consider

1. Why would a mayor cut the education budget rather than tax wealthy individuals and businesses?
2. Do you support the priorities of the "People's Budget"?

On Friday, May 6, 2011, New York City Mayor Michael Bloomberg announced a proposed budget that required teachers and students to pay for the economic problems of the city, state, and nation. He called for the elimination of over six thousand teaching positions: two thousand by attrition and four thousand by lay-off. The United Federation of Teachers responded with a radical counter-proposal, a "People's Budget" for New York City, and organized mass protests including a march through Wall Street.

The teachers union declared: "All around us, teachers, public employees, poor and working people are under attack like never before. Here in New York City, the assault is being led by Mayor Bloomberg, and his weapon of choice is the budget. The mayor is proposing drastic cuts in his budget that would savage our city's most vulnerable citizens. All while protecting the only people in New York who could afford to give back and who aren't paying their fare share—Wall Street bankers and other millionaires."[10]

According to the coalition that supported the Wall Street march, "The Big Banks crashed our economy, destroying jobs, foreclosing on millions of homes and wrecking city and state budgets across the country. After trillions in taxpayer funded bailouts, Wall Street is making billions in profits and giving away record bonuses to CEOs. But our communities are still hurting. Here in New York City, tens of thousands have lost their homes and their jobs. Now, Billionaire Mayor Mike Bloomberg is proposing devastating budget cuts as the only solution to the economic crisis that Wall Street caused. Enough is Enough."[11]

The People's Budget included the following demands:

1. Save $120 million by ending special tax deductions for the city's five thousand millionaires.
2. Save over $100 million by regulating bank practices and eliminating "toxic interest rate swaps."
3. Save $185 million by preventing mortgage foreclosures that take property off of the tax rolls.
4. Save $120 million by terminating or renegotiating inappropriate municipal contracts with the banks.
5. Eliminate the $139 million in funding to privately operated charter schools.

Notes

1. http://www.aft.org/newspubs/press/weingarten072213.cfm.
2. www.ctunet.com/blog/president-lewis-statement-on-the-boards-decision-to-close-50-schools.
3. www.uft.org/news-stories/where-curriculum.
4. www.wsws.org/en/articles/2010/01/pers-j12.html.
5. www.ctunet.com.
6. http://www.commondreams.org/view/2012/09/10.

7. Ibid.
8. http://extranews.net/chicago-teachers-union-responds-to-fact-finding-report.html.
9. http://cnsnews.com/news/article/chicago-teachers-union-president-strike-about-very-soul-public-education.
10. www.uft.org/campaigns/fight-back-may-5-and-may-12.
11. www.onmay12.org.

5

BUSINESS, POLITICS, AND SCHOOL DEFORM

Words are very important. They shape the way we think about ideas. During federal budget debates political opponents on the right and left argued over whether Americans should think of social security as an entitlement that has negative connotations because it is undeserved, or as an insurance policy that all working people contributed toward. Reform and reformer are other terms people fight over because we generally view reform as something that is positive. But reform loses its meaning when it is only a synonym for change, because we might not agree on which changes are actually good. I refuse to allow opponents of public education to capture the vocabulary of reform so I frequently call their proposals "so-called reforms" or school deform.

A major battle over school deform was fought out in Los Angeles, California (Los Angeles Times,[1] when an anti-teacher political action committee spearheaded by Mayor Antonio Villaraigosa received sizeable donations from around the country for its school board candidates. Money poured in from a number of the most prominent school deformers including New York City Mayor Michael Bloomberg, who gave $1 million; the California Charter Schools Association; the misnamed StudentsFirst, founded by former District of Columbia Schools Chancellor Michelle Rhee; and a subsidiary of Rupert Murdoch's News Corp.

Topics in this chapter include the presidential education agenda, connections between school and work, and the responsibility of schools for college and career readiness. In many ways the for-profit edu-corporations and their not-for-profit allies resemble a giant octopus with tentacles reaching into every facet of public education. A number of the essays in this chapter in one way or another address the pernicious influence of the corporate giant Pearson on education policy in the United States.

At the end of an episode of the television series "The Big Bang Theory," Dr. Sheldon Cooper is outfoxed by one of his archrivals, minor television celebrity Will Wheaton from "Star Trek: The Next Generation." Sheldon's face clenches into a twisted tree gnarl and as the camera zooms out so viewers feel they are inside a version of Google Earth, he lets out an eternal scream "W-H-E-E-E-A-T-O-N!!!!" that can be heard galaxies away. Sometimes that is how I feel about the educational mega-giant Pearson. P-E-A-R-S-O-N!!!!

A. Matt Damon Can't Save the Schools
B. Opposition Grows to School Deform
C. Higher Education for the Twenty-First Century
D. Hacking Away at the Pearson Octopus
E. Pearson "Education"—Who Are These People?
F. Los Angeles Students Outfox Apple, Pearson, and the School Board

A. Matt Damon Can't Save the Schools

Based on an essay published on the *Huffington Post*, August 1, 2011
www.huffingtonpost.com/alan-singer/saving-public-education_b_915337.
html

Questions to Consider

1. Why was the Save Our Schools rally disappointing?
2. What do you think of John Kuhn's speech?
3. Would you participate in direct action to defend education in the United States?

Matt Damon gave a great speech at the July 2011 Save Our Schools Rally in Washington, DC. Matt's mom, a teacher educator from the Boston area, told the crowd she was very proud of him. Diane Ravitch, Debbie Meier, Jonathan Kozol, who have been involved in what Ravitch calls the "Great School Wars" for decades, and John Kuhn, a superintendent of schools at a microscopic North Texas school district (two schools and 397 students) also spoke well. Kuhn, particularly, gave a rousing speech. But great speeches are not enough to build a social movement. Even John Stewart's humorous pre-taped comments won't do it. It was very hot on Saturday. But while I am glad I attended the rally, listened to the speeches, and marched around the White House, I was also very disappointed. Five thousand participants will not save the public school system.

The demands of the rally were actually quite moderate and reasonable, and that was part of the problem. People were not angry enough. They asked for equitable funding for all public school communities, an end to high-stakes testing for student, teacher, and school evaluation, curricula developed for and by local school communities, and teacher and community leadership in forming public education policies.

Public school advocates face a powerful coalition willing to dismantle public education in the United States for a variety of reasons. Teachers and teachers unions, branded as over-paid, liberal, and obstructionist in the right-wing media, make easy targets.

Desperate parents grasp at "reform" straws hoping to offer a better future to their own children, even if others are left behind. Right-wing and religious ideologues want to operate their own schools. Clueless politicians, including President Obama, who send their own children to fancy and expensive private schools, are eager to assign blame but short on solutions. Technology companies and publishers hope to de-professionalize teaching so they can market their "wonders" to ill-prepared parents without interference. Anti-union/anti-teacher business groups, hedge fund operators, and pseudo-philanthropists wanted to privatize education on a business model so that they and numerous assorted corporate vultures can pick at the carcass of public education. It is going to be hard to defeat this coalition.

John Kuhn, superintendent of the Perrin-Whitt Consolidated Independent School District in Texas was especially inspirational at the rally and his speech can help empower the resistance to school deform:

> I stand before you today proudly bearing the label of unacceptable because I educate the children they will not educate. . . . Public school teachers, you are the saviors of our society and always have been. You are the first responders standing in this rubble while they sit in their offices and write judgmental things about you on their clipboards. . . . Bail out the bankers and bankrupt the teachers. We will still teach. I'm not in it for the money. I'm not in it for the benefits. I'm in it because it is right. I'm in it because the children . . . need somebody like me in their lives. I will teach these kids.[2]

Post-It Note: I have a suggestion for future actions. I propose an annual day of absence the day before election day when all the teachers in the United States call in sick. People could go to the doctor during the day for appointments and absence notes and then gather at four in the afternoon in every town square to demand respect for schools, students, and teachers. Teachers could leave substitute lessons for students explaining why they were missing and why learning is important.

B. Opposition Grows to School Deform

Based on an essay published on the *Huffington Post*, January 24, 2013
    www.huffingtonpost.com/alan-singer/opposition-grows-to-schoo_b_2533623.html

Questions to Consider

1. Why are high-stakes tests continually used for purposes other than the ones for which they were designed?
2. Should schools be closed without taking into account the wishes of a community and the broader impact of the closing?

In his recent 2013 State of the Union address, President Barack Obama promised "A country that leads the world in educating its people." In his second inaugural address he promised to "reform our schools" as part of his administration's effort to promote "equality" and defend this country's "most ancient values and enduring ideals." But despite these promises, a growing number of parents and teachers are unhappy with his showcase program, Race to the Top. They argue it is the antithesis of the education, justice, and equality he claims is central to his ideas and American values.

In January 2013, the battleground in the debate over whether Obama-initiated school reforms actually deform education in the United States was Garfield High

School in Seattle, Washington. At Garfield, teachers organized a boycott of standardized tests, the Measures of Academic Progress (MAP), used to evaluate students and teachers. The governing board of the Seattle Public Schools system also decided to review MAP and other tools used for assessing students and teachers. The school district uses MAP tests to track student progress and as part of its evaluation of teacher performance. Garfield High School teachers called the MAP testing regime useless at best and even harmful to many students. In 2013, MAP tests were being used by six thousand school districts across the country in grades Kindergarten through ninth. Garfield teachers argued that the tests were not aligned with school curricula so they did not measure what is actually taught in classes. In addition, the tests, designed and marketed by the Northwest Evaluation Association, were never intended for use in evaluating teachers. The test boycott was endorsed by the National Center for Fair and Open Testing (FairTest) and the American Federation of Teachers. An online petition signed by leading educators in the United States supported the boycott.

At the same time, pressure was growing to oppose what are considered the arbitrary and discriminatory closing of public schools because of Race to the Top mandates. Students, parents, and advocacy representatives from eighteen major United States cities testified at a hearing before the United States Department of Education in Washington, DC, on January 29, 2013, and rallied in front of the building and at the Martin Luther King, Jr. Memorial. They demanded that the Department of Education declare a moratorium on school closings and design a plan to support community school improvement. Organizers also requested, but did not receive, a meeting with President Obama. According to organizers, at least ten cities filed or were in the process of filing Title VI Civil Rights complaints with the United States Department of Education Office of Civil Rights arguing that school closings discriminated against low-income, minority communities.

C. Higher Education for the Twenty-First Century

Based on an essay published on the *Huffington Post*, July 3, 2012
www.huffingtonpost.com/alan-singer/higher-education-for-the-_b_1642764. html

Questions to Consider

1. What does a twenty-first century job look like?
2. What should the role of schools be in preparing students for future work?
3. How do you view my proposals?

I do not know what a twenty-first century job looks like. As much as they talked about education preparing young people for twenty-first century jobs, I do not think the 2012 presidential candidates Barack Obama and Mitt Romney had a clue either. Based on the impact of technological change on the workforce during the last century, I do not think anyone really knows for sure.

Image a debate between William McKinley (Republican) and William Jennings Bryan (Democrat), major party presidential candidates in 1900. When the discussion came to jobs, they would have promised to better prepare Americans for twentieth century jobs. But the jobs they were most familiar with would have mostly been on farms and in factories. And the workers would have been as young as ten years old. In 1900 there were about thirty million working people in the United States counting everyone over the age of ten. While some states had begun to restrict child labor, there were no federal restraints on child labor until 1916 and those were overturned two years later by the Supreme Court.

Virtually none of the jobs they would have wanted schools to prepare American young people to perform even exist in the United State anymore. Common jobs at the beginning of the twentieth century included hod carriers, rail straighteners, blacksmiths, moulders, turners, wire drawers, pick miners, shot firers, glass blowers, and mule drivers; jobs that soon disappeared. Seven thousand children worked as newsboys in 1900. There were ten million skilled and unskilled manual workers. The largest groups of manual workers included 1.5 million factory workers and over 600,000 coal miners. Two and a half million people worked as service workers in 1900, which included housekeepers and laundresses. Almost eleven million people worked on farms.

According to the Historical Statistics of the United States prepared by the Bureau of the Census,[3] in 1900 there were 134,000 stenographers/typists/secretaries but no computer designers, programmers, or operators—because there were not any computers. By 1950 there were 1.6 million stenographers/ typists/ secretaries and in 1970 3.9 million. These were major sources of employment for women entering the work force up until the last couple of decades of the twentieth century. But with the development of computers and new audio and recording technologies stenography has disappeared, typing is a lost art, and secretaries are becoming less necessary.

All this is the long-way-around of saying that higher education cannot just be about preparing people for specific jobs, because those jobs might not be around much longer. One futuristic website predicts the key areas for job growth during the next decade as biomedical engineers, data communications analysts, and home health aides and attendants.[4] The first two sound like you can build a career in the field, unless of course it becomes outsourced to another country where the work can be done more cheaply. The second two are low skill and low wage.

Higher education is going to have to be about preparing people to think and problem solve so they can adapt to change. It is also going to have to be about preparing people to be thoughtful participants and activists in a democratic society.

Unfortunately, right now higher education in the United States is trapped in a series of crises, many of which are related to cost and some to corporate raiders looking to privatize the more profitable pieces.

If higher education is going to prepare Americans for any type of future, reform is desperately needed. These are my short-term changes and long-range proposals.

Short-Term Changes:

1. Empower the federal Office of Post-Secondary Education in the United States Department of Education to actively regulate post-secondary public, private, and proprietary schools.
2. Immediate federal regulation of all post-secondary, for-profit proprietary schools that engage in interstate commerce to ensure the quality of programs, graduation and job placement rates, and honest advertising. Close proprietary programs that do not meet federal post-secondary standards.
3. Immediate federal regulation of all higher-education colleges, community colleges, and universities who want their students to be eligible for federal Pell grant loans and loan guarantees (FAFSA) to ensure the quality of programs, graduation and job placement rates, and honest advertising.
4. Immediate federally financed cancellation of all public and private students loans—interest and principal. Student debt now exceeds one trillion dollars and is a crippling anchor on the American future.[5]
5. Investigation of online programs and courses to determine whether they provide students with quality college-level education on par with regular college programs.
6. Apply guidelines similar to No Child Left Behind and Race to the Top to ensure that all demographic groups are served by post-secondary school programs.

Long-Range Proposals:

1. Free public higher education for all qualified students modeled on the old CUNY system and systems in Scandinavian countries, especially the program in Denmark that provides students with a monthly stipend while they continue their higher education.
2. Voluntary integration of private non-profit colleges into a federal public college system.
3. Direct federal aid to state and federal public universities to replace student loan system.
4. No public money to remaining private universities.
5. Federal employment programs with private partners to fully utilize the skills of college graduates.

D. Hacking Away at the Pearson Octopus

Based on an essay published on the *Huffington Post*, May 8, 2012
    www.huffingtonpost.com/alan-singer/hacking-away-at-the-pears_b_1464134.html

Questions to Consider

1. Should a conservative group in Texas be able to determine what is included in textbooks across the country?
2. How much, if any, influence should for-profit companies and private foundations have on education policies?
3. Where are the checks on Pearson's influence over education in the United States?

In many ways the for-profit edu-corporations and their not-for-profit allies resemble a giant octopus with tentacles reaching into every facet of public education in the United States. I am reminded of the book *The Octopus* (1901) by Frank Norris that detailed the way railroads at the start of the nineteenth century controlled every facet of business and individual life. There is also a famous political cartoon from 1904 that portrays the Standard Oil monopoly as a giant octopus controlling state and national governments.

This giant octopus is strangling public education in both blatant and subtle ways. For example, on the surface the 2000 and 2003 editions of the popular middle school United States history book *The American Nation* barely differ. Both editions list the publisher as Prentice-Hall in association with American Heritage magazine. However, in the 2003 edition Prentice-Hall was listed as a sub-division of Pearson.

What does it mean that Prentice-Hall became a sub-division of Pearson and that *The American Nation* was a Pearson publication?

The 2000 edition of *The American Nation* was reviewed by a committee of eleven middle school teachers, including one from New York State and two, or 18%, from Texas. For the 2003 Pearson edition, the review committee was expanded to twenty-two classroom teachers, with seven, or 32%, from Texas. In addition, there was one representative each from Virginia, Arkansas, Georgia, Tennessee, Alabama, and Idaho and still only one from New York State.

Anyone familiar with coverage of the 2008 and 2012 presidential elections knows that this review committee leans heavily toward teachers from the most conservative "Red" or Republican states. What Pearson is doing is tilting the coverage of United States history to win approval from school boards in these states, and in doing this, allowing the most conservative school boards in the nation to determine what gets taught in American schools.

The seven Texas teachers on the review board teach in a state where the ideologically-driven state curriculum requires them to teach about Judeo-Christian influences of the nation's Founding Fathers, but not the reasons they supported the

principle of separation of church and state. It describes the United States government as a "constitutional republic" instead of a "democratic" system. Texas standards promote the idea that the United States is somehow different from all other
countries, a point of view known as of "American exceptionalism," and champions unregulated free enterprise without what it considers excessive government
interference. A *New York Times* editorial charged that the "social conservatives
who dominate the Texas Board of Education" had created an ideologically driven
curriculum.[6]

Teachers and parents could recommend that their school districts use a different middle school United States history textbook. However, Pearson has been
expanding voraciously and controls what used to be the independent school textbook publishing companies Scotts Foreman, Longman, Addison-Wesley, Allyn &
Bacon, Silver, Burdette & Ginn, and the Macmillan Company, all in partnership
with Colonial Williamsburg, the Smithsonian Institute, the Discovery Channel,
MapQuest, and Inspiration Software. Partnership in these cases generally means the
other organizations get paid or receive donations to let Pearson use their names.

Pearson's influence over American education goes much deeper and it empowers right-wing forces in other ways as well. In the *New York Times,* columnist Gail
Collins reported that Pearson, "the world's largest for-profit education business,
which has a $32 million five-year contract to produce New York standardized
tests," also had "a five-year testing contract with Texas that's costing the state
taxpayers nearly half-a-billion dollars."[7] Because Pearson used the same questions
on different state exams, and because Pearson's contract with Texas was so much
larger than its contract with New York, that meant New York State assessments
were designed to satisfy requirements established by the very conservative Texas
Education Agency. That may be why the 2012 eighth-grade reading test had
questions about a race between a pineapple and a hare, rather than real issues such
as the arms race or the continuing impact of race in the United States.

Pearson's contract with New York State requires it to provide twenty to twenty-
five nationally normed multiple-choice questions per grade that are supposed to
meet a national educational standard. This permits New York State Education to
compare the performance of children from New York with children from other
states. According to a column that appeared on the *Washington Post* website,[8] "the
pineapple passage was part of this stipulation. The material was drawn from Pearson's item bank—material that had been seen in several other states handled by
the vendor." Pearson was obligated to provide New York State with "120–150
nationally-normed ELA and math items" on future exams, which means it will be
double-booking, making "money re-using previously developed items and selling
them to Albany. Afterward, the vendor can sell them to other states, having banked
a wealth of data showing how over one million more kids fared on its questions."

Pearson is also a key partner of the National Governors Association (NGA) and
Council of Chief State School Officers. In this capacity, it promoted the Common
Core standards, pushing Singapore as a model for education to the United States,

and promoting conferences for educational officials where they had the opportunity to explore emerging international methods, best practices, and policies with an eye to the ways in which they may apply to their local education contexts.[9] A number of state governments, including Illinois, investigated whether trips to exotic locations paid for by Pearson were actually attempts to buy influence. Pearson had $130 million worth of contracts with the state of Illinois alone. The NGA also partnered with the Pearson Foundation to create study guides that promoted the organization's role and the historical role played by state governors in the classroom.

The boundary between Pearson the foundation and Pearson the company is difficult to identify. The Pearson Foundation promoted the Common Core standards. Pearson the company marketed material to implement them. Pearson, it is not clear which one, and Kentucky collaborated to create the "first digital learning repository aligned to the Common Core State Standards. Kentucky, the first state to adopt the standards, uses Pearson's EQUELLA software to embed the standards in the Kentucky Learning Depot, the state's digital library and learning community. The EQUELLA software currently powers the Depot."[10]

In *Twenty Thousand Leagues Under the Sea* by Jules Verne (1870), Captain Nemo and the Nautilus were attacked by what is either a giant squid or octopus (depending on how you translate from the original French). Nemo and the crew had to chop off its tentacles with axes and harpoon the beast to escape. If public schools are going to survive the current attack by the for-profit edu-corporations and their not-for-profit allies, the United States will need a new Nemo with a bold crew of parents, teachers, and students to hack away at the corporate octopus.

Post-It Note: Susan Aspey, vice president for Media Relations at Pearson Public Affairs responded via email to two of my Huffington Post *essays.[11] On one occasion she said "my Pearson colleagues would welcome the opportunity to contribute to the discussion about the many salient issues facing parents, teachers and students today. I'd like to extend an invitation to meet in the near future in New York and introduce you to some of our researchers and experts who are working daily with educators to improve learning." I did not hear from Ms. Aspey again and the meeting never took place.*

E. Pearson "Education"—Who Are These People?

Based on an essay published on the *Huffington Post*, September 4, 2012
www.huffingtonpost.com/alan-singer/pearson-education-new-york-testing-_b_1850169.html

Questions to Consider

1. Should public education be a "for-profit" enterprise?
2. Are Pearson's managers qualified to make educational decisions or even recommendations?
3. Is it dangerous that the Pearson footprint seems to be everywhere in American education?

According to an article in *Reuters*,[12] an international news service based in Great Britain, "investors of all stripes are beginning to sense big profit potential in public education. The K–12 market is tantalizingly huge: The U.S. spends more than $500 billion a year to educate kids from ages five through 18. The entire education sector, including college and mid-career training, represents nearly 9 percent of U.S. gross domestic product, more than the energy or technology sectors."

Pearson, a British multi-national conglomerate, is one of the largest private businesses maneuvering for United States education dollars. The company had net earnings of £956 million or approximately $1.5 billion in 2011.

Starting in May 2014, Pearson Education will take over teacher certification in New York State as a way of fulfilling the state's promised "reforms" in its application for federal Race to the Top money. The evaluation system known as the Teacher Performance Assessment (TPA and edTPA) was developed at Stanford University with support from Pearson, but it will be solely administered and prospective teachers will be entirely evaluated by Pearson and its agents. Pearson advertised for current or retired licensed teachers or administrators willing to evaluate applicants for teacher certification. It was prepared to pay $75 per assessment.

The Pearson footprint appears to be everywhere and taints academic research as well as government policy. For example, the Education Development Center (EDC), based in Waltham, Massachusetts, is a "global nonprofit organization that designs, delivers and evaluates innovative programs to address some of the world's most urgent challenges in education, health, and economic opportunity." EDC works with "public-sector and private partners" to "harness the power of people and systems to improve education, health promotion and care, workforce preparation, communications technologies, and civic engagement."[13] In education, it is involved in curriculum and materials development, research and evaluation, publication and distribution, online learning, professional development, and public policy development. According to its website,[14] its funders include Cisco Systems, IBM, Intel, the Gates Foundation, and of course, Pearson Education, all companies or groups that stand to benefit from its policy recommendations.

EDC sponsored a study on the effectiveness of new teacher evaluation systems,[15] "an examination of performance-based teacher evaluation systems in five states," that Pearson is promoting, but there are two very big flaws in the study. First, of the five states included in the study, Delaware, Georgia, Tennessee, North Carolina, and Texas, four, Georgia, Tennessee, North Carolina, and Texas, are notorious anti-union states where teachers have virtually no job security or union protection, and Delaware used the imposition of new teacher assessments to make it more difficult for teachers to acquire tenure. In Texas, North Carolina, and Georgia collective bargaining by teachers is illegal. Tennessee, Texas, and North Carolina used the new assessments to make it easier to fire teachers and Georgia used the assessments to determine teacher pay. The second flaw is that the study draws no connection between the evaluation system and improved student learning.

According to the *Financial Times* of London,[16] a Pearson owned property, in what I consider a conflict-of-interests, Susan Fuhrman, the president of Teachers

College at Columbia University, has been a "Non-Executive Independent Director of Pearson PLC" since 2004 and a major stockholder in the company. Fuhrman also is "president of the National Academy of Education, and was previously dean of the Graduate School of Education at the University of Pennsylvania and on the board of trustees of the Carnegie Foundation for the Advancement of Teaching."

In official Pearson PLC reports available online,[17] Susan Fuhrman, president of Teachers College-Columbia University, is listed as a non-executive director of Pearson. As of February 29, 2012, she held 12,927 shares of Pearson stock valued at $240,000. As a non-executive director she also receives an annual fee of 65,000 or almost $100,000. Fuhrman has been a non-executive director since 2004 and has received a substantial sum, but not the $20 million I initially reported.

There has been resistance to Pearson's influence over American education. In May 2012, students and teachers in the University of Massachusetts Amherst campus School of Education launched a national campaign challenging the forced implementation of Teacher Performance Assessment. They argued that the field supervisors and cooperating teachers who guided their teaching practice and observed and evaluated them for six months in middle and high school classrooms were better equipped to judge their teaching skills and potential than people who had never seen nor spoken with them. They refused to participate in a pilot program organized by Pearson and to submit the two ten-minute videos of themselves teaching and a take-home test. They were supported by United Opt Out National, a website that organized a campaign and petition drive to boycott Pearson evaluations of students, student teachers, and teachers.[18]

The question that must be addressed is whether the British publishing giant Pearson and its Pearson Education subsidiary should determine who is qualified to teach and what should be taught in the United States? I don't think so! Not only did no one elect them, but when people learn who they are, they might not want them anywhere near a school—or a government official.

From what I can make out from its website,[19] the three key players at Pearson and Pearson Education have been Glen Moreno, chairman of the Pearson Board of Directors, Dame Marjorie Morris Scardino, formerly the overall chief executive for Pearson, and William Ethridge, chief executive for North American Education. The largest stockholders are a British investment firm called Legal & General Group PLC that controls thirty-two million shares or 4% of the company and the Libyan Investment Authority with twenty-four million shares or 3% of the company. According to the *Financial Times of London*,[20] the Libyan Investment Authority was founded in January 2007 by Libyan dictator Muammar Gaddafi's son Seif al-Islam, his heir apparent until the regime's collapse.

Glen Moreno is wealthy, powerful, influential, and highly suspect. According to Wikipedia,[21] Moreno was born in California in 1943 and has a law degree from Harvard University. He worked for eighteen years at Citigroup in Europe and Asia, running the investment banking and trading divisions. Moreno was a director of Fidelity International Ltd. and became chairman of Pearson, the publisher of the British newspaper *Financial Times*, in October 2005.

Moreno was chairman of UK Financial Investments, the group set up by the British government to protect public funds used to bail-out banks after the 2008 global economic collapse. He was forced to resign in 2009 when it was revealed that he was a trustee of Liechtenstein Global Trust (LGT), a private bank accused of aiding tax evasion. Moreno was also deputy chairman of Lloyds Banking Group, Great Britain's largest mortgage lender, but stepped down from there in May 2012.

Among the Pearson troika, Moreno is the lowest paid, although he apparently has other resources. According to *Forbes*,[22] his total compensation in 2011 was a little over $600,000. He did however own a home in London and a cattle farm in Virginia and according to the *Times of London*,[23] managed to contribute £500,000 to the British Conservative Party in 2009, and purchased 200,000 shares of Lloyds stock in 2010.

Dame Marjorie was also originally an American but became a British citizen. She was CEO of Pearson from 1997 to 2012. Before becoming CEO of Pearson she was a lawyer in Georgia and a newspaper publisher. In 2007, *Forbes* magazine placed her seventeenth on its list of the one hundred most powerful women in the world.[24] She was named a "Dame of the British Empire" in 2010. According to *Forbes*,[25] her total compensation in 2011 was $2,455,000. But that represented a tiny fraction of her compensation, which included stock options. At the time, Scardino held 1.5 million shares of Pearson stock.

William Ethridge became chief executive of Pearson's North American Education division in 2008. He has what Pearson considers educational experience because he previously worked for Prentice Hall and Addison Wesley. At Pearson he was previously head of its Higher Education, International and Professional Publishing division and chairman of CourseSmart, a Pearson sponsored consortium of electronic textbook publishers. According to *Forbes*,[26] his total compensation in 2011 was $1,390,000. He also held a half million shares of Pearson stock.

According to ILSE or London South East,[27] which reports British stock market transactions, on July 30 and 31, 2012, Dame Marjorie and William Ethridge were heavily involved in Pearson stock transfers and sales on the London exchanges earning them millions of dollars. If I read the ILSE report correctly, the percentage of their holdings that Ethridge and Scardino sold seemed to be a bit less than 4% of their total holdings. The sales brought Ethridge alone approximately $323,500 in United States dollars.

This was at a time when financial observers, including the influential Nomura Group, were questioning whether Pearson stock was overvalued. ILSE reported that "Pearson had warned in April that its adjusted operating profit would be down in the first half of 2012. . . . Sales at Penguin dropped 4%, with profits falling 48% to £22 million, which management said was caused by lower sales in its more profitable U.S. market. Uncertainty over potential national and local government spending cuts in the US continues to cast a shadow over the group's Education business."[28]

In other words, Pearson's chief operating officers, who are also heavily invested in the company, were busy trading stocks and racking up dollars and pounds while the corporation's financial situation was shaky. And their solution is to sell, sell, sell their products in the United States.

Are these the people we want designing tests, lessons, and curricula for our students and deciding who is qualified to become teachers?

Post-It Note: Charles Goldsmith, head of Corporate Communications at Pearson was particularly incensed by this blog: "The blog post published by Alan Singer in the Huffington Post *on September 4th contains numerous serious factual inaccuracies about Pearson and its directors."[29] I did make an embarrassing mistake while evaluating British stock prices, which I corrected. The* Huffington Post, *to its credit, insisted that I correct factual inaccuracies but supported my right to be critical of the Pearson operation.*

F. Los Angeles Students Outfox Apple, Pearson, and the School Board

Based on an essay published on the *Huffington Post*, September 27, 2013
    www.huffingtonpost.com/alan-singer/la-students-outfox-apple-_b_4003489.
html

Questions to Consider

1. Are iPads and online instruction the best way to educate students?
2. Should teachers be required to use Pearson software, curricula, and assessments?
3. Are Los Angeles students really smarter than the government officials and business people involved in this issue?

> Following news that students at a Los Angeles high school had hacked district-issued iPads and were using them for personal use, district officials have halted home use of the Apple tablets until further notice.
> —*Los Angeles Times*, September 25, 2013

It turns out students in Los Angeles really are smarter than school board members and business people from two of America's largest and most powerful corporations.

At the start of the 2013–2014 school year, the Los Angeles school district planned to start distributing iPads to all students in the district, the second-largest school system in the United States. Forty-seven school campuses across Los Angeles are scheduled to receive 640,000 iPads by the end of 2014. The initiative is ultimately supposed to cost $1 billion. The iPads come with a three-year warranty.

In August, 1,500 teachers from forty-seven schools received their own iPads and staff development to use for lesson plans, class assignments, homework, and tests. The iPads came preloaded with software developed by Pearson Education that is supposed to be aligned to the national Common Core standards.

The iPads cost $678 each. They have a case and software, but no keyboard. The Los Angeles school district hired fifteen facilitators and paid for teacher training and technical support. Teachers will be provided with packaged lesson plans and material. Students are supposed to use their iPads to access online lessons, read digital texts, and take exams aligned with the lessons.

The purchase of the iPads was approved by the Los Angeles school board by a vote of 6–0 with one school board member abstaining because he owns stock in Apple. District Superintendent John Deasy did not participate in deliberations because he also is an Apple stockholder. School board member Tamar Galatzan declared the decision marks "an amazing adventure we're about to embark on. . . . Nothing is perfect, but we've made the best choice possible."[30]

Rejected bids were made by Dell and HP. All three finalists included Pearson Education software as part of their proposal. Apple claims there are "nearly 10 million iPads already in schools today."[31]

One week after students started receiving their iPads, students attending at least three Los Angeles high schools had figured out how to disarm a built-in security lock that was supposed to limit what they could do with the devices. This freed them to use the iPads to surf the Internet, send tweets, socialize on Facebook, stream music through Pandora, and who knows what else besides homework and school assignments. Student access to social networks and tweets will of course invalidate any of the online exams.

All the students had to do to trick the system was to delete their personal profile information and then they were free to use the I-Pads any way they wanted to. They can download their own programs and music onto the iPads and enjoy themselves while they are supposed to be rigorously and vigorously learning the Pearson way.

A different question, but I think an even larger question, is whether teachers should be using scripted online Pearson lessons and assessments. I do not remember any public discussion over whether Pearson should decide what gets taught in American schools.

When the news broke that students had unlocked iPad security, Los Angeles school Superintendent John Deasy declared that "as student safety is of paramount concern, breach of the . . . system must not occur."[32] The school district police chief recommended to senior staff that the district delay further distribution of the devices because "once this hits Twitter, YouTube or other social media sites explaining to our students how to breach or compromise the security of these devices," it will be impossible to "prevent a 'runaway train' scenario."[33]

Unfortunately, it appears that neither the school superintendent nor the head of security consulted with tech-savvy students before initiating the Apple-Pearson iPad rollout. Maybe Apple and Pearson should hire the Los Angeles students to test out their products. In the meantime, Los Angles officials are exploring ways to use the warranty to get their money back.

Post-It Note: The close ties between school officials, foundations promoting "educational reform," and companies doing business with school districts is disturbing. Los Angeles school Superintendent John E. Deasy was previously the superintendent of Prince George's County Schools, the second-largest school system in Maryland. He resigned after two years to become deputy director of education at the Bill and Melinda Gates Foundation. When Deasy left Prince George he was being investigated for misrepresenting educational and professional credentials on his resume and for a potential conflict of interest. One of his chief advisors in Los Angeles, Superintendent of Instruction Jaime Aquino, resigned in September 2013 after the Apple-Pearson contract was awarded. In an interview, Aquino claimed he left his position because of stalled reform efforts. Between 2008 and 2011, Dr. Aquino worked for America's Choice, a Pearson subsidy. There is no evidence of illegal activity by Deasy or Aquino in Los Angeles, but their connections with Gates, Apple, where Deasy was a stockholder, and Pearson, should raise flags.

Notes

1. Howard Blume, "N.Y. Mayor Gives $1 million to Back L.A. School Board Slate," *Los Angeles Times* (February 12, 2013), http://articles.latimes.com/2013/feb/12/local/la-me-bloomberg-lausd-20130213; http://dianeravitch.net/2013/03/06/l-a-upset/.
2. http://carlaranger.blogspot.com/2011/03/supt-john-kuhn-at-save-texas-schools.html.
3. www.census.gov/prod/www/statistical_abstract.html.
4. http://future-jobs.findthedata.org.
5. NPR, "Student Loan Debt Exceeds One Trillion Dollars" (April 24, 2012), www.npr.org/2012/04/24/151305380/student-loan-debt-exceeds-one-trillion-dollars.
6. Editorial, "Politicized Curriculum in Texas," *New York Times* (May 26, 2010), www.nytimes.com/2010/05/26/opinion/26wed4.html.
7. Gail Collins, "A Very Pricey Pineapple," *New York Times* (April 28, 2012), www.nytimes.com/2012/04/28/opinion/collins-a-very-pricey-pineapple.html.
8. Fred Smith, "Pearson and how 2012 standardized tests were designed," on *The Answer Sheet* by Valerie Strauss, April 27, 2012.
9. Michael Winerip, "New Questions about Trips Sponsored by Education Publisher," *New York Times* (January 2, 2012), www.nytimes.com/2012/01/02/education/inquiry-into-school-officials-travels-paid-for-by-pearson.html.
10. Press Release: Kentucky, Pearson Aim to Create First Digital Learning Repository Aligned to Common Core State Standards, February 14, 2011.
11. Email response on April 4, 2013 to my Huffington Post essay "Pearson and the Atlanta School Mess," www.huffingtonpost.com/alan-singer/pearson-and-the-atlanta-s_b_3005867.html.
12. Stephanie Simon, "Private Firms Eyeing Profits from U.S. Public Schools," *Reuters* (August 2, 2012), www.reuters.com/article/2012/08/02/usa-education-investment-idUSL2E8J15FR20120802.
13. www.edc.org/about.

14. www.edc.org/about/funders.
15. http://ies.ed.gov/ncee/edlabs/regions/northeast/pdf/REL_2012129.pdf.
16. http://markets.ft.com/Research/Markets/Tearsheets/Directors-and-dealings?s= PSON:LSE.
17. www.macroaxis.com/invest/manager/PSON.L—Susan_Fuhrman.
18. http://unitedoptout.com/boycott-pearson-now/.
19. www.pearson.com/about-us/board-of-directors.html.
20. Lina Saigol and Cynthia O'Murchu, "After Gaddafi: A Spent Force," *Financial Times of London* (September 8, 2011), www.ft.com/intl/cms/s/0/1b5e11b6-d4cb-11e0-a7ac-00144feab49a.html#axzz2r91hOSeJ.
21. http://en.wikipedia.org/wiki/Glen_Moreno.
22. www.forbes.com/profile/glen-moreno/.
23. Elizabeth Judge, "Business big shot: Glen Moreno," *The Times* (February 11, 2009), www.thetimes.co.uk/tto/business/industries/banking/article2160598.ece. "Moreno buys Into Lloyds," *The Sunday Times* (March 31, 2010), www.thesundaytimes.co.uk/sto/business/money/article253188.ece.
24. www.forbes.com/profile/marjorie-scardino/.
25. http://lt.hemscott.com/SSB/tiles/company-data/forecasts-deals/major-shareholders.jsp?epic=PSON&market=LSE.
26. Ibid.
27. www.lse.co.uk/about-us.asp.
28. www.lse.co.uk/SharePrice.asp?SharePrice=PSON; www.advfn.com/nasdaq/StockNews.asp?stocknews=NWS&article=53615866
29. Blog comment, March 20, 2013, www.huffingtonpost.com/alan-singer/pearson-education-profits_b_2902642.html.
30. Barbara Jones, "LAUSD Spending $30 Million to Buy 30,000 iPads for Students," *Los Angeles Daily News* (June 17, 2013), www.dailynews.com/general-news/20130618/lausd-spending-30-million-to-buy-30000-ipads-for-students.
31. www.apple.com/pr/library/2013/06/19Apple-Awarded-30-Million-iPad-Deal-From-LA-Unified-School-District.html.
32. Howard Blume, "L.A. Students Breach iPads'Security," *Los Angeles Times* (September 24, 2013), http://articles.latimes.com/2013/sep/24/local/la-me-lausd-ipads-20130925.
33. Ibid.

6

WHO MAKES EDUCATION POLICY?

The federal government didn't write them, didn't approve them, and doesn't mandate them. And we never will. Anyone who says otherwise is either misinformed or willfully misleading.

—Arne Duncan, American Society of News Editors Annual Convention, Capital Hilton, Washington, DC, June 25, 2013 (www.ed.gov/news/speeches/ duncan-pushes-back-attacks-common-core-standards)

This statement by United States Secretary of Education Arne Duncan may be techni-cally accurate, but it is fundamentally misleading. Common Core is not the law of the land, but its advocates have close ties to government decision-makers and the Obama/Duncan educational regime has been among its principal promoters. David Wakelyn, who navigated Common Core through the Nation Governors Association (NGA), moved on to become an education advisor to New York State Governor Andrew Cuomo. Before Dan Crippen became executive director of the NGA, he was director of the Congressional Budget Office. Richard Laine, director of the education division at NGA had close ties with Arne Dun-can when Laine was director of education at the Wallace Foundation and associated with the Illinois Business Roundtable and Duncan was working with foundations, with charter schools, and as head of the public school system in Chicago. Perhaps the greatest impetus for adoption of Common Core standards was the federal Race to the Top grant program that requires states to adopt "internationally benchmarked standards and assessments that prepare students for success in college and the work place," which in effect meant they had to adopt the Common Core.

The real questions are "Why didn't Duncan just tell the whole truth?" and "Who is making educational policy in the United States?" These are not rhetorical questions; I really do not know the answers. I am not sure anyone does.

I am in my sixties and can remember all of the presidents since Dwight Eisenhower: eleven of them. As best as I can remember, they all claimed to be the "education president" with improving education one of their highest priorities. Presidential initiatives included Eisenhower's response to the launching of Sputnik by the Soviet Union with a push for math and science education, John F. Kennedy's promotion of physical fitness in the schools and expanded federal aid to education, Lyndon Johnson's support for the Head Start pre-school program, George W. Bush's "No Child Left Behind policy," and Barack Obama's "Race to the Top."

But despite decades of education presidents, there does not appear to be any clear educational direction coming from the federal government, and there is a lot of state resistance. Part of the problem is that the United States Constitution reserved control over education to the states, but at least since the 1950s they have been more and more dependent on the national government to set a direction. At the same time, state governments have resisted calls for racial desegregation, higher and equal funding for all schools as well as targeted funding for high-needs communities, and efforts to impose standards.

One reason these essays often discuss educational initiatives in New York City is because I find numerous similarities between educational policies of the Bloomberg regime that governed the city from 2002–2013 and the Obama administration in Washington, DC, especially in their attitudes toward teachers and public schools. Obama sends his children to private school. Bloomberg sent his daughters to private schools when they were younger. Both Obama and Bloomberg value loyalty and smarts and believe that the key to success is management. But neither seems to value honest and open criticism, actually knowing something about the issue or job, and real life experience in the field.

A. Pretending to Confront the Global Achievement Gap
B. Obama, Duncan, and the Public Schools
C. Thank You, Arne Duncan
D. Race to the Top Mandates Impossible to Implement
E. Empty Promises in the Obama Mis-Education Agenda
F. What Is a Twenty-First Century Job?
G. Guest Essay: Governor Christie's War against New Jersey Public Employees by Norman Markowitz

A. Pretending to Confront the Global Achievement Gap

Based on an essay published on the *Huffington Post*, November 24, 2010
www.huffingtonpost.com/alan-singer/pretending-to-confront-th_b_787237.
html

Questions to Consider

1. How will the United States recruit new talent into teaching if starting salaries remain uncompetitive?
2. Is it legitimate to compare education in the United States with education in countries such as Denmark and Finland?
3. What must be done to achieve goals in education for the twenty-first century?

In a *New York Times* op-ed piece,[1] columnist Thomas Friedman joined the growing list of people who know nothing about education but feel they have all of the solutions. Freidman, in his columns, often has interesting ideas, but he generally takes them in the wrong direction. "Teaching for America" was no exception. In the essay, Friedman strongly endorsed Secretary of Education Arne Duncan and Barack Obama's vision of an educational future for the United States, especially their Race to the Top program.

To bolster his case, Friedman reported on ideas about education taken from *The Global Achievement Gap* by educator Tony Wagner.[2] Wagner, who co-directs the Change Leadership Group in the Harvard University School of Education, argued there are three basic skills that students need if they are going to thrive in a twenty-first century knowledge-based economy. They must have the ability to think critically and solve problems. They must be able to communicate effectively. They also must be able to work collaboratively. Unfortunately, Friedman failed to explain how any of these goals would be achieved by the Duncan/Obama test-driven initiative.

In this column, Friedman, who emphasizes his agreement with Arne Duncan, is especially enamored by countries like Finland and Denmark whose students are supposedly "leading the pack in the tests that measure these skills." They invest heavily in recruiting, training, and supporting teachers and are able "to attract and retain the best." Friedman and Duncan also sing the praises of Singapore and South Korea where they "don't let anyone teach who doesn't come from the top third of their graduating class."

Duncan hopes to replicate their success with a "national teacher campaign" to recruit new talent and a new National Education Academy modeled on the United States military academies.[3] But it is not likely that either intense recruitment or a national academy will be magic bullets. Among other problems, according to a study published by the Economics Policy Institute,[4] "Compared to other countries, U.S. flunks in teacher pay." In 2008, the starting salary earned by teachers in South Korea was 141% of the per capita Gross Domestic Product. In Finland, teachers earn 95%, but in the United States they earn only 81%. In 2010, the United States per capita GDP was $46,400, which would mean to be competitive with South Korea, starting teachers would have to be paid $65,425 a year instead of approximately $42,000.

Friedman and Duncan are either willfully ignorant or consciously misleading about the countries they want the United States to emulate. I would like American students to achieve the highest levels of education, and I would like higher teacher pay, but these countries are hardly examples to follow or that can be followed. Essentially these are all small, homogeneous societies that have found a comfortable niche in the global economy that has made it possible to pay teachers higher salaries and provide a high quality education for most of their young people.

South Korea is among the world's most ethnically homogeneous nations and was a military dictatorship for much of the second half of the twentieth century. Its economy is largely dependent on foreign trade, especially to the United States. Without this trade it would be hard pressed to remain either prosperous or a democracy and to maintain its school system.

In Finland and Denmark, not only are populations homogenous, but the countries are tiny. The populations of each are a little over five million people or about the combined population of Chicago and Los Angeles. Finland and Denmark are also well known for the scope of their social service programs, free public higher education and health care, and worker pensions, programs I support, but which are not likely to be implemented in the United States.

Singapore, an island city in Southeast Asia, has a population under five million. A major financial center, it functions more as a corporation than as a country and has been rated as the most business-friendly economy in the world by the World Bank. Although it has an elected parliament, it is essentially a one-party state. Nearly half of its population is made up of foreign workers and students with no political rights.

If the United States is going to educate all of its children like these countries apparently do, it will have to finally come to terms with its racial, ethnic, and class divisions. Not only will it have to pay teachers significantly more, but it will have to provide an array of social services to families, and ensure students that if they do perform well and graduate from college they will be able to secure well-paying jobs and have decent lives. Otherwise Freidman and Duncan are just pretending to support improved teacher preparation and higher student performance.

Post-It Note: In November 2009, President Obama announced that American schools needed to look more like schools in South Korea. He told a meeting of the United States Hispanic Chamber of Commerce "Our children spend over a month less in school than children in South Korea every year. That's no way to prepare them for a 21st-century economy. We can no longer afford an academic calendar designed for when America was a nation of farmers who needed their children at home plowing the land at the end of each day. That calendar may have once made sense, but today it puts us at a competitive disadvantage."[5] *Obama's remarks came as a surprise to many South Koreans because the country's education system was being increasingly criticized in Korea for its lack of creativity and heavy dependence on private tutoring. In addition, Dr. Samuel Kim, a research scholar at Columbia University,*[6] *reported that 44% of Korean students who entered "top" American universities dropped out before graduating, a much higher rate than for students from China (25%), India (21%), and even the 34% dropout rate for American students at the same universities. Years of extra tutoring had prepared Korean students for college entrance exams but not for acquiring a college education.*

B. Obama, Duncan, and the Public Schools

Based on an essay published on the *Huffington Post*, October 26, 2009
www.huffingtonpost.com/alan-singer/obama-duncan-and-the-publ_b_333910.
html

Questions to Consider

1. Why does it take three to five years of experience to become an effective teacher?
2. What kind of support helps new teachers, especially teachers working in high-needs communities?
3. Does data-driven assessment help anyone?
4. Which revolution do you believe in?

The people who did not win the wars in Iraq and Afghanistan and could not rebuild the economy after it collapsed in 2007 decided to turn their attention to cleaning up what they saw as the education mess in the United States and they found an easy target—schools of education.

Arne Duncan, Barack Obama's basketball pal from Chicago and the educator-in-chief, who was never a teacher and apparently never worked with children or in schools in any capacity, claimed he could revamp public school education by overhauling the schools of education. Duncan demanded "revolutionary change" so teachers were better prepared to work with kids with high needs and to use data-driven assessment to improve instruction. (Didn't they use data-driven assessment to manage industry, banks, and their wars so successfully?)

Before I go any further, in the name of openness and honesty, I am one of the targeted professors of education that Duncan and Obama apparently wanted to shake up. I guess I am the problem.

On the other hand, I did teach in some of New York City's more difficult schools for fourteen years before becoming a teacher educator.

I am not a fan of professors of education who profess, but who have little or no experience in schools. Even while based at Hofstra University, I spend at least two mornings a week working with teachers in public schools. Most of these schools have large minority populations with many high-needs children. But changing schools of education is going to change very little.

According to an article in *USA Today* (October 22, 2009), Duncan wants states and school districts to "link the performance of teachers to their education schools" so they can identify which programs prepare teachers well and which ones do not.[7] He claimed he talked to hundreds of great young teachers while serving as Chicago schools chief and they had two complaints about education schools. They said they did not get the "hands-on teacher training about managing the classroom that they needed, especially for high-needs students" and "were not taught how to use data to improve instruction and boost student learning."[8] Curiously, just the answers he was looking for. Also, not surprising answers from middle-class teachers who are grappling with the culture shock of teaching in inner-city communities with little support from school administrators.

The first problem with the Obama/Duncan plan is that nothing short of experience in schools is going to prepare middle-class aspiring teachers to work with students and communities that have high social and academic needs. Even if they understand and empathize with the students, it takes three to five years of hard work to develop the judgment to become an effective teacher in any setting, let alone in hard-pressed urban and minority schools. No one can be inoculated to become a successful teacher while in a teacher education program. Change will require ongoing support and training for teachers while they are working and much smaller classes. These revolutionary changes will be much more expensive than futile attacks on schools of education and local, state, and federal governments have been unwilling to spend the money.

They are also unwilling to make the investment in improving conditions in the lives of students. Increasing numbers live in poverty with little hope for the future, despite Obama's election and fine speeches. If Obama/Duncan want to improve schools they will need to rebuild neighborhoods, provide jobs, and help stabilize families.

The United States has a capitalist economy. Businesses try to make a profit. Governments are concerned with the bottom line. Why don't our schools work better? It has little to do with schools of education. The reality is that it is cheaper to import car mechanics from Jamaica and Pakistan and computer technicians from India and China than to improve conditions in inner cities in the United States and provide students with real educations.

I agree with Obama/Duncan. Our schools need revolutionary change. We just believe in different revolutions.

C. Thank You, Arne Duncan

Based on an essay published on the *Huffington Post*, April 8, 2010
    www.huffingtonpost.com/alan-singer/thank-you-arne-duncan_b_529977.
html

Questions to Consider

1. How did some states qualify for Race to the Top money?
2. Can school reforms that ignore broader economic and social issues succeed?

Politicians like to focus on test scores and place blame on teachers, but the real problem is that American schools have been devastated by a national economy that has been stalled in recession and near recession since 2007. Not only is funding for schools sharply reduced in real dollars (the money you have available to spend), but problems faced by students, teachers, and families are much greater.

It is difficult to preach hope to students and convince them to study harder when parents are unemployed, homes are in foreclosure, and the future looks bleak. It is also difficult for teachers to preach hope when they are totally demoralized. Maybe Barack Obama and Arne Duncan can understand it if I explain in basketball-speak. Think of how difficult it is to motivate players on a sub −.500 team with no chance of making the playoffs who are just going through the motions.

After 2007, banks and big companies were bailed out by the federal government, but not state governments and social service programs. State budgets remain deep in the red and school budgets are being cut, cut again, and cut deeper. Thousands of teachers continue to face layoffs. No government official has projected a figure nationwide, the numbers are too scary, but a decline of 100,000 teachers through attrition and layoffs might not be off the mark.

Faced with a budgetary disaster of historic proportions, state governments turned in desperation for federal help. But instead of confronting the reality facing education, the Obama/Duncan Dream Team offered the states the opportunity to compete for federal "Race to the Top" grant money. The payoffs were so small, even for the "winners," it amounted to little more than pissing in the ocean.

But at least "Race to the Top" makes it clear how Obama/Duncan see the future. I never thought of Tennessee and Delaware as models for anything, except it seems their bureaucrats are really good at filling out paper work. They beat out thirty-eight other states and the District of Columbia to win an initial share of $4 billion in federal education grants, because they convinced Barack and his friend Arne that they had "bold plans" for overhauling their public school systems. Georgia and Florida came in third and fourth, two more states with far from championship quality school systems, but neither won any money.

So what did Barack Obama see as the solution to what plagues the schools? He tried to force states to expand the number of charter schools, to evaluate teachers based on student test scores, and to computerize data to magically turn around low-performing schools. The highlight of Delaware's winning proposal was a new state law that allowed teachers rated as "ineffective" for three years to be removed from the classroom, even if they had tenure. I do not believe in protecting the incompetent, but does anyone really believe that firing a few teachers will ensure that every student in the United States receives a twenty-first century education?

Tennessee secured its award by passing a law that allowed the state to intervene in failing schools, another unlikely solution. Has anyone ever heard of Roosevelt, New York, or Newark, New Jersey? New York and New Jersey have been intervening in their schools for decades, but have made little improvement. It seems there is no magic pill that improves test scores in districts where students live is dire poverty and have immense needs that the schools can only begin to address.

The New York State application was graded poorly partly because there was a legal cap on the number of charter schools run with public money but exempt from many union and curricular rules. That also clarifies things. To get the grant you needed to pass rules but remove oversight. Wait a minute! Aren't rules without oversight what allowed the banks to act irresponsibly and caused the entire economic mess?

That brings us to the unions. I have had my differences with the leadership of the New York City United Federation of Teachers over the years, but as a teacher and parent I knew we depended on them to keep city officials in line. The only thing that stopped the city's Department of Education from stuffing more kids into rooms was the teacher contract, and believe me the city tried to raise class size repeatedly in the past. The union may protect some incompetents by demanding due process from a mayor committed to arbitrary authoritarianism, but the same rules that protect them also protect tens of thousands of excellent teachers from administrative harassment.

Upper-middle-class professional families with children in public schools may be worried that all the talk of equity and opportunity for everyone will interfere with the special privileges and little niche programs with extra funding they have received from so-called reformers like Michael Bloomberg and Joel Klein in New York City. But do not worry. Arne Duncan understands your pain. When he was Chicago school chief he had an assistant maintain a top-secret list of the well-connected families whose children were helped to get into the best schools. The list was maintained by a Duncan aide who was rewarded for his service by being made chief of staff to the president of the Chicago Board of Education. According to a *Chicago Tribune* article,[9] the initials "AD" appeared on the list fifty times next to the names of people seeking special favors.

I was blind, but now I see. All I can say is thank you, Arne Duncan.

Post-It Note: At the end of the novel Animal Farm, *the animals were confused. They could no longer tell the pigs from the human farmers. I have a similar problem. When it comes to education policy, I can no longer tell Bloomberg/Klein and Obama/Duncan apart. That is why I wanted to thank Arne Duncan for clarifying things for me. There really is not much of a difference.*

D. Race to the Top Mandates Impossible to Implement

Based on an essay published on the *Huffington Post*, November 22, 2012
    www.huffingtonpost.com/alan-singer/race-to-the-top-mandates-_b_1105092.
html

Questions to Consider

1. Why do politicians, the wealthy, and other non-educators think they have the
    right and the expertise to mandate school policy?
2. How should government decision-makers respond when experienced school
    and district administrators say mandates will not work?

In the 2012 Republican Party presidential debates candidates like Mitt Romney
and Herman Cain touted their business executive experience and claimed expertise at job creation. Former Governors Rick Perry and John Huntsman promoted
their management experience as the CEOs of state governments. Whatever you
may think of their proposals for stimulating the economy and ending unemployment, there is no question that these candidates believed, and they believed their
audiences believed, that knowledge and experience are important leadership qualities. However, when it comes to educational leadership, it seems that knowledge
and experience do not count for very much.

In 2011 Tennessee was awarded a federal Race to the Top grant worth over
$500 million based on a proposal that required teachers to be rated based on stu-
dent test scores and extensive evaluations by school administrators. Arne Duncan,
Barack Obama's education czar, highly praised Tennessee for its "courage" and
"commitment to turn their ideas into practices that can improve outcomes for
students." Tennessee Governor Bill Haslam called his state "the focal point of
education reform in the nation" and declared Tennessee's new motto to be "First
to the Top."[10]

It turned out however that Tennessee, which ranked near the bottom of the
country on the National Assessment of Educational Progress, may not be getting to the top any time soon. One middle school principal, who was originally
a big supporter of Tennessee's Race to the Top proposal, described it as a disaster.
According to Will Shelton,[11] principal of Blackman Middle School in Murfrees-
boro, the new rules required repeated observations of the school's best teachers
and forced principals to complete enormous volumes of paperwork. The result
was that they never had time to work with either the students or the teachers who
actually needed the help.

Shelton accused Tennessee of agreeing to micromanage schools in order to get
the federal Race to the Top funds. He called the four observations a year of his
strongest teachers "an insult to my best teachers" and a "terrible waste of time."
He is required to have a twenty-minute pre-observation conference with each
teacher, observe the teacher in the classroom for fifty minutes, hold a twenty-
minute-long post-observation conference, and complete an evaluation rubric with

nineteen variables and assign teachers a score of from one to five on each variable. In addition, the state required he keep completed copies of his evaluations for every visit to every teacher on file to show any visiting state assessors.

The situation in Tennessee has become so absurd that elementary school teachers of subjects that are not tested find themselves evaluated based on student scores on tests in completely unrelated subjects. Music teachers are evaluated based on student writing samples and first-grade teachers are evaluated based on how their former students perform on tests they take as sixth-graders. According to *Education Week*,[12] the situation in Tennessee was so convoluted and impractical that the entire Race to the Top program was in jeopardy.

You would think the problems in Tennessee would make national leaders and the media pause a moment to rethink Race to the Top mandates. However, an editorial in the *New York Times* declared that Tennessee had made "significant headway in turning itself into a laboratory for education reform" and called on state lawmakers and educational officials to "resist any backsliding."[13]

New York State, which secured $700 million in the Race to the Top competition, developed a new teacher evaluation process that it promised to implement in order to receive the grant. The evaluation process for teachers and schools is so complex that the city and state Departments of Education had to hire expensive consultants to go into schools and explain the criteria and formulas for evaluation to teachers.

Experienced New York State school principals are saying the emperor is naked. Based on what is happening in Tennessee and other states, concern over the impact of unproven practices on the education of young people, and a realistic appraisal of the educational reforms that is rooted in knowledge and experience, a number of school principals challenged the race to test and assess. Led by the Long Island Principals Association they issued an open letter to state officials and the public that questioned the validity of the proposed Annual Professional Performance Review (APPR). The letter was signed by thousands of principals, district administrators, and teachers from a wide spectrum of school districts across the state. It is a systematic examination of educational research and best practice that concludes:

> the proposed APPR process is an unproven system that is wasteful of increasingly limited resources. More importantly, it will prove to be deeply demoralizing to educators and harmful to the children in our care. Our students are more than the sum of their test scores, and an overemphasis on test scores will not result in better learning. According to a nine-year study by the National Research Council, the past decade's emphasis on testing has yielded little learning progress, especially considering the cost to our taxpayers. We welcome accountability and continually strive to meet high standards. We want what is best for our students. We believe, however, that an unproven, expensive and potentially harmful evaluation system is not the path to lasting school improvement. We must not lose sight of what matters the most—the academic, social and emotional growth of our students.[14]

You do not want a doctor operating on patients without knowledge or experience, you do not want engineers building bridges without knowledge and experience, and we need to value the knowledge and experience of these school-based educators before we establish educational policies that will undermine education in the United States.

Maybe instead of repeatedly testing teachers and students, what the nation really needs is a series of new tests to establish qualifications before people are allowed to run for government office or serve in government administrative capacities.

E. Empty Promises in the Obama Mis-Education Agenda

Based on an essay published on the *Huffington Post*, February 13, 2013
www.huffingtonpost.com/alan-singer/obama-education-policy_b_2677689.html

Questions to Consider

1. Were the Obama educational proposals more than empty promises?
2. What can the federal government do to ensure better quality education?

I am a lifetime teacher, first in public schools and then in a university-based teacher education program. I think I do an honest job and that students benefit from being in my classes. I was hoping to hear something positive about the future of public education in President Obama's 2013 State of the Union speech. But I was so disturbed by what Obama said about education that I had to turn him off. In the morning I read the text of his speech online, hoping I was wrong about what I thought I had heard. But I was not. There was nothing there but shallow celebration of wrong-headed policies and empty promises.

For me, the test question on any education proposal always is, "Is this the kind of education I want for my children and grandchildren?" Obama, whose children attend an elite and expensive private school in Washington, DC, badly failed the test.

Basically Obama was looking to improve education in the United States on the cheap. He bragged that his signature education program, Race to the Top, was "a competition that convinced almost every state to develop smarter curricula and higher standards, for about 1 percent of what we spend on education each year."[15] I am not sure why Obama felt entitled to brag. Race to the Top had been in place for four years and its major impact seemed to be the constant testing of students, high profits for testing companies such as Pearson, and questionable reevaluations of teachers. It is unclear to me what positive changes Race to the Top actually achieved.

In the 2013 State of the Union Address, Obama made three proposals, one for preschools, one for high schools, and one for colleges.

Obama on preschools: "Study after study shows that the sooner a child begins learning, the better he or she does down the road. But today, fewer than 3 in 10 four-year-olds are enrolled in a high-quality preschool program. . . . I propose working with states to make high-quality preschool available to every child in America. . . . In states that make it a priority to educate our youngest children, like Georgia or Oklahoma, studies show students grow up more likely to read and do math at grade level, graduate high school, hold a job, and form more stable families of their own."

I am a big supporter of universal pre-kindergarten and I like the promise, but Georgia and Oklahoma are not models for educational excellence. Both states have offered universal pre-K for more than a decade and in both states students continue to score poorly on national achievement tests. Part of the problem is that both Georgia and Oklahoma are anti-union, low-wage Right-to-Work states. In Oklahoma City, the average salary for a preschool teacher is $25,000 and assistant teachers make about $18,000, enough to keep the school personnel living in poverty. Average preschool teacher salaries for job postings in Oklahoma City are 17% lower than average preschool teacher salaries for job postings nationwide. The situation is not much better in Georgia. In Savannah, average preschool teacher salaries for job postings are 12% lower than average preschool teacher salaries for job postings nationwide.

Obama on secondary schools: "Let's also make sure that a high school diploma puts our kids on a path to a good job. Right now, countries like Germany focus on graduating their high school students with the equivalent of a technical degree from one of our community colleges, so that they're ready for a job. At schools like P-Tech in Brooklyn, a collaboration between New York Public Schools, the City University of New York, and IBM, students will graduate with a high school diploma and an associate degree in computers or engineering. . . . I'm announcing a new challenge to redesign America's high schools so they better equip graduates for the demands of a high-tech economy. We'll reward schools that develop new partnerships with colleges and employers, and create classes that focus on science, technology, engineering, and math—the skills today's employers are looking for to fill jobs right now and in the future."

Unfortunately, P-Tech in Brooklyn, the Pathways in Technology Early College High School, is not yet, and may never be, a model for anything. It claims to be "the first school in the nation that connects high school, college, and the world of work through deep, meaningful partnerships, we are pioneering a new vision for college and career readiness and success."[16] Students will study for six years and receive both high school diplomas and college associate degrees. But in September 2013, the school was only in its third year of operation, had only about 320 students, and had no graduates or working alumni.

According to a *New York Times* report that included an interview with an IBM official,[17] "The objective is to prepare students for entry-level technology jobs paying around $40,000 a year, like software specialists who answer questions from IBM's business customers or 'deskside support' workers who answer calls from PC users, with opportunities for advancement."

The thing is, as anyone who has called computer support knows, those jobs are already being done at a much cheaper rate by outsourced techies in third world countries. It does not really seem like an avenue to the American middle class. The IBM official also made clear, "that while no positions at I.B.M. could be guaranteed six years in the future, the company would give P-Tech students preference for openings."

Obama on the cost of a college education: "[S]kyrocketing costs price way too many young people out of a higher education, or saddle them with unsustainable debt. . . . But taxpayers cannot continue to subsidize the soaring cost of higher education. . . . My Administration will release a new "College Scorecard" that parents and students can use to compare schools based on a simple criteria: where you can get the most bang for your educational buck."

As a parent and grandparent I agree with President Obama that the cost of college is too high for many families, but that is what a real education costs. If the United States is going to have the high-tech twenty-first century workforce the President wants, the only solution is massive federal support for education. There is a way to save some money, however I did not hear any discussion of it in the president's speech. Private for-profit businesses masquerading as colleges have been sucking in federal dollars and leaving poor and poorly qualified students with debts they can never repay. These programs should be shut down, but in the State of the Union Address President Obama ignored the problem.

The *New York Times* documented the way for-profit edu-companies, including the massive Pearson publishing concern, go unregulated by federal education officials.[18] These companies operate online charter schools and colleges that offer substandard education to desperate families at public expense.

President Obama, celebrating mediocrity and shallow promises are not enough. You would never accept these "solutions" for Malia and Sasha. American students and families need a genuine federal investment in education.

F. What Is a Twenty-First Century Job?

Based on an essay published on the *Huffington Post*, April 18, 2011
www.huffingtonpost.com/alan-singer/what-is-a-21st-century-jo_b_850081.html

Questions to Consider

1. What does a twenty-first century job look like?
2. Should K–12 public education be organized to train students for specific employment opportunities?
3. What happens to a dream deferred?

According to the White House website, "President Obama will reform America's public schools to deliver a 21st century education that will prepare all children for success in the new global workplace." In addition, President Obama's "first priority" in confronting the current economic crisis is "to put Americans back to work."[19]

The president made clear the connection between education and work in the 2011 State of the Union address where he explained that, "nearly half of all new jobs will require education that goes beyond a high school education." On another recent occasion the president declared, "If we want more good news on the jobs front then we've got to make more investments in education."[20]

If President Obama is right about the importance of education for improving national competitiveness, you would expect teaching to be a twenty-first century growth industry. Yet teachers continue to face layoffs across the country and the population of students in schools of education is declining. In addition, teacher unions and professional associations are under attack and seniority rights that protect our most experienced teachers may soon disappear.

Evidently this is really not a nation that values education, certainly not mass public education. Who would choose a career that is at best temporary and where PowerPoint slides marketed by textbook and testing companies may soon replace teachers in the classroom? College graduates may be faced with the choice between earning a minimum wage flipping burgers at McDonald's or flipping pre-packaged slides at a "school" near you.

Paul Krugman, Nobel Prize-winning economist at Princeton University and a *New York Times* columnist,[21] has warned that twenty-first century jobs may not be tied to higher education and improved skills at all. For example, new software has simplified legal searches and wiped out entry-level middle-class jobs in the legal profession. Software has also been replacing highly skilled, well-educated computer engineers who specialize in chip design.

According to Krugman, rather than expanding in recent decades, the type of work that supports a strong middle class has lagged behind the rest of the economy since the 1990s. Krugman cited studies by economists David Autor, Frank Levy, and Richard Murnane who argued that computers excel at "cognitive and manual tasks that can be accomplished by following explicit rules." Jobs that primarily include searching and maintaining research databases (such as the work done by paralegals and medical and insurance personnel), information sorting (book keepers and accountants), and information delivery (teachers?) may disappear or just be de-professionalized with a parallel collapse in salary.

Krugman concluded, "the notion that putting more kids through college can restore the middle-class society we used to have is wishful thinking. It's no longer true that having a college degree guarantees that you'll get a good job, and it's becoming less true with each passing decade."[22]

So where should the ambitious student look for twenty-first century jobs? The April 17, 2011, "Education Life" section of the *New York Times* made specific recommendations listing the top ten growth fields.[23] Unfortunately, there are relatively few jobs available in these fields or they are low-paid, low-skill work.

The number one field was biomedical engineering with a projected growth rate of 72%. The mean salary for someone with a master's degree in science or engineering was projected at $82,500. Unfortunately, they only anticipated 12,000 new slots by 2018, or about 1,500 a year. If you want a job in this field, you better start lining up now. Network and data analysts (number two) get paid a little less (mean of $76,500), but they anticipate more jobs in the field (over 50,000), that is until they are all outsourced to India and the Philippines.

Number five (financial examiner, 11,000 jobs) and number seven (physician assistant, 29,000 jobs) are also the types of jobs where the more skilled work will be quickly outsourced. That leaves medical scientist (44,000 jobs) and biochemist/biophysicist (9,000 jobs) for American Ph.D. students.

Low-wage jobs were the big boom area as the baby boomer population ages. College graduates can find plenty of minimum wage work as home health aides (anticipated 461,000 jobs), as less demanding personal care attendants (anticipated 376,000 jobs), pushing skin care products to the aged (15,000 jobs), and helping them in the gym (6,000 jobs).

Maybe President Obama is right and Paul Krugman and the *New York Times* are wrong? If that is the case, I need him to be more specific. I would like to be able to tell my students where they can find the twenty-first century jobs.

If Obama and his economic team and the budget-cut Republicans who control the House of Representatives are wrong however, they should reread a clever little poem written by Langston Hughes called "A Dream Deferred" (1951). Will a dream deferred explode like a "raisin in the sun?"

G. Guest Essay by Norman Markowitz: Governor Christie's War against New Jersey Public Employees

Based on an essay published on the *Huffington Post*, September 15, 2010
www.huffingtonpost.com/alan-singer/christies-war-against-new_b_718775.html

Post-It Note: This article was written by Rutgers University Professor Norman Markowitz based largely on material compiled by Peter Guzzo, who represents various trade unions and other groups to the New Jersey legislature. With Norman's permission it was published on the Huffington Post, *September 15, 2010.*

Questions to Consider

1. How was Governor Christie engaging in class war against working people?
2. What can public- and private-arena unions do to fight back against this type of assault?

A day after he was inaugurated as governor of New Jersey, Chris Christie issued an executive order that reduced the state's maximum contribution to public employee pension funds. This was not a surprise. In his campaign for governor,

Christie had blamed public workers for the state budget deficit. Trade unions knew through leaked memoranda even before Christie was inaugurated that his advisors were planning to divide the labor movement, which has historically been strong in New Jersey, by pitting public employees against other workers.

Christie proclaimed his own version of a "class war" with the comment that there are "two classes of people in New Jersey: Public employees who receive rich benefits and those who pay for them."[24] Christie's demagoguery has most sharply been directed against teachers and their unions. He called the National Education Association (NEA) the "National Extortion Association." His style, which is both crude and extreme, is reminiscent of Senator Joe McCarthy's verbal attacks during the Red Scare of the 1950s.

The reality of course is that New Jersey public employees are neither living high through their pension benefits, nor are they the cause of the state's complex fiscal crisis. In terms of income, public sector employees earn less than their counterparts in the private sector. This, however, is balanced out by their health and pension benefits, what many Europeans called "social incomes." The pension "crisis" in New Jersey, as in other states, has been the result primarily of the larger stock market crisis and the raiding of pension funds. States and communities have been "skipping" payments to these funds in order to balance budgets. As of 2009, when Christie took office, all public pension funds in New Jersey were under-funded by $46 billion.

When Governor Christie's executive order was thrown out by the State Court of Appeals because he had usurped the powers of the legislative branch, he began to seek other ways to implement it, including the passage of new legislation. This required him to seek allies among Democrats who controlled the majority in both houses.

With the help of strategically placed Democrats and with a united Republican party behind him, Christie succeeded in passing "reform" legislation that would limit the pension system to full-time employees who work thirty-five hour weeks at the state level and thirty-two hour weeks at the local level, base pensions for new employees and teachers on their five highest-salary years rather than their three highest years, change the formula used to determine pensions for new employees, and push new employees as much as possible into 401K plans. In addition, new state workers would have to work a minimum of thirty-five hours a week to receive health benefits and municipal and school employees would have to work at least twenty-five hours.

Governor Christie also signed into law a 2% annual "cap" on property tax increases for communities, although Democrats were able to have health care, pensions, debt repayment, and existing contracts with public employees exempted from this cap. Although Christie routinely denounces "big government," he has demanded that communities "renegotiate" existing contracts with public employees and threatened them with cutoffs of state aid.

In response, the Democratic Party has pursued a policy of retreat. Their leaders seemed to hope that Christie would overextend himself and that the disastrous consequences of his policies would lead voters to turn against Christie and the

Republican Party. The consequences of waiting for Christie's failure may be disastrous. New Jersey may experience the breakdown of education and social services. It may lose through retirement or exodus outstanding teachers, police, and other municipal employees, who see their pension and health care rights eroding.

Among other anti-union and anti-worker proposals Governor Christie has made is calling for a 30% co-pay for health benefits for all public employees and retirees covered by the New Jersey State system. This would mean thousands of dollars in out of pocket expenses for employees and constitute a large de facto wage cut and extreme hardship for many older people.

Governor Christie also come forward with a series of reform proposals called a "tool kit" that would devastate the civil service system, eliminate gains that public employee unions have made over decades, and lead to major income and benefit reductions for public employees. It is feared that he plans to replace full-time employees with part-time employees so new hires would not be eligible for pension or health care benefits. This would probably have the greatest impact on lower-income employees. If Christie has his way, New Jersey will be transformed from a state that currently has the highest per capita income in the nation into a cheaper labor state. How such a work force can run schools, police forces, municipalities, and state agencies does not seem matter to him.

Meanwhile, Governor Christie's policies offer no solution to the pension problem in New Jersey or the crazy quilt system of pensions funded by regressive payroll taxes that we have in the United States. A comprehensive solution to these questions has to be carried forward at the federal level.

Christie used the pension and health care fiscal crisis in an attempt to divide and conquer the labor movement. In response, the New Jersey labor movement fought him in the courts, in elections, and in the communities at every level. Defeating Christie's economic proposals in New Jersey was essential not only to the defense of teachers and other public workers, but as a lesson to all of the "little Christies" that the policies of the Reagan-Bush eras that produced the present economic crisis would not be recycled as a phony solution to that crisis.

Post-It Note: According to legend, in 1920 a young boy approached baseball star "Shoeless" Joe Jackson, who was accused of participating in a betting scandal during the 1919 World Series. The boy pleaded with him, "Say it ain't so, Joe." But there was nothing Joe could say. I wish I could say it ain't so, but Chris Christie was reelected governor of New Jersey in November 2013 and he is now a leading contender for the 2016 Republican Party nomination for president.

Notes

1. Thomas Friedman, "Teaching for America," *New York Times* (November 21, 2010), www.nytimes.com/2010/11/21/opinion/21friedman.html.
2. Tony Wagner, *The Global Achievement Gap, Why Even Our Best Schools Don't Teach the New Survival Skills Our Children Need—and What We Can Do About It* (New York: Basic Books, 2010), www.tonywagner.com/resources/the-global-achievement-gap.

3. Thomas Friedman, "Teaching for America," *New York Times* (November 21, 2010), www.nytimes.com/2010/11/21/opinion/21friedman.html.
4. Joydeep Roy, "Compared to Other Countries, U.S. Flunks in Teacher Pay," Economic Policy Institute (April 1, 2008), www.epi.org/publication/webfeatures_snapshots_20080402/.
5. www.whitehouse.gov/the_press_office/Remarks-of-the-President-to-the-United-States-Hispanic-Chamber-of-Commerce.
6. http://newpol.org/content/why-korean-school-system-not-superior.
7. "Duncan: 'Revolutionary Change' Needed in Teachers Colleges," *USA Today* (October 22, 2009), http://usatoday30.usatoday.com/news/education/2009-10-22-obama-teachers_N.htm.
8. Ibid.
9. Azam Ahmed, "How VIPs Lobbied Schools," *Chicago Tribune* (March 23, 2010), http://articles.chicagotribune.com/2010–03–23/news/ct-met-cps-admissions-0323—20100322_1_schools-chief-arne-duncan-principals-david-pickens.
10. Michael Winerip, "In Tennessee, Following the Rules for Evaluations Off a Cliff," *New York Times* (November 7, 2011), www.nytimes.com/2011/11/07/education/tennes sees-rules-on-teacher-evaluations-bring-frustration.html?ref=opinion.
11. Ibid.
12. Liana Heitin, "Teacher-Evaluation Rush May Jinx Other States' Efforts," *Education Week* (October 18, 2011), www.edweek.org/ew/articles/2011/10/19/08eval.h31.html.
13. Editorial, "Tennessee's Push to Transform Schools," *New York Times* (November 12, 2011), www.nytimes.com/2011/11/12/opinion/tennessees-push-to-transform-schools.html.
14. www.newyorkprincipals.org/appr-paper.
15. "Obama's 2013 State of the Union Address," *New York Times* (February 12, 2013), www.nytimes.com/2013/02/13/us/politics/obamas-2013-state-of-the-union-address.html?_r=0.
16. www.ptechnyc.org/site/default.aspx?PageID=1.
17. Al Baker, "At Technology High school, Goal Isn't to Finish in 4 Years," *New York Times* (October 22, 2012), www.nytimes.com/2012/10/22/nyregion/pathways-in-tech nology-early-college-high-school-takes-a-new-approach-to-vocational-education.html?hpw&_r=0.
18. Stephanie Saul, "Profits and Questions at Online Charter Schools," *New York Times* (December 13, 2011), www.nytimes.com/2011/12/13/education/online-schools-score-better-on-wall-street-than-in-classrooms.html?hp.
19. www.whitehouse.gov/issues/education; Deborah White, "President Obama's Education Policy 'Guiding Principles,'" About.com (April 7, 2010), http://usliberals.about.com/od/education/a/ObamaEdcuationPolicies.htm.
20. www.whitehouse.gov/the-press-office/2011/01/25/remarks-president-state-union-address.
21. Paul Krugman, "Degrees and Dollars," *New York Times* (March 7, 2011), www.nytimes.com/2011/03/07/opinion/07krugman.html.
22. Ibid.
23. Cecilia Capuzzi Simon, "Top 10 List: Where the Jobs Are," *New York Times* (April 17, 2011), www.nytimes.com/2011/04/17/education/edlife/edl-17conted-t.html?pagewanted=all.
24. "Gov. Christie to Propose Permanent Caps on Salary Raises for Public Workers," NJ.com (May 8, 2010), www.nj.com/news/index.ssf/2010/05/gov_christie_to_propose_public.html.

7

WHERE IS THE CHART FOR CHARTER SCHOOLS?

Charter schools are publically funded but privately operated and are often exempt from many educational regulations. According to the National Center for Educational Statistics there were over five thousand public charter schools with 1.7 million students operating in the United States during the 2010–2011 school years. Approximately 20% were in California, while Texas and Florida each had about 10% of the charters. The number of charter schools is rapidly increasing and there were almost six thousand in the school year 2012–2013.

Radio, television, and print ads show a very unlikely and powerful coalition supporting the demand for new charter schools—Barack Obama, Arne Duncan, JPMorgan Chase, assorted hedge funds, New York City Mayor Michael Bloomberg, and Black activist Reverend Al Sharpton. The impression they are trying to give in the advertisements is that everybody whose opinion we trust thinks it is a good idea and that the teachers and their evil unions want to block reform that will benefit children.

On May 27, 2010, JPMorgan Chase ran a full-page advertisement in the New York Times *with the headline "The Way Forward, Investing in Our Children's Future." It cost the bank approximately $180,000. This is the same JPMorgan Chase that received a $25 billion bailout from Congress as part of the federal Troubled Assets Relief Program (TARP). Just because the bank cannot manage its own affairs, does not mean it should not manage ours.*

A New York Times *editorial on October 16, 2013,[1] perhaps inadvertently, gave some clues to why these groups so adamantly support charter schools. According to the Times, "a vast majority of them are not unionized, and they have real financial advantages because their work force is younger and more transient and their payrolls, pensions and medical costs are lower."*

The reality is that most middle-class suburban parents in the United States are very happy with the public schools their children attend. Inner-city schools with working-class and poor minority student populations have not had the same levels of success or satisfaction, but as far as I can tell there is no magic bullet to transform these schools.

My fear is that once charter schools open the door, private school vouchers will rush in, and the entire public school system will be dismantled. Then we can hire Walmart and McDonald's, or maybe Halliburton and AIG, to run our schools. But do not worry, they may not do a very good job educating children, but they will be "too big to fail."

A. Charter Schools Are the Wrong Answer
B. What Happens If the Charter School Companies Win?
C. Charter Schools Don't Do Miracles
D. Schools Enter Chartered Waters

A. Charter Schools Are the Wrong Answer

Based on an essay published on the *Huffington Post*, June 18, 2010

www.huffingtonpost.com/alan-singer/charter-schools-are-the-w_b_617054.
html

Questions to Consider

1. Can benefits supposedly offered by charter schools be provided in public schools?
2. Who makes money from charter schools?
3. What is the answer to poor education in inner-city communities?

On June 14, 2010, the *New York Times* ran a front-page article about kindergarten children at the Clara E. Coleman Elementary School from Glen Rock, New Jersey, who were learning about the principles of engineering through hands-on activities before they even knew how to read.[2] Their task was to design housing that would protect the three little pigs from the big, bad wolf.

This was a wonderful project, in a wonderful classroom, with an excellent teacher, in an affluent suburban school district. Pictures that accompanied the article showed that the children in this class and school were almost all White. According to real estate estimates and the 2000 census report, in the borough of Glen Rock, about twenty miles from New York City, the median household income was over $100,000 a year, about 60% of adults are college graduates, houses sell for about $500,000, and the population was 90% White, 6% Asian, 3% Latino, and 2% African American. For the high school graduating classes of 2004 through 2006, over 95% of students indicated that they would move on to a two-year or four-year college.

The *New York Times* article also highlighted a program in Manassas, Virginia, which has a thriving biotech industry, where the local school district had spent $300,000 on a children's engineering program since 2008 for projects like "making musical instruments from odds and ends, building bridges with uncooked spaghetti and launching hot-air balloons made from trash bags and cups." There was also a science technology program at the Midway Elementary School of Science and Engineering in Anderson, South Carolina, where kindergarten children "celebrated Groundhog Day by stringing together a pulley system to lift a paper groundhog off the floor."

In fact, these are all wonderful projects, in wonderful classrooms, with excellent teachers, in affluent, White, suburban school districts. My point is that public education and teacher preparation in the United States is not failing the American people. What is failing is education in inner-city minority communities and it is failing, not because of minority parents, their children, or teachers and their unions, but because government on every level, corporations, and White suburban taxpayers, do not want to pay what it will cost to rebuild inner-city communities and create decent living conditions for children and their families.

Inner-city minority children do not need charter schools that will have a limited impact at best, they need their parents to have decent jobs and they need to live in decent homes. There is only one miracle cure for urban poverty and it is spelled J-O-B-S!

In many American cities, the charter school movement is basically an alliance between national foundations philosophically antithetical to public education, local politicians who are building political machines, and business speculators. High-quality education is at best an afterthought. According to the New York City Department of Education,[3] the student population in the city's elementary and middle-level charter schools was 60% Black and 33% Latino in 2010. White and Asian families overwhelmingly preferred to send their children to the city's higher-performing designer mini-schools.

Examples of what will happen to public education if the charter school movement succeeds in privatizing education in the United States are the for-profit proprietary "colleges" and the empires of church groups such as the one headed by the Reverend Floyd Flake in St. Albans, Queens. The federal government is trying to rein in, without success, the rip-off proprietary programs that make millions of dollars by accepting any "student" eligible for federal loans, training them for nonexistent jobs, and then leaving the students saddled with thousands of dollars of debt that they can never pay back.

In Queens, New York, Floyd Flake has become a very wealthy man parlaying political connections in both major parties with his church-related charitable activities. The *New York Times* reported that Flake and his partners earned over $1 million by transferring a church-owned senior citizens housing complex into private for-profit housing that they will manage and milk for even more money.[4] Flake, either with or without his church, has his tentacles into casinos, real estate, the delivery of government services, and of course, they run a private school. A former Congressman, Flake was investigated for income tax evasion and embezzlement, but walked when a judge threw out the government's case against him and his wife. Just wait until the Reverend Flake and the proprietary "colleges" get into the charter school business.

B. What Happens If the Charter School Companies Win?

Based on an essay published on the *Huffington Post*, November 8, 2010
www.huffingtonpost.com/alan-singer/what-happens-if-the-chart_b_780000.html

Questions to Consider

1. Do charter schools represent a flowering of public educational choice or are they an actual threat to public education in the United States?
2. Are online classes for elementary and secondary school students legitimate educational practice?

3.   Are charter schools really efforts by edu-businesses to maximize profits at the expense of the public?

One of the arguments made by advocates for charter schools is that they expand consumer choice and that, given the state of education in many inner-city minority communities, experimentation with alternatives can only help the situation. As buzz words, choice and experimentation always sound good. After all, we know about the disappointing performance of many students in inner-city schools under the current educational system, so why not try something else?

Unfortunately, we already know what will happen if private, for-profit charter school companies take over K–12 education in the United States because for-profit proprietary companies have already successfully invaded what used to be called "higher education." These companies have defrauded the government, left families deep in un-repayable debt, and cheated students out of an education.

In 2010 the federal Department of Education published a list of suspect businesses masquerading as colleges and issued new rules to protect students from aggressive and misleading recruitment by private, for-profit institutions. For-profit colleges received $26.5 billion in government-funded student aid in 2009. Tax dollars insure student loans and the government must pay them if students default.

One of the worst offenders is the so-called University of Phoenix, a "university" in name only, operated by the Apollo Group. Phoenix currently enrolls over 280,000 students nationwide. It makes its money by recruiting students who are eligible for federal Title IV financial aid programs. Over 90% of Apollo's net revenue in 2009 came from federal money.

Phoenix advertises that it offers flexible degree programs for "working learners" who have jobs or other obligations that keep them from attending school full-time, but who want to garner credentials that will improve their income and employment possibilities. However, according to its 2008–2009 records, only 9% of its customers "graduated," the average debt per customer is over $13,000, less than half of its customers repay loans, and 13% of them are currently in official default on loan payments. Phoenix's parent company, the Apollo Group, is also under investigation by the Securities and Exchange Commission for illegal insider trading in company stocks.

Another large proprietary school accused of misrepresentations and under investigation is Kaplan University with 138,000 customers, a loan repayment rate of only 28%, and a default rate of 17%. Kaplan, which is the largest and fastest-growing division of the Washington Post Company, boasts, "We build futures." It is unclear, however, what kind of futures the company actually builds.

Kaplan started as the American Institute of Commerce in 1937, changed its name to Quest College, and became Kaplan College when purchased by Kaplan, Inc., in 2000. It changed its name again, to Kaplan University, when it was granted permission to offer graduate-level degree programs. It is currently based in

Davenport, Iowa, has offices in Fort Lauderdale, Florida, and online student support centers in Florida, Illinois, and Arizona.

Almost all of Kaplan's customers take online courses of dubious quality. For a while California's public community colleges allowed students to take some courses at Kaplan and transfer credits that would count toward their degrees. However, in 2009 the University of California and Cal State University systems, concerned about the quality of Kaplan courses, canceled their agreement with the company.

Kaplan University has an open admissions policy, which means there are no admissions standards other than eligibility for federal Pell grants and student loans. Kaplan was one of fifteen for-profit colleges cited by the Government Accountability Office for malfeasance, and three former academic officers have filed a federal lawsuit accusing the "university" of defrauding the United States government out of more than $4 billion. They allege that Kaplan enrolled unqualified students, inflated student grades so they could stay enrolled, and falsified documents to obtain accreditation. The company's response is that the lawsuit should be dismissed because it lacks the specificity required in a federal fraud case.

In the movie *Waiting for "Superman,"* cute kids and desperate families plead for access to charter schools. But the movie is little more than propaganda for a well-financed campaign to undermine public education in the United States so edu-businesses can pick up the more profitable pieces. They need to divert us with the cute kids and their families because few people would buy their product if they realized it was being pushed by companies like Phoenix and Kaplan.

Post-It Note: The Washington Post Company sold its newspapers and held onto Kaplan because charters and proprietary schools are more profitable than the newspaper business.[5]

C. Charter Schools Don't Do Miracles

Based on an essay published on the *Huffington Post,* June 30, 2010
www.huffingtonpost.com/alan-singer/charter-schools-dont-do-m_b_627600.html

Questions to Consider

1. Is it possible to reorganize all public schools using the Locke model?
2. Is the United States willing to pay what it costs to have a top educational system?

Charter schools are not the magic bullet that will transform urban minority public schools. As you peel away layers of the charter onion, the inevitable problems come to the surface.

Locke High School in Los Angeles was touted as a charter school miracle. I wish it were true, but it is not. In 2008, Locke was notorious as one of the worst failing schools in the United States. It had a high crime rate and a low graduation rate, the opposite of what schools should be. At one point a race riot involving six hundred students made the national news.

According to the *New York Times*,[6] two years after a charter school group named Green Dot took over management of the school, gang violence was down, attendance was improved, and performance on standardized tests was inching up. The school had become one of the number one stops on the charter school reform bandwagon tour, as corporate and government "education reformers," including federal Department of Education bigwigs, got photo-ops in its newly tree-lined courtyard and issue pronouncements about how wonderful everything has become.

But a closer look at the Locke miracle, way down in the *Times* article, exposed what has actually taken place there. In 2007, a former principal complained that Locke was the Los Angles dumping ground for problem students. Only 15% of its students could pass the state standardized math test. The first thing Green Dot did was get rid of all the troubled students and bring in a fresh supply. It also dumped most of the teachers—keeping those prepared to work longer hours for less pay, what it defined as enthusiasm. Locke reopened in Fall 2008 with a new freshman class. Green Dot also fixed up the place to make it attractive for the photo ops.

The big problem was cost, although Green Dot is a non-profit company, its administrators do get paid. The four-year turnaround at Locke cost $15 million over budget. This does not include part of a $60 million grant from the Gates Foundation to support state development, which makes the actual cost of the turnaround much higher. Unfortunately, the federal government has set a $6 million cap for the reorganization of an individual school. Green Dot is now more than 150% over budget. The rest of the money, $9 million, was covered by donations from foundations, supposed charities, but often business groups hoping to make lucrative profits from the dismantling of public education.

Locke is actually a good model of what educational change will really cost. The school has additional administrators, security, two psychologists, busing, and health services for students, in addition to staff development provided by the Gates Foundation. None of this has anything to do with being a charter school. This is just the real cost of educating inner city children.

D. Schools Enter Chartered Waters

Based on an essay published on the *Huffington Post*, May 10, 2010
    www.huffingtonpost.com/alan-singer/schools-enter-chartered-w_b_569501.html

Questions to Consider

1. Given the realities of charter schools, why does President Obama continually support them?
2. Why has the myth of charter school success taken root?

Why should facts dictate government policy? The Obama/Duncan Department of Mis-Education apparently does not think they should. Just because charter schools do not make a difference does not mean we cannot force them on the states as the latest mis-educational panacea.

In 2010, the New York Senate passed a bill that would more than double the number of privately run, but publicly financed, charter schools in the state to 460. Why? To help the bankrupt state secure up to $700 million in federal "Race to the Top" grant money. This version of the bill was backed by charter school advocates and mysteriously eliminated restrictions on where the new charter schools could be placed and removed provisions for the state comptroller to audit the schools. Not surprisingly, the bill was strongly opposed by the state teachers union.

Among those pushing hard for charter schools in the United States are President Obama, Secretary of Education Arne Duncan, the Bill and Melinda Gates Foundation, the New Schools Venture Fund founded by investors who helped start Google and Amazon, and the Walton family of Walmart. In New York State, a group called Education Reform Now ran a massive radio campaign pushing for charter schools. The group is financed by hedge fund financiers from Hawkshaw Capital, Gotham Capital, SAC Capital, and Maverick Capital who made a lot of money while the world economy tanked during the last few years. Apparently, since they were so successful in ruining the economy, they felt they should lend their expertise to set school policy. Education Reform Now's three-member staff of educational experts includes an investment fund manager, a former investigator for the NYC Civilian Complaint Review Board, and someone who previously worked in the entertainment industry.

The problem with the charter school movement is that the majority of the approximately five thousand to six thousand charter schools in the United States are no better, and in many cases worse, than local public schools. Stanford University researchers from the Center for Research on Education Outcomes found that less than 20% of charter schools offered a better education than comparable local schools and about half offered an equivalent education. However, in more than a third of the charter schools, 37%, educational achievement was significantly worse than in local public schools.

Operators of some of the more successful charter schools include Uncommon, KIPP, and Aspire Public Schools. But they have created only about 350 schools during the last ten years and are heavily dependent on $500 million in philanthropic support and a lot of unpaid work hours. In a *New York Times* interview,[7] David Levin, co-founder of the KIPP charter school network and superintendent of KIPP's New York City schools, described how he works seventy-five to ninety hours a week training teachers, raising money, and shuttling among six schools. He does reserve Sundays for his wife, whom he met speed-dating. Levin taught fifth grade in Houston, Texas, for three years but then left the classroom because he could not sustain the pace. The point should have been you cannot operate a national or state school system based on hyperactive individuals who eventually burn out.

Celebrities and philanthropists want to take credit for the roughly one hundred charter schools that have been successful, but ignore the other 4,900 schools. According to a *New York Times* report,[8] the Cleveland Arts and Social Sciences Academy, which is "not the kind of charter school that celebrities visit" is "close to the norm for urban Ohio, where 60 percent of charter school students in the eight largest districts attend a school that earned a D or F on its last state report card."

Is this what Obama/Duncan mean by "Race to the Top"?

Notes

1. Editorial, "Thinking Sensibly about Charter Schools," *New York Times* (October 16, 2013), www.nytimes.com/2013/10/16/opinion/thinking-sensibly-about-charter-schools.html.
2. Winnie Hu, "Studying Engineering Before They Can Spell It," *New York Times* (June 14, 2010), www.nytimes.com/2010/06/14/education/14engineering.html?pagewanted=all.
3. www.nyccharterschools.org/about.
4. Russ Buettner, "Sale of Property Positioned Queens Pastor to Gain," *New York Times* (June 18, 2010), www.nytimes.com/2010/06/18/nyregion/18flake.html?pagewanted=all.
5. James O'Toole, "Amazon's Bezos Buys Washington Post for $250 million," CNNMoney (August 5, 2013), http://money.cnn.com/2013/08/05/news/companies/washington-post-bezos/.
6. Sam Dillon, "School Is Turned Around, but Cost Gives Pause," *New York Times* (June 25, 2010), www.nytimes.com/2010/06/25/education/25school.html?pagewanted=all.
7. Elissa Gootman, "Six Days of School, and Then a Day Not of Rest," *New York Times* (May 9, 2010), www.nytimes.com/2010/05/09/nyregion/09routine.html.
8. Trip Gabriel, "Despite Push, Success at Charter Schools Is Mixed," *New York Times* (May 2, 2010), www.nytimes.com/2010/05/02/education/02charters.html?pagewanted=all.

8

COMMON CORE—WHAT IS IT GOOD FOR?

National Common Core standards promise to transform and upgrade education in the United States, however many parents and teachers remain dubious. Part of the problem is that the standards have been connected to both new high-stakes assessments for students and the evaluation of teachers. My point of view about the national Common Core standards has evolved over time as I have tried to help teachers and school districts develop curricula, units, and lesson plans that address Common Core skills. While the Common Core standards ignore content and provide little in the way of specific guidelines for teaching, they do encourage systematic planning, conscious decision-making, and vertical (across grade-levels) and horizontal (across subject areas) integration.

A number of companies, organizations, and academics are busy marketing themselves as experts on Common Core so they can get paid by school districts for staff development workshops and products. This has certainly clouded debate over the value of the Common Core standards. Pearson is a major promoter of Common Core and a source for instructional materials and programs supposedly aligned with the standards. The company also sells staff development workshops to districts.

A. Common Core, What Is It Good For?
B. Can Common Core Turn On the Math and Science?
C. The Third-Grade Science Fair: A Common Core Conundrum
D. Common Core: The Good, the Bad, and the Ugly
E. What's Missing from Common Core Is Education for Democracy

A. Common Core, What Is It Good For?

Based on an essay published on the *Huffington Post*, April 19, 2012
   www.huffingtonpost.com/alan-singer/common-core-what-is-it-go_b_1434
012.html

Questions to Consider

1. Why is the New York State Council for the Social Studies concerned about the national Common Core standards?
2. Why are curriculum choices so politically sensitive?
3. Should private corporations be allowed to use philanthropic foundations to influence educational policies that will benefit their business interests?

At its 2012 annual meeting the New York State Council for the Social Studies passed five resolutions condemning the national and state Common Core standards for marginalizing social studies. The resolutions charged that attention to math and reading left little time or money in K–12 classrooms for effective instruction in social studies, citizenship, and history and demanded that the state develop a new set of core standards. The position taken by the NYSCSS is one of a number of reasons to question whether the much ballyhooed national Common Core standards will deliver promised improvements in education.

An article in *Newsday* reported on Long Island, New York, schools trying to implement Common Core standards.[1] The article asked us to "Think of it as America's first national lesson plan—coming soon to a public school near you." But as you read the article, more questions arise about the Common Core than are answered. For example, "English classes are tackling more works of nonfiction from Common Core's recommended lists, which include the philosophical writings of Ralph Waldo Emerson and Henry Thoreau, along with speeches by George Washington, Abraham Lincoln and Ronald Reagan."

While I hate to be picky, I cannot think of any speeches by George Washington. There are two big problems. First, Washington was barely literate. Letters that he is known to have written are spiced with examples of invented spelling. John Adams called him "too illiterate, too unlearned, too unread for his station and reputation" and according to Thomas Jefferson, he was "chiefly in action, reading little."[2]

Second, Washington did not like to speak in public, partly because of ill-fitting false teeth. His famous "Farewell Address" was largely written by James Madison and Alexander Hamilton and published as a written report rather than delivered as a speech.

I also wonder which speeches delivered by Ronald Reagan students should concentrate on. Reagan was a decent actor who could deliver his lines and his speeches offer solid sound-bites: "Mr. Gorbachev, tear down this wall;" "A people free to choose will always choose peace;" and "It's morning in America again."

There is also his declaration that the Soviet Union was an "evil empire." But the speeches overall are less than memorable and Reagan wrote none of them. Instead, he had a coterie of speechwriters including Peggy Noonan, Ken Khachigian, and Peter Robinson. I can only guess that Reagan speeches are included because the Common Core must present teachers with conservative Republican alternatives.

It will also be interesting how teachers address the religious connotations in some of the "Reagan" speeches. At the time President Reagan made the "evil empire" speech in 1983, I thought he was drawing a connection between the popular *Star Wars* movie series and the Cold War struggle between the United States and the Soviet Union. What I did not realize was that the speech was delivered at a meeting of the National Association of Evangelicals, probably not a group overtly familiar with the movies, but definitely a group that knew the Book of Revelation from the New Testament where John calls on Christians to hasten the coming of the Kingdom of God by doing battle with the Roman evil empire.

But more important than historical gaffes is the substance of what Common Core asks teachers to do. The *Newsday* article reported on an eleventh-grade English class at Ward Melville High School in Setauket, New York, where an "English class recently spent five days studying Lincoln's Gettysburg Address—a speech just three paragraphs long." I asked a class of working teachers what they would teach if they spent five days on the Gettysburg Address. They had some interesting replies, including using the Gettysburg Address as a model and having students write funeral addresses about people who died as a result of other mass deaths such as Hiroshima and 9/11 that they would connect to broader historical and moral points. However, none of them could figure out how you would spend more than one or two days on the speech. Their general conclusion was that this effort to implement the Common Core wasted a lot of time.

I did find two useful pieces of information in the article. The author noted that the Common Core standards "are a creation of the National Governors Association, working together with the Council of Chief State School Officers, which represents state education commissioners." What he left out however is that much of the work of these groups is funded by foundations related to companies like Microsoft and Pearson that stand to make a lot of money selling new products to school districts if the standards are implemented.

In 2010, the National Governors Association received a significant portion of its operating budget from foundation grants and contracts, corporate fellows, and other contributions. The NGA and CCSSO have received millions of dollars from the Gates Foundation. Its over one hundred corporate partners include Educational Testing Service, Apple, Pearson, Cisco, College Board, DeVry, Houghton Mifflin, IBM, Intel, Microsoft, and Scholastic, all companies that stand to benefit from its policy recommendations. Recent corporate award winners include Walmart (2011), Intel (2010), and Microsoft (2009).

The *Newsday* article also mentioned that "many educators wonder where school districts will find the extra money to buy Common Core textbooks that are being rushed out by publishers eager to capture an expanding national market. New textbooks are just one of the budget expenses, along with new commercial tests and teacher training, that local administrators say are being pushed on their districts in the drive for education reform." It quoted an adjunct math professor from Hofstra University that the standards provide publishers "an unprecedented opportunity to print mountains of textbooks and piles of cash."

The Gates and Pearson foundations have a number of shared initiatives centering around the development of the "Common Core curriculum" adopted by over forty of the states. Grover J. "Russ" Whitehurst, a former director of the United States Department of Education's research arm said the Pearson-Gates arrangement represents an "interesting intertwining" of non-profit and for-profit motives and will undoubtedly prompt questions about "who profits from the common core."[3]

Pearson also partners with Apple and has been implicated in the suit the United States Justice Department has brought against Apple and five publishers including the Penguin Group, which is owned by Pearson, for conspiring to raise the price of e-books in violation of anti-trust laws. After all, the business of business is profit, not education.

B. Can Common Core Turn On the Math and Science?

Based on an essay published on the *Huffington Post*, June 29, 2012
www.huffingtonpost.com/alan-singer/can-common-core-turn-on-t_b_1619 130.html

Questions to Consider

1. Does the memorization of formulas actually interfere with the development of conceptual knowledge?
2. Can learning by problem solving be applied in other academic areas?
3. To what extent is the unleashing of creative imagination the key to learning and teaching?

The Common Core standards, if they separate the learning of skills from content and understanding, point teachers in the wrong direction.

Critiques posted on a Common Core mathematics blog examining the standards make similar points.[4] A comment on the calculation of area argues that the National Assessment of Educational Progress (NAEP)'s "stark revelation of the extent to which students fail to understand the concept of area and lack basic problem solving skills warrant not a simple tweaking of current methodology, but a complete rethinking of how the topic of area is presented." The authors of the post explains that "mathematics curricula compartmentalize math skills into discrete chunks" because "it's easier to teach and easier to write tests." However, this "math bite approach to imparting skills . . . institutionalizes a testing regime, at the expense of developing students' thinking skills." The authors conclude, "Even if they [students] learn every standard, the parts remain disjointed without students gaining the real math wisdom that comes from synthesizing parts into a whole." Unfortunately, when the authors "examined CCSSI Mathematics' [Common Core State Standards Initiative Mathematics] approach to the topic of area," they found "little that holds promise . . . CCSSI completely overlooks the value of emergent learning through requiring a sequence of problems of ever-increasing complexity."

I found an ally in my campaign to morph content, skills, and understanding in online videos by Dan Meyer, a former high school math teacher based in the San Francisco Bay Area. Meyer argues in "Math class needs a makeover" that math classes need to focus on conceptualizing and solving problems rather than memorizing what are for students meaningless formulas.[5]

Meyer's ideas fit in nicely with *The Algebra Project*,[6] an approach developed by Bob Moses, a Civil Rights activist from the 1960s, who promoted the idea that all children can master math. In *The Algebra Project*, Moses laid out a five-step approach:

1. Students participate in a *physical experience*, like a trip, where they see examples of what they are studying (e.g., arches, geometric shapes, suspension bridges).
2. Following the trip, students draw *pictorial representations* or construct models of what they have observed.
3. Next, they discuss and write about the event in their everyday dialect or intuitive language. Moses calls this stage *"People Talk."*
4. Their oral and written reports are then translated into the standard dialect or structured language as part of *"Feature Talk."*
5. In the last step, students develop *symbolic or algebraic representations* that describe what they have learned. They present these representations in class and explore how they can be used to describe other phenomena.

The Dan Meyer video reminded me of "math" experiences I had with my own now adult children and a project I participated in at a summer work camp for neighborhood teenagers from Brooklyn in the 1970s and 1980s.

When my son was a high school junior, I got a call from the school telling me that he was failing chemistry. I asked if there was anything I could do to help him and was told that unless I could teach him the missed work myself his fate was already sealed. My son and I decided to take up the challenge, but the problem remained that I had not learned much chemistry in high school and remembered nothing other than that I hated both the subject and my teacher. One glance at the textbook and the periodic table just brought back nightmares.

We tried doing some homework problems together and then somehow we realized, I do not recall whether it was him, me, or some kind of collaborative insight, that chemistry was really algebra. Instead of memorizing formulas, which is what they were doing in class and had completely alienated him, we had to solve the problems. In chemistry the addition of energy or some kind of reagent "balanced" the two sides of the equation. Our goal was always to establish the BALANCE. Our discovery was a little like the scene in the movie *Stand and Deliver* about math teacher Jaime Escalante where the student realizes that the entire point of math was to "fill the hole" by balancing both sides of the equation.

Another time, my stepdaughter was planning to return to graduate school and was practicing for the standardized test known as the GRE. She kept getting stumped by the math and called me for help with one particular sample problem:

> Thirty people are at a costume party. Sixteen are dressed as Dracula and fourteen are dressed as Wolfman. If all the Wolfmen stay at the party, how many additional Draculas have to arrive before they make up two-thirds of the guests.

I told her give me five minutes and I would call her back. I set up a table and began to add. There are sixteen Draculas and thirty people. If four more Draculas arrive there will be twenty and thirty-four people, still short of two-thirds. If another four arrive there will be twenty-four Draculas and thirty-eight people, which is still short. But if another four, or a total of twelve arrive, we will have twenty-eight Draculas and forty-two guests, which is exactly two-thirds.

My step-daughter was glad to get the answer, but wanted a formula to memorize so she could use it for other problems. I replied the key was not to memorize formulas but to solve problems. That night I had Draculas, Wolfmen, and Bob Moses running through my head and in the morning I called her back. Once you solved the problem you could construct the formula to describe your solution.

Originally you have sixteen Draculas among the thirty people. Sixteen plus something equals thirty. The kicker is we want the Draculas to be two-thirds of the party-goers. Sixteen plus some unknown number is equal to two-thirds of thirty plus the same unknown number. Make X the unknown number.

$$16 + X = 2/3(30 + X)$$

Whatever you do to one side of the equation you have to do to the other to maintain BALANCE.

Multiply both sides by three.

$$3(16 + X) = 2(30 + X)$$

$$48 + 3X = 60 + 2X$$

Subtract twenty-eight from both sides.

$$3X = 12 + 2X$$

Subtract 2X from both sides.

$$X = 12$$

I think these two examples just represent good standard school teaching that can be applied in any classroom.

The summer camp work project was a little different and illustrates the importance of real world problem solving. I was working with teams of six teenagers and our goal was to re-roof cabins in the woods. We had to load ninety-pound rolls of three-foot-by-fifty-foot tar paper on a flatbed truck, drive as close to the cabin as possible, carry the ninety-pound rolls of tar paper to the cabin, and then carry the ninety-pound rolls of tar paper up the ladder to the roof. I think you get my point. These were heavy rolls of tar paper.

I asked my work team how many rolls of tar paper they thought we needed for the roofing job and suggested we could calculate the amount we needed using math. They did not want to be bothered. It would be easier to carry the tar paper up to the roof than it would be to solve the problem, or so they thought.

By the time we got the rolls of tar paper to the work site they were rethinking their decision. It was hot and the tar paper was heavy. The first teen struggled getting up a few rungs of the ladder but finally made it. He called down "This is too hard. We better learn the math." We measured the roof and then calculated exactly how many three-foot-wide by fifty-foot-long rolls of tar paper we needed for the job. It was still hard getting them up the ladder, but we only took as many as we actually needed. Real world math had triumphed over student resistance.

Maxine Greene, a twentieth-century educational philosopher based at Teachers College in New York City,[7] wrote about "creative imagination" as the key to learning and called on teachers to unleash the "creative imaginations" of their students. Greene argues that "teaching and learning are matters of breaking through barriers—of expectation, of boredom, of predefinition." She believes "to teach . . . is to provide persons with the knacks and know-how they need in order to teach themselves" and "put into practice in their own fashion what they need to join a game, shape a sonnet, or devise a chemical test." To me, Greene's ideas mean teachers have to help students identify problems and support their efforts to create their own solutions.

As a teacher, I feel I am at my best when I identify problems and search for solutions along with my students. Recently, I was working with a class of social studies teachers examining Social Darwinism and late nineteenth and early twentieth century pseudoscientific justifications for racism. The discussion got a little technical as the teachers grappled with what Charles Darwin, the founder of modern evolutionary biology, and Herbert Spencer and Andrew Carnegie, Social Darwinists who believed human evolution justified social inequality and capitalist society, actually knew about the mechanisms of biological evolution.

The answer is really very little. Most of our current scientific knowledge about genetics came long after they died.

Somehow I got involved in explaining the differences between "trait" or "structural" genes and "regulator" genes. Based on my reading of the work of Stephen J. Gould, especially *Ontogeny and Phylogeny*,[8] a trait gene, what we commonly just call genes, provides the instructions that determine most aspects of biological development, such as the existence of nervous systems that provide for the possibility of intelligence or for the existence of melanin or skin pigment. The regulator genes interact with the trait genes and "tell" them how fast to operate and when to turn on or shut off. The on-and-off and rate of operation affects the extent of brain development and intelligence as well as the depth of skin color.

The trait genes that produce the human brain and nervous system are not fundamentally different from the trait genes operating in other mammals, however the regulator genes that control the trait genes in humans turn down the growth rate much more slowly. This process, which allows for the retention of juvenile or even prenatal rates of growth as organisms mature, is called neoteny and explains both human intelligence and why in some groups of people more melanin is produced and they have darker skin color.

One of my great joys as a teacher is that I get to learn and problem-solve along with my students. In this case, I was getting a lot of blank looks from my class when I hit upon an idea that would help me solve my problem and explain the difference between trait and regulator genes. We had a sink in the classroom. I stopped the drain, turned the water on full throttle, and the sink began to fill. The sink and the water supply represented the structural genes. I gradually turned the spigot and shut off the water flow. The spigot represented the regulator genes that control the water flow. If these genes turn off at birth there is no water in the sink. If they turn off gradually, water accumulates. If they don't turn it off at all, the water overflows.

I worry that with the Common Core standards' focus on mastering skills through repetitive practice, students will never learn to find their own solutions to chemistry or geometry problems, challenge established authority, imagine creatively, and adjust the flow of water. Most students will not learn very much and what they do learn, they will not learn better.

C. The Third-Grade Science Fair: A Common Core Conundrum

Based on an essay published on the *Huffington Post*, June 4, 2013
www.huffingtonpost.com/alan-singer/the-3rd-grade-science-fai_b_3384601.html

Questions to Consider

1. What does scientific thinking look like in an eight-year-old?
2. What happens when teachers are evaluated based on student created artifacts?

My eight-year-old grandchildren Sadia and Gideon worked very hard on their third-grade science projects and at first I was very impressed with their tripartite boards and their ability to explain what they were testing. I got to see more of Gideon's project because his team worked at his house with Gideon's father. Sadia and her team worked with one of the other parents. At the end, both Sadia and Gideon were able to explain their hypothesis, procedure, and conclusions, a pretty good explanation of the scientific method for third-graders.

My son-in-law, a professional architect, constructed a two-channel ramp by splitting a cardboard tube. Gideon and his teammate raced and timed spheres, marbles, balls, and a series of round objects of different sizes and densities down the ramps to test whether size and density impacted on velocity. They were very involved with the project, largely because they had an exceptional dad to work with. They loved doing the marble races, although I am not sure how much science they learned.

Sadia's team tested whether fruits and vegetables could conduct electricity using a voltmeter. But when she demonstrated the project to me I realized two things. She did not know what electricity was, although she knew it had something to do with "electrons;" where the electricity came from; and whether the fruits and vegetables created the electricity or it came from another source. At one point she tested the voltmeter by connecting it to a AA battery and it registered negative current. She thought the voltmeter was broken until I suggested she change the wires to the other side of the battery, reverse polarity, and take a new reading. Sadia is a very good student who follows directions to the letter. But what she had not done was actually experiment; play around with the voltmeter, battery, and fruits and vegetables to actually try to figure out what was happening. It was science without science.

And then I went to view the third-grade science fair on parents' night and saw about one hundred other impressive, but nearly identical, tripartite boards explaining the hypothesis, procedure, and conclusions for different experiments downloaded from the Internet. What I realized is that there was little evidence of any of the students having actually conducted experiments or having any real knowledge of what they were presenting. This was a beautifully done Common Core presentation of academic vocabulary with little context or understanding.

I do not blame the teachers who were following Common Core academic guidelines to promote the use of academic vocabulary. I do not blame the parents who helped the children to the best of their abilities. I certainly do not blame the children who worked hard to create lovely projects and learn complex vocabulary.

The culprit is the Common Core conundrum. I believe Common Core goals are useful for teachers because they help define what students should be able to do at different stages in school. But the Common Core does not detail what students should actually know about content and concepts or how they should be taught.

In fact, in a section called, "What Is Not Covered by the Standards," it makes clear that the standards do not address "how teachers should teach. For instance, the use of play with young children is not specified by the Standards, but it is welcome as a valuable activity in its own right and as a way to help students meet the expectations in this document. Furthermore, while the Standards make references to some particular forms of content . . . they do not—indeed, cannot—enumerate all or even most of the content that students should learn. The Standards must therefore be complemented by a well-developed, content-rich curriculum consistent with the expectations laid out in this document."[9]

In theory, "a great deal is left to the discretion of teachers and curriculum developers." But that, unfortunately, is only in theory, because teachers are under tremendous pressure to prepare students for standardized assessment that will be used to evaluate students, teachers, administrators, schools, and districts. Third-graders will be tested on whether they can define hypothesis, procedure, and conclusion, not whether they actually understand electricity, conductivity, density, velocity, or science, and certainly not whether they can actually organize a scientific experiment.

To satisfy promises made in its Race to the Top grant application, the New York State education commissioner imposed a new formula for evaluating teachers in New York City schools. Because teachers are being evaluated based on student performance, a whole new breed of standardized exams will be developed to test students in a variety of subjects previously untested including art, music, and gym. It will be a financial bonanza for testing companies like Pearson, but will sorely impact on what students learn.

Expect children, including kindergarten and pre-school children, to be tested on the technical vocabulary of a subject, not how to dribble a ball, draw a family, or sing a song. Science will mean memorizing vocabulary for the test, not actually learning science.

D. Common Core: The Good, the Bad, and the Ugly

Based on an essay published on the *Huffington Post*, May 22, 2013
    www.huffingtonpost.com/alan-singer/common-core-the-good-the-_b_3319687.html

Questions to Consider

1. What does it mean to be "college and career ready"?
2. Can any curriculum or standards package ensure that every student develops the skills and knowledge needed to graduate from high school "college and career ready"?
3. Is it possible to fight for the "good" in Common Core while opposing the imposition of the less useful and destructive parts?

> From our highest-performing districts to our most challenged, the Common Core lights the way along that path; the Common Core standards will help us to ensure that each of our students—regardless of zip code or family

income—develops the skills and knowledge needed to graduate college- and career-ready.

—New York State Educational Commissioner John B. King, Jr.,
New York State Education Department, "News and Notes,"
May 2013[10]

I have been very critical of the national Common Core standards developed by the National Governors Association and the Council of Chief State School Officers with money from Pearson and the Bill and Melinda Gates Foundation for a number of reasons. I believe they are partly a ploy by major publishers and media companies to sell new material to schools that is actually the same old stuff marketed with different labels. I think the stress on skill acquisition in reading and math at the expense of content understanding in other subject areas has the potential to eviscerate instruction in history, social studies, science, health, literature, the arts, and language. And I think pairing the Common Core standards with high-stakes tests for students and new forms of teacher evaluation has the potential to undermine effective instruction and learning. However, unlike some conservative columnists, I do not believe it is a secret federal (Obama) plan to nationalize education in the United States.

I am a big Clint Eastwood fan and I think his career is a good metaphor for Common Core. Eastwood has been good (if not great), bad, and unfortunately, very ugly. In the good category I count *Unforgiven*, *Million Dollar Baby*, *Pale Rider*, and I loved *Space Cowboys*. There is a lot of bad in a five-decade career, but *The Bridges of Madison County* and *Heartbreak Ridge* stand out. Although the "Dirty Harry" movies and the Spaghetti westerns probably belong in the ugly category, the ugliest moment, and certainly the most bizarre, was Clint debating an empty chair at the 2012 Republican National Convention.

Despite John King's enthusiastic report quoted above, with Common Core, it is easiest to document the bad and the ugly. Students are being tested and teachers are being evaluated based on material that has never been taught and curricula that is still to be written. Randi Weingarten, president of the American Federation of Teachers, is calling for a moratorium on high-stakes tests based on Common Core until students and teachers actually have a chance to see and to master new material and skills.

Jamie Gass, director of the Center for School Reform at the Pioneer Institute for Public Policy in Boston, has kept me up to date on growing national opposition to the Common Core standards, especially from conservative groups. While People for the American Way has the Pioneer Institute on its right-wing "watch list," Jamie has certainly done an effective job of both reporting on and marshaling opposition to Common Core from the right and left ends of the political spectrum.

In Indiana, Republican Governor Mike Pence halted implementation of Common Core because of opponents who believe the standards are not as good as

Indiana's old ones and others who want educational decisions made on the local level. In Pennsylvania, Democratic state legislators complained that Common Core was a $300 million "unfunded education mandate" and charged that the assessments tests required under Common Core would undermine "traditional instruction" and be "devastating to fiscally challenged schools."

In "The Ballad of John and Yoko," the Beatles reminded listeners that change "ain't easy." They were not singing about American schools but they well could have been. When right-wing conservative groups and state governments stake out a position against Common Core, it makes me suspicious.

Rather than teachers and parents just harping on the bad and the ugly, we need to look at what is good, or at least useful in Common Core. I have tried to do this in conversations I have had with teachers at Hofstra University and in local schools. When discussing Common Core, I stress four things:

1. Common Core calls on teachers to plan systematically to ensure that skill development is embedded throughout the curriculum. For example, in United States history classes, if a class does not get to spend time on map analysis during study of European settlement and the revolutionary era, teachers need to make sure they include a lot of map study when students learn about westward expansion and the Civil War.

2. Common Core calls on teachers to make conscious decisions about what to focus on in each lesson. Teachers must be curriculum planners rather than curriculum consumers. They have to design lessons that address the particular academic needs of their students rather than relying on textbooks or scripted, pre-packaged, lessons. This is a major reason I am opposed to many of the private for-profit companies trying to use Common Core to sell material to schools.

3. Common Core calls on schools to reorganize to promote vertical and horizontal integration. Vertical integration means that curriculum and skill acquisition should be coordinated so that teachers can build on prior student learning and have a sense of final academic goals. For example, in economics, normally a subject studied in the senior year of high school, students should be able to read, analyze, evaluate, and draw conclusions about articles, charts, graphs, and political cartoons from newspapers like the *New York Times* and the *Wall Street Journal*. Common Core is at its best (see the Post-It Note at the end of this essay), when it helps teachers, parents, and students understand what it means to be college and career ready.

4. Horizontal integration means that grade-level teachers from different subject disciplines need to meet and plan regularly so that they have a better understanding of where and why students are having academic difficulty, can develop material targeting the needs of individual students, and can work together to support skill acquisition and content understanding. Science teachers can give students word problems that deepen their understanding

of math. English teachers should have students read historical literature that supports social studies instruction by helping students develop a sense of time, place, and people.

I think the John King statement quoted above is ridiculous. In no way does Common Core "light the way." But that does not mean it is not useful. Common Core standards need to be separated from the push by publishers to sell material, the high-stakes testing of children, and from the evaluation of teachers. We need to recognize that the standards are limited because they focus on skills while ignoring the content of what children should learn in school. In addition, teachers and school districts need time to develop lessons, units, and institutional models that support Common Core goals. But none of these things mean the goals are invalid.

Parents, teachers, and students need to fight for the good in Common Core while challenging the bad and the ugly.

Post It Note: According to the national Common Core standards,[11] *students who are college and career ready should "demonstrate independence;" "comprehend and evaluate complex texts;" "discern a speaker's key points, request clarification, and ask relevant questions;" "articulate their own ideas;" "become self-directed learners;" "read purposefully;" "assess the veracity of claims and the soundness of reasoning;" "value evidence;" "understand other perspectives and cultures;" and "evaluate other points of view critically and constructively." No wonder right-leaning state education departments want nothing to do with Common Core. I suspect politicians who support it never read it or did not read it with the critical perspective required of high school students, otherwise they would all be running for the hills.*

E. What's Missing from Common Core Is Education for Democracy

Based on an essay published on the *Huffington Post*, July 30, 2013

www.huffingtonpost.com/alan-singer/whats-missing-from-common_b_3673 244.html

Questions to Consider

1. Why are citizenship and education for democracy left out of the Common Core?
2. What happens to a society when education ignores citizenship?

Something is missing in Common Core's single-minded focus on skill acquisition—education for democracy—and this is a serious lapse.

According to its mission statement,[12] "The Common Core State Standards provide a consistent, clear understanding of what students are expected to learn, so teachers and parents know what they need to do to help them. The standards are designed to be robust and relevant to the real world, reflecting the knowledge and skills that our young people need for success in college and careers. With American students fully prepared for the future, our communities will be best positioned to compete successfully in the global economy."

Common Core standards are supposed to "provide a consistent, clear understanding of what students are expected to learn" and be "relevant to the real world." But "real world" expectations are defined as preparing students for "success in college and careers" and "to compete successfully in the global economy." As best as I can ascertain, in the entire document, there is no real discussion of life in a democratic society and the role of education in promoting democratic processes and democratic values.

The view of education promoted in Common Core, devoid of substance and disconnected from life in a democratic society, was endorsed by President Barack Obama at a meeting with United States governors in 2010 and is at the heart of the federal Race to the Top program.

Unfortunately, President Obama seems unaware of the consequences of this type of narrowly focused education.

Democracy is hard to build as we are witnessing around the world. It requires a sense of shared community, respect for democratic values such as minority rights, concern for the well-being of others, freedom of expression, and the right to be actively involved in the political process. It requires a sense of being part of an inclusive and diverse body politic, of citizenship. White man's democracy supported by the enslavement of Africans broke down in the United States in the 1850s and led to civil war. Despite the collapse of communism, the countries that emerged from the former Soviet Union remain far from democratic. In India, which calls itself a democracy, government is largely corrupt and most of the population is impoverished. China, the most populous country in the world, is more capitalist than communist, but it still has an authoritarian state.

Without a sense of shared community based on democratic values, democratic processes can be meaningless. In 1933, Adolph Hitler became chancellor of Germany and the Nazi Party rose to power through constitutional means. In Egypt recently, as happened in Iran in the 1980s, a religious party without a commitment to a broader sense of community and democratic values that respect the rights of minorities and an open exchange of ideas, used democratic processes to achieve power and then used power to suppress the rights of others. In Libya and Syria, both countries without a sense of national community and shared democratic values, the collapse of dictatorships brought civil war, not democracy, and the rise of anti-democratic forces.

Although President Bush promised to export freedom to Iraq and Afghanistan when the United States invaded those countries, and that they would become democratic models for the entire Middle East, anti-democratic forces either control them or are on the verge of acquiring power.

Meanwhile, in Washington, DC, the democratic process is continually stalemated by a lack of commitment to democratic values by the Republican Party, which would rather bring the whole house of cards down than compromise. The Republican Party has a voting majority in the House of Representatives. Under the so-called Hastert Rule it refuses to even allow proposed laws to be discussed and voted on unless a majority of the Republicans agree to the proposal in advance.

This rule, which does not appear in the United States Constitution or the House of Representatives' own procedures, allows 118 House Republicans to veto any action no matter what a majority of the House wants. It is a Republican Party dominated by a more rural, more White south and west, so the wishes of the rest of the country, more urban, more diverse, and more populated, are completely ignored while the country plunges deeper and deeper into economic malaise and social decay.

The national Common Core standards are NOT responsible for current and future civil wars in Egypt, Syria, and Afghanistan. They are NOT responsible for the political stalemate in Washington, DC, that has virtually incapacitated the Obama administration, preventing it from dealing with pressing economic, environmental, and social issues. But Common Core does share something with disasters overseas and at home. They all have roots in a mistaken concept of what it means to live in a democratic society.

The sad thing is that citizenship, democratic values, and preparation for an active role in a democratic society are at the core of many earlier state standards and are prominent in the curriculum goals of the National Council for the Social Studies (NCSS). But these are ignored in the Common Core push for higher test scores on math and reading exams.

In response to the marginalization of content, including social studies and history content, in the Common Core, the NCSS released what it called the "College, Career, and Civic Life (C3) Framework for Social Studies State Standards" in defense of social studies and citizenship education. Their C3 framework is aligned with the Common Core standards for English Language Arts and Literacy in History/Social Studies. However, it argues for the value of education as preparation for "civic life" and emphasizes "skills and practices as preparation for democratic decision-making."[13] According to the NCSS, "Active and responsible citizens are able to identify and analyze public problems, deliberate with other people about how to define and address issues, take constructive action together, reflect on their actions, create and sustain groups, and influence institutions both large and small. They vote, serve on juries when called, follow the news and current events, and participate in voluntary groups and efforts. Implementing the C3 Framework to teach students to be able to act in these ways—as citizens—significantly enhances preparation for college and career."[14]

Democracy requires that Americans see themselves as citizens, not just as consumers or employees. Common Core, by ignoring the fundamental values that make democracy possible, does education and the United States a tremendous disservice.

Notes

1. John Hildebrand, "LI Schools Start Using Common Core Plan," *Newsday* (April 1, 2012), www.newsday.com/long-island/education/li-schools-start-using-common-core-plan-1.3636770.

2. Both quoted in John Taylor Gatto, *The Underground History of American Education,* 2nd edition (New York: Oxford Village Press, 2001), http://johntaylorgatto.com/chapters/1s.htm.

3. Catherine Gewertz, "Gates, Pearson Partner to Craft Common Core," *Education Week* (April 27, 2011), www.edweek.org/ew/articles/2011/04/27/30pearson.h30.html?tkn=WNPFBe2J3.

4. http://ccssimath.blogspot.com/2012/06/concept-of-area-part-2.html.

5. www.ted.com/talks/dan_meyer_math_curriculum_makeover.html.

6. www.algebra.org/.

7. Maxine Greene, *Releasing the Imagination: Essays on Education, the Arts, and Social Change* (San Francisco: Jossey-Bass, 2000); see http://socialimagination.wikischolars.columbia.edu/quotes.

8. Stephen Jay Gould, *Ontogeny and Phylogeny* (Cambridge, MA: Harvard University Press, 1977).

9. www.schoolimprovement.com/common-core-360/blog/What-is-Not-Covered-by-the-Standards/.

10. http://myemail.constantcontact.com/News-and-Notes-from-Commissioner-King.html?soid=1110847617454&aid=z3DoOkmOaY0.

11. www.corestandards.org/ela-literacy/introduction/students-who-are-college-and-career-ready-in-reading-writing-speaking-listening-language.

12. www.corestandards.org.

13. www.socialstudies.org/c3.

14. Ibid.

9

HIGH-STAKES TESTING

I sometimes joke with students that my super-power is test taking; I can pass any test on any subject without studying as long as the test is written in English. All super-heroes have limitations and my kryptonite is a decided lack of ability in languages. My skill at test taking did not translate into being a consistently good student. In fact it became an excuse not to study or work hard in classes I did not enjoy. At least in my case, and I suspect in most cases, high-stakes standardized tests are not very accurate predictors of a student's academic performance. While girls are generally better students than boys, boys are disproportionally represented in schools where admission is based on high-stakes assessments. This may be because many immigrant families make heavier investments in the education of their sons or to what Claude Steele, a social psychologist,[1] calls "performance anxiety" resulting from "stereotype threat." Studies conducted by Steele demonstrate that apprehension caused by the feeling you are suspected of intellectual inferiority can lead to poorer test scores.

Reliance on high-stakes assessment has produced a backlash from parents and teachers who see the tests as undermining both education and social values. Pearson Education has been a particular target because of its role in designing and marketing high-stakes assessments. Essays in this chapter explore many of the controversies surrounding the high-stakes testing craze. They include tests for admission to selective schools, standardized tests used to evaluate students and teachers, the validity of the tests, the role of testing companies in promoting their products, and how high-stakes testing encourages cheating.

A. What Do the Tests Test?
B. Do These Tests Have Educational Value?
C. Cheating Students Who "Pass" the Test
D. The "Wisdom" of Pearson's Pineapple Passage
E. Pearson and the Atlanta School Mess
F. Did the "Melk Man" Learn to Cheat at Stuyvesant High School?
G. Cheating on the Test—I May Be Guilty Also!

A. What Do the Tests Test?

Based on an essay published on the *Huffington Post*, April 29, 2013
www.huffingtonpost.com/alan-singer/what-do-the-tests-test_b_3177684.
html

Questions to Consider

1. How do results on standardized tests mirror inequalities in American society?
2. If girls are in general better students, why are the high-stakes test schools disproportionally male?
3. Are there ever truly objective and fair tests?
4. Who benefits from the present system?

My eight-year-old grandchildren, Sadia and Gideon, survived the Spring 2013 third-grade ELA and math tests without being scarred for life. From their perspective it was "Much Ado about Nothing" and they were more concerned about the start of the little league baseball season.

For me, the bigger question remains the value of these tests in the education of children, especially the impact they have on what gets taught (curriculum), how it is taught (pedagogy), and how learning is accurately measured (assessment).

Based on his study of student performance on standardized tests from 1960 to 2010, Sean Reardon found that "Students growing up in richer families have better grades and higher standardized test scores."[2] The gap continues to rise, and according to Reardon, family income is a better predictor of student performance on these tests than any other factor. All the high-stakes standardized tests measured was the socio-economic status and earnings of parents and not how much students know or how well they will perform in school.

Rather than waste all this time and money on testing, an alternative is to just throw out the standardized tests and assign students to classes, schools, and colleges based on their parents' income tax forms. While this may not be fair to students from poorer families, tax revenues would probably rise. The wealthy would be less inclined to search for loopholes or cheat on their taxes if they thought their children would be denied admission to elite high schools and colleges because their reported income was too low.

In 2012, a federal civil rights complaint charging bias in the New York City specialized high school application process was brought against the city by a number of Civil Rights organizations.[3] They charged that "racial disparities" in admission to the city's select high schools resulted "in large part from admissions policies that rely too heavily or even exclusively on standardized tests" and on a "marked failure to provide African Americans and Latinos with opportunities to learn the material or otherwise prepare to meet the admissions standards."

As recently as 1999, the student body at prestigious Brooklyn Technical High School was about one-quarter African American, but since then the percentage has dropped to about 10%. There has been a similar decline at Stuyvesant High School where the percentage of Black students dropped from nearly 13% Black in 1979 to about 1% now.

Once again, in 2013, the number of African American and Latino students admitted to the selective high schools fell sharply. According to a report on the website Gotham Schools,[4] "Of the 5,229 students accepted to the city's eight Specialized High Schools this year, 618 were black or Hispanic, according to data the Department of Education released today, the day that eighth-graders learned their high school placement. Last year, the schools accepted 733 black and Hispanic students." The figures were most disturbing at Stuyvesant High School where just nine African American and twenty-four Latino students were admitted. Meanwhile, at Brooklyn Tech, the number of African American and Latino students who were admitted dropped by 22% from the previous year.

New York City Mayor Michael Bloomberg defended the admission procedure claiming these selective high schools were "designed for the best and the brightest" and that he saw no need to change the admissions policy or state law. The mayor declared, "I think that Stuyvesant and these other schools are as fair as fair can be. . . . There's nothing subjective about this. You pass the test, you get the highest score, you get into the school—no matter what your ethnicity, no matter what your economic background is. That's been the tradition in these schools since they were founded, and it's going to continue to be."

However, another report cast serious doubts on whether the high school admission test identified the "best and brightest" as the mayor claimed. According to an article in the *New York Times*, "Girls Excel in the Classroom but Lag in Entry to 8 Elite Schools in the City,"[5] "In the United States, girls have outshined boys in high school for years, amassing more A's, earning more diplomas and gliding more readily into college, where they rack up more degrees—whether at the bachelor's, master's or doctoral levels." But when it comes to admission to New York City's selective high schools, boys make up about 60% of the students at the most prestigious schools. In 2013, 51% percent of the middle school students who took the Specialized High School Admissions Test were girls, but girls made up only 45% of the students who were admitted to the schools.

This is surprising for two reasons. Nationally, enrollment in highly competitive high schools is 55% female. In addition, when schools use multiple criteria for admission, including school performance, girls do significantly better than boys. The *Times* reported that at LaGuardia High School of Music and Art and Performing Arts, where admission is based on grades, auditions, and portfolios, the study body is nearly three-quarters female.[6] Other elite programs that weigh-in school performance in their admission process have similar population imbalances favoring girls. At Bard, Millennium, Beacon, and Townsend Harris high schools girls outnumber boys by at least three to two. The principal at Bard said he has had to work to find ways to recruit more qualified male students.

If girls are in general better students, why are the high-stakes test schools disproportionally male? The best answer I can come up with is that the admission test, which is designed by Pearson, does not accurately measure the ability to perform in high school at the highest levels. More likely, the results reflect a decision by immigrant families to invest in their sons by paying for them to take expensive test prep classes at private cram schools where tuition costs can run to thousands of dollars. Students who do not have access to these courses because they are girls, from poorer families, or African American and Latino are then discriminated against by the testing process. If this is the case, and I strongly suspect it is, we are once again looking at money as the key to success, not desire to excel or performance in school.

B. Do These Tests Have Educational Value?

Based on an essay published on the *Huffington Post*, August 15, 2013
www.huffingtonpost.com/alan-singer/tests-designed-so-student_b_3739487.html

Questions to Consider

1. In your view, why were the results on the initial Common Core aligned tests so poor?
2. Why were respected school administrators so critical of the tests?
3. How did you do on the sample problems?

The results are in and the news is bad. Student scores plummeted dramatically on New York State math and reading tests administered in Spring 2013 that were supposedly aligned with new national Common Core standards. Statewide, about a third of the students passed the reading or math exam. The previous school year, on a different series of tests, 55% of the state's students were considered proficient in reading and 65% in math.

The airwaves and the Internet were abuzz with explanations, apologies, and outrage. For months, state and local education officials tried to prepare parents for the anticipated low scores. State Education Commissioner John B. King sent an open letter to "New York State Parents and Families" acknowledging that "students struggled on this year's test" but this was because the state had introduced higher standards and more difficult tests so "every single one of our students" would be on track for college and careers by the time they graduate from high school.[7] At a press conference, King, said the test scores should not be seen as a reflection on districts, schools, and teachers, but as a new "baseline" for future student performance. He was also confident that the scores on tests developed by the private Pearson Education corporation, a subdivision of the global Pearson media conglomerate, accurately assessed student mastery of Common Core standards.

New York City Mayor Michael Bloomberg rejected criticisms of the tests and actually called the results "very good news."[8] He blamed the media for focusing on declines in student performance. Meanwhile United States Secretary of Education Arne Duncan argued the drop in scores was because "too many school systems lied to children, families and communities." He believes that with the new Common Core standards and tests "finally, we are holding ourselves accountable as educators."[9]

An editorial in the *New York Times* took a similar position.[10] It claimed: "Over the last decade or so, most states deceived the public about the dismal quality of public schools by adopting pathetically weak learning standards that made children appear better prepared than they actually were. Not surprisingly, when states like Kentucky dropped the charade and embraced more challenging standards, scores dropped precipitously. That same scenario is playing out in New York State, which, this week, released the first round of scores from tests linked to the rigorous Common Core learning standards, which have been adopted by all but a handful of states."

While test scores were down all across New York State, the results were definitely uneven.

- In New York City, test scores fell in every school district, but were more pronounced in poorer communities. In nine New York City schools no students at all passed the math exams.
- In Rochester, New York, an overwhelmingly minority upstate urban school district located in a city abandoned by industry and where middle-class White families fled to the suburbs, only 5% of students passed either the reading or math tests.
- Statewide, only 15% of Black students and 19% of Hispanic students passed the math exams, compared with half of White students and over 60% of Asian students.
- Only 6% of students with learning disabilities passed English.
- Students whose first language is not English did even worse. Only 3% of non-native speakers were proficient.

Other New Yorkers were less sanguine (sanguine is a good Common Core vocabulary word, for any high school readers that means cheerfully optimistic), especially on Long Island where the opposition to Common Core and the new assessments was more intense. A growing Opt-Out movement of parents who do not want their children's educations directed by high-stakes assessments argued "The test results help our cause by forcing districts to publicly acknowledge the flaws in the state's testing policy, instead of defending them."[11]

In two districts, school superintendents spearheaded the opposition to the testing regime. William Johnson of Rockville Centre called the data provided by the tests "uninterpretable," adding that the test scores did not have much meaning for his district.[12] John Rella, superintendent of schools in the Comsewogue School District on Long Island, charged that these tests were part of a campaign to "shake confidence in public education" at a time when school budgets are being slashed and the media is creating a "toxic environment towards public education." He described the message being delivered by the testing regime as "unconscionable" and "hurtful to children."[13]

Carol Burris, the principal of South Side High School in Rockville Centre, compared "data-driven, test-obsessed reforms" being promoted by the New York State Department of Education and the Obama administration with depressing scenes from a Charles Dickens novel about nineteenth-century schools in industrial Great Britain.[14]

According to Burris, "Because of the Common Core, our youngest children are being asked to meet unrealistic expectations. New York's model curriculum for first graders includes knowing the meaning of words that include 'cuneiform,' 'sarcophagus,' and 'ziggurat.' Kindergarteners are expected to meet expectations that have led some early childhood experts to worry that the Common Core standards may cause young children harm. If we are not careful, the development of social skills, the refinement of fine motor skills, and most importantly, the opportunity to celebrate the talents and experiences of every child will be squeezed out of the school day."

Burris argued that the so-called curriculum reforms are being pursued without evidence that higher tests scores actually signal that students will be more ready to perform in college.

Burris also charged that tremendous financial interests" were "driving the agenda about our schools—from test makers, to publishers, to data management corporations—all making tremendous profits from the chaotic change. When the scores drop, they prosper. When the tests change, they prosper. When schools scramble to buy materials to raise scores, they prosper. There are curriculum developers earning millions to created scripted lessons to turn teachers into deliverers of modules in alignment with the Common Core (or to replace teachers with computer software carefully designed for such alignment). This is all to be enforced by their principals, who must attend "calibration events" run by "network teams."

I agree with Johnson, Rella, and Burris. Common Core standards and the New York State assessments are supposed to emphasize deep analysis and creative problem solving, but I saw none of it on sample math problems published in the *New York Times*.[15]

This is a sample grade seven math question.

Carmine paid an electrician x dollars per hour for a 5-hour job plus $70 for parts. The total charge was $320. Which equation can be used to determine how much the electrician charged per hour?

1. $5x = 320 + 70$
2. $5x = 320 - 70$

3. $(70 + 5)x = 320$
4. $(70 - 5)x = 320$

I gave this problem to a group of teacher education students and many had the same trouble that the seventh graders had. They knew that cost equals labor (5X) plus materials ($70) or $5X + 70 = 320$. But the choices with 320 on one side of the equation are incorrect. You have to take a second step and translate the equation into $5X = 320 - 70$. THEY HAD A RIGHT ANSWER BUT THEIR RIGHT ANSWER WAS NOT ONE OF THE CHOICES.

As far as I can tell, these were poorly designed tests, a consistent problem with Pearson tests. New York State should demand its money back. A well-designed test has a range of difficulty and starts with easier questions so students feel comfortable taking the test and do their best. As a result it produces a range of grades and gives teachers a sense of the level where individual students are performing. This test seemed to only have difficult questions so anxious students panicked and did poorly and teachers had no idea what they actually know.

For an eighth-grade reading passage titled "Jason's Gold," questions had multiple correct answers and students were asked to figure out which ones the test writers thought were best. These were opinion questions presented as if they had factual answers. It is also unclear to me how knowing the meaning of the word "momentous" in line eighteen or understanding a comparison of people to iron-filings demonstrates readiness to start a career or go to college.

The tests were also unfair because students in higher grades were tested on work from earlier grades that they were never taught. It was even worse for non-English speakers—BECAUSE THEY DON'T SPEAK ENGLISH. Imagine how you would perform on a test on a subject you never studied or administered in a language you do not know.

Based on past experience we know that students always score lower when a new test is introduced because they were taught, and teachers reviewed, for the previous series of tests. This happens every time and scores rebound when teachers have copies of the new tests and students study from them. Next year New York State, if the testing regime continues, can claim miraculous improvement when nothing has changed except that teachers and students are familiar with the tests. My guess is that savvy school administrators will concentrate test prep on students who scored closest to the next highest level. It will be easiest to get them over the threshold so it looks like schools, teachers, and test review materials are making a difference.

As with many standardized tests, these assessments most accurately reflect the social conditions of the lives of students. Except that no one in political power wants to address the growing social inequality gap in the United States. All they seem to want to do is give harder and harder tests.

I think the tests are really being used as weapons against teachers and schools to force them to adopt questionable but expensive curricula being marketed by test prep companies that seem to have enormous influence over politicians. Instead of buying packaged test prep and curriculum programs, a state can get the best bang for its buck by having students memorize a few simple lower-order thinking rules.

1. Remember the order of operation when solving math problems and to ADD exponents.
2. These are two-step problems. Do the second step before you look at the choices.
3. If the problem does not have an answer have confidence in your ability, the problem probably does not make sense.
4. The reading tests are asking for opinions not facts and they want their opinions not yours.
5. Remember *The Hunger Games*! "May the odds be ever in your favor."

C. Cheating Students Who "Pass" the Test

Based on an essay published on the *Huffington Post*, February 10, 2012
www.huffingtonpost.com/alan-singer/english-regents-exam_b_1268007.
html

Questions to Consider

1. Must everybody enjoy reading the same books and about the same topics?
2. Is it possible to devise high-stakes standardized tests that do not pervert instruction and will accurately measure student concept learning and skill mastery?
3. Should teachers and schools be evaluated based on student performance on tests?

We are now learning that with all the pressure on teachers, administrators, and schools to lift student test scores, standardized exams actually measure very little. Many high school teachers, especially in urban and minority communities in New York City and State, have long wondered why scores on the state high school English exit exam (the regents) were higher than in other subject areas. English teachers thought it was just because they were better at what they do, although other content area teachers had their suspicions.

Thanks to an article by Michael Winerip in the *New York Times*,[16] we now know why students score much better on the English regents. The exam is much easier than the others. In fact it is so easy that it does not even measure basic student literacy. It also calls into question the reliability of standardized tests to measure anything about schools, let alone teacher performance, and the whole federal Race to the Top program.

In its current iteration, the English regents, which takes three hours to complete, includes twenty-five multiple choice questions, an essay, and two short response questions that require a paragraph-long answer. Winerip examined the rubric posted online by New York State for evaluating student essays.[17] He found acceptable answers were full of spelling and grammatical errors, conceptual mis-understanding, and often simply restated the question.

Fortunately for Winerip's sanity, he did not analyze the short-answer part of the test, probably because it has not yet been posted on the state website. However, the August 2011 exam is available and it suggests the problem is even greater than Winerip recognized. For part one, a teacher reads a passage to students about an individual concerned with recycling paper. Students then must answer eight multiple-choice questions about the passage. A typical question is "The speaker uses less paper in her kitchen by purchasing . . ." The choices are silverware, plastic bags, sponges, and pot holders. For the rest of the test, students read three one-page passages and a poem and answer questions about the content. In August, the first passage was about camping and comfort, the second offered brief biographies of Peter Roget and George and Charles Merriam, and the third was an excerpt from a novel.

None of the passages were on technical material. None of the passages were on the difficulty level of the sports coverage in the *New York Times*. None of the passages in any way demonstrated the ability to do college-level work. Neither the reading passages nor the questions utilize high school, let alone college, level vocabulary. There were no questions about vocabulary, grammar, or books. Shakespeare remains in the high school English curriculum but not on the regents. In more affluent suburban districts, middle-school students should easily pass this test.

Based on Michael Winerip's analysis of the scoring rubric on the most recent New York State English regents, and my examination of the August 2011 reading passages and multiple-choice questions, not only are New York State students who pass this test ill-prepared to do college-level work, but those who are going on to college are being exempted from remedial programs they desperately need.

Lying to students about the level of their work—that is the real crime with the inflation of English regents grades.

D. The "Wisdom" of Pearson's Pineapple Passage

Based on an essay published on the *Huffington Post*, May 10, 2012
  www.huffingtonpost.com/alan-singer/the-wisdom-of-pearsons-pi_b_1505897.html

Questions to Consider

1. Why did the hare defeat the pineapple?
2. Why did Pearson feel obligated to defend its test?
3. Why did state education defend Pearson?

Pearson Says Its Tests Are "Valid and Reliable"
Anemona Hartcollis, *New York Times*,
May 5, 2012, A21

In a letter to the New York State Education Department, mega-test and textbook publisher Pearson Education defended a controversial reading passage and questions on the 2012 administered eighth-grade reading assessment. Pearson claimed the passage was a reliable measure of student understanding of "character traits, motivation and behavior."[18] New York State, which paid Pearson $32 million to develop assessment tests, announced that it would not count these questions or questions on a recent fifth-grade math test that required prior knowledge of material not taught in the fifth-grade curriculum.

Pearson claimed that answers to questions based on the reading passage the "Pineapple and the Hare" could be derived from "evidence" available in the text. One question asked students which was the wisest animal. According to Pearson, "The owl declares that 'Pineapples don't have sleeves,' which is a factually accurate statement. This statement is presented as the moral of the story, allowing a careful reader to infer that the owl is the wisest animal."

Merryl Tisch, chancellor of the New York State Board of Regents, had an interesting twist on the controversy. She thought the pineapple question "made sense in context," but did not think it should have been used because "it added fuel to arguments by those who oppose using testing in teacher evaluations."[19]

Tisch told the *New York Times* that the Pearson exams were in no way invalidated by the plethora of errors plaguing them: "I take full responsibility for all of these errors, I do, I do, do. . . . And I would hope that Pearson as a producer of these exams would join me in this responsibility." She added, "Does it invalidate the test? Definitely not." She also dismissed critics as people who are "really just trying to push back, not only against the test, but against testing in general and against teacher evaluations in specific." An Internet petition protesting against high-stakes standardized tests was launched by a coalition of over one hundred organizations, and United Optout organized a national boycott of Pearson to combat the privatization of education in the United States.

What was missing from much of the debate over the wisdom of the Pearson pineapple passage was discussion of what wisdom actually is and what the curriculum standards that are supposed to be the basis for instruction and assessment are. Clearly Pearson and Tisch need some lessons in classical philosophy. I decided to read up about wisdom in the University of Chicago's *The Great Ideas, A Syntopicon of Great Books of the Western World*,[20] which identifies wisdom as one of the 102 great ideas of Western Civilization.

According to the *Syntopicon*, Plato did not believe human philosophers could actually achieve wisdom because this was a property reserved for the gods. People, but not pineapples, hares, or owls, could only hope to be lovers of wisdom, contemplating truth and using whatever understanding they managed to acquire to direct their conduct.[21] Aristotle, unlike Plato, believed humans could acquire wisdom through intellectual excellence, but he did not believe wisdom necessarily provided philosophers with moral virtue.[22] Aristotle also believed in practical wisdom, which he defined as concern with "things about which it is possible to deliberate."[23] The *Syntopicon* describes Roman Catholic theologian and philosopher Thomas Aquinas, who lived from 1225 to 1274, as an Aristotelian, or follower of Aristotle. Aquinas believed the essential quality of a wise man was his capacity to "order and to judge."[24]

Based on my understanding of Plato, Aristotle, and Thomas Aquinas, the owl, at least in this passage, would not be wise. The owl announced the fact that the pineapple did not have sleeves, but it did not explain, draw conclusions based on the observation, or make choices. The only animal that displayed any "wisdom" in the classical sense in this story is probably the hare, who decided to race the pineapple because of his knowledge that the pineapple could not run. The moral of the story of course is that it is a good thing the eighth-graders don't read Plato, Aristotle, and Thomas Aquinas.

Pearson and Tisch probably also need to familiarize themselves with the state learning standards. The social studies learning standards require that middle school students who took this reading assessment should be able to gather, organize, classify, know, describe, understand, explore, investigate, consider, explain, analyze, and interpret information in order to be considered "wise." Teachers are expected to be familiar with "Bloom's Taxonomy," which outlines higher-level thought-provoking questions and is required to ask questions that encourage students to help understand and use information on a more sophisticated level.

If Pearson and Tisch were teachers being evaluated based on the lesson of the pineapple, the hare, and the owl, because of their misapplication of the concept of wisdom and their failure to ask higher-order thinking questions, they would both be rated "UNSATISFACTORY."

E. Pearson and the Atlanta School Mess

Based on an essay published on the *Huffington Post*, April 3, 2013
www.huffingtonpost.com/alan-singer/pearson-and-the-atlanta-s_b_3005867.html

Questions to Consider

1. Who checks when school districts and testing companies report miraculous results?
2. Should Pearson be allowed to advertise itself as a promoter of school reform and student achievement?

On March 29, 2013, a Fulton County, Georgia, grand jury charged Beverly L. Hall, the former superintendent of Atlanta schools and thirty-four other

former and current school officials with racketeering, theft, influencing wit-
nesses, conspiracy, and making false statements in connection to a school testing
scandal that was exposed in 2011. Dr. Hall had been highly honored and well
paid because of supposedly miraculous improvements in student test results in
Atlanta. In 2009, she was named "School Superintendent of the Year" by the
American Association of School Administrators and hosted at a White House
reception by United States Secretary of Education Arne Duncan. In addition,
she received more than $500,000 in performance bonuses while superintendent
of the Atlanta school system.

The Atlanta testing scandal has broader implications for education in the
United States as politicians, including President Barack Obama, and private corporations and foundations push for increased testing of students and the evaluation
of teachers based on student scores on high-stakes standardized tests. The push for
increased testing has reshaped what happens in classrooms across the country and
may be a poison that ultimately threatens the survival of our public schools.

The Atlanta scandal initially broke when the *Atlanta Journal-Constitution* published studies in 2008 and 2009 that found "suspiciously high gains" on the state
Criterion-Referenced Competency Test (CRCT) and a large number of erasures
on answer sheets with wrong-to-right corrections at fifty-eight Atlanta schools.[25]

In a press release issued in July 2011, the governor of Georgia summarized the
findings of the state's investigation of Atlanta schools. According to the governor,
"the 2009 CRCT statistics . . . allow for no conclusion other than widespread
cheating in APS [Atlanta Public Schools]," a finding that was confirmed by a
decline in erasures on the 2010 test. The governor reported, "There were warnings
of cheating on CRCT as early as December 2005/January 2006. The warnings
were significant and clear and were ignored." He also stated there was evidence of
cheating as early as 2001. Investigators "found cheating in 44 of the 56 schools"
they examined. "There were 38 principals of those 56 schools (67.9%) found
to be responsible for, or directly involved in, cheating." Of 178 school personnel
implicated, "82 confessed to this misconduct." Sadly, the report notes, "Thousands
of children were harmed by the 2009 CRCT cheating by being denied remedial
education because of their inflated CRCT scores."

While the suspect test, the Georgia Criterion-Referenced Competency Test
was designed by McGraw-Hill, other companies, especially Pearson Education,
may bear some responsibility for what happened in Atlanta. Pearson designs and
administers a number of standardized tests in Georgia, including writing tests
for grades three, five, eight, and eleven; the EOCT (End of Course Tests)/ and
the GHSGT (Georgia High School Graduation Tests) in English/Language Arts,
Mathematics, Science, and Social Studies.[26] It also runs school "improvement"
programs in Atlanta schools through its Achievement Solutions division.

I want to make this very clear: I am NOT accusing Pearson or any of the other
testing and tutorial companies marketing their products to the Atlanta school
system of cheating on these exams. But given their involvement in these schools

and the promotion of their products based on data they reported from the Atlanta school system, they have a responsibility to clarify their role.

Pearson's program in Atlanta was especially important to its marketing efforts because the fifty-one thousand students in the Atlanta public schools were 92% Black and Latino and 70% received free or reduced price lunch, a designation for poverty. These are the groups that both the federal No Child Left Behind and Race to the Top programs are targeting for academic improvement. Pearson argued that success in Atlanta with its student population would translate into success anywhere.

According to a Pearson Achievement Solutions document entitled "School Progress/Atlanta Public Schools," Pearson Achievement Solutions worked with eleven schools in Atlanta Public Schools starting in the 2000–2001 school year. "Prior to working with Pearson Achievement Solutions, all 11 schools were not meeting Adequate Yearly Progress (AYP) goals. In the 2002–03 school year, after just two years working with Pearson Achievement Solutions, all 11 schools achieved AYP. All 11 schools also met the AYP goals in the 2003–04 school year. Since then, Pearson Achievement Solutions has continued work with eight of those schools. All eight schools have achieved their AYP goals every year through the 2005–06 school year."[27]

The Pearson document highlighted student performance at Grove Park Elementary School, which in 2004 was named a "Georgia School of Excellence" recognized for recording continuous gains in student achievement in reading, language arts, and math over a three-year period, and East Lake and Walter White Elementary schools, which were declared Pearson Achievement Solutions National Demonstration Schools for 2006–2007.

The 2011 Georgia criminal investigation report also highlighted these schools. Investigators found the level of cheating at Grove Park to be "moderate." However, at East Lake the cheating was described as "severe." Investigators charged that the school principal and testing coordinator "directed efforts including changing answers and arranging easier tests for some students." The principal also "threatened retaliation against teachers who 'slandered' her to investigators."[28]

The cheating was also reported as "severe" at White Elementary where teachers were accused of giving answers to students and correcting CRCT answer sheets.

Again, I want to make very clear that *I am not accusing Pearson or any of the other testing and tutorial companies marketing their products to the Atlanta school system of cheating on these exams.* But given their involvement in these schools and the promotion of their products based on data they reported from the Atlanta school system, there is much they have to answer for. If they want to continue marketing their high-stakes tests, tutorials, and curriculum packages to United States schools, they have an obligation to explain their role.

For example, how did Pearson, which claims to have checkpoints "built into the process to ensure consistent progress in achieving school improvement goals," attempt to establish the validity of the Atlanta school district's claims for off-the-charts improvement on test scores before taking credit for the results? I would also like to know why the Pearson Achievement Solutions website was down for updating while the indictments were being released and whether any material was deleted.

Pending a full and satisfactory response from Pearson and the other testing and support companies, I recommend that the federal government, states, localities, and school districts place a moratorium on all further business dealings with companies marketing high-stakes tests, tutorials, and curriculum packages. I also recommend they look into suspending existing contracts until there is full disclosure.

F. Did the "Melk Man" Learn to Cheat at Stuyvesant High School?

Based on an essay published on the *Huffington Post*, August 20, 2012

www.huffingtonpost.com/alan-singer/did-the-melk-man-learn-to_b_1796446.html

Questions to Consider

1. Do American institutions create an environment that promotes cheating?
2. Is extra help for those who can afford it a form of cheating?
3. Did you ever cheat? Why?

Cheating scandals break in the media every day. Finding a competitive edge, even if it involves bending or breaking rules you consider arbitrary in the first place, is endemic to American society. Most of us "cheat" when we drive above the posted speed limit. According to one study, seven out of ten motorists speed. Baseball players "cheat" using performance-enhancing drugs. Cyclists "cheat" by blood doping. The wealthy, including presidential candidates, "cheat" by finding loopholes that let them avoid paying their fair share of income taxes. The Republican Party "cheats" by trying to block voting in minority communities. Apparently, the crime is not cheating, only getting caught.

Melky "the Melk Man" Cabrera did not attend Stuyvesant High School in Manhattan, an elite institution renowned for Nobel Prize winners and students who cheat on standardized tests. He grew up in Santo Domingo Oeste in the Dominican Republic and started playing professional baseball there at age seventeen.

Melky was born in a country where the vast majority of people living below the official poverty line, which is over 40% of the total population, lack indoor plumbing and running water, 20% do not have electricity, and most people do not complete primary school. Two-dozen United States major league baseball teams have training and recruitment facilities in the Dominican Republic and the country supplies more major league baseball players than any other country outside the United States, so it is not surprising that Melky and many of his contemporaries turned to baseball as a way of escaping conditions in the Dominican Republic.

The story of Melky's downfall and the test scandal at Stuyvesant have painful similarities. In both cases, cheating offered a very high payback for relatively low risk and seemed consistent with the culture of the institution and society.

Cabrera, a former New York Yankee and San Francisco Giant, was suspended for fifty games starting on August 15, 2012, following a positive test for the performance-enhancing steroid/hormone testosterone, which is banned by Major League Baseball. Cabrera, an average player who suddenly blossomed as a star, was the Most Valuable Player in the 2012 All-Star game. He issued a statement acknowledging his guilt and apologizing for using a banned substance.

Melky joined a long list of baseball players who were accused of using performance-enhancing drugs. Alphabetically they include Barry Bonds, the all-time home run champion; Ken Caminiti, who died of a drug overdose in 2004; Jose Canseco, who has admitted to using banned drugs and testified against other players; Roger Clemens, who was twice tried for lying to Congress about drug use but never convicted; Jason and Jeremy Giambi; home run champion and former record holder Mark McGuire; David Ortiz; Rafael Palmeiro; Andy Pettitte; the twice-suspended Manny Ramirez; Yankee third baseman Alex Rodriguez, a twelve-time All-Star and three-time Most Valuable Player; and Sammy Sosa, who hit 609 home runs, number eight on the all time baseball list.

Melky and these players "cheated" because apparently they believed all their competitors were, because the rewards for cheating were contracts worth tens of millions dollars, and because even if they were caught, they still made mega-bucks. Cabrera was scheduled to be paid $6 million in 2012 and even with the fifty-game suspension from baseball he collected over $4 million from the San Francisco Giants. If he had not been caught taking testosterone, Cabrera was in line to sign a multi-year $50 million contract that would have started the next year

At Stuyvesant High School in June 2012, a student was caught photographing a statewide Spanish exam using a cell phone and texting the images to approximately eighty other students. The incident led to the resignation of the school's principal. Cheating at Stuyvesant was probably widespread. In 2010, an editorial in the school's student newspaper charged that "academic dishonesty" at Stuyvesant was "firmly entrenched" but rarely punished.[29] Among other things, "If you walk down any hallway in the building you are almost guaranteed to see students copying homework."

Part of the problem is that it may be difficult for Stuyvesant students to distinguish between legal and illegal forms of cheating. Few would consider it cheating to study for the New York City Specialized High School Admissions Test (SHSAT) using a Barron's Review book (list price $16.99), even though it contains three full-length practice tests based on past exams.

But is it cheating when families pay thousands of dollars for private tutors to prepare children for the test by having them review old tests over and over again? Admission to Stuyvesant is so competitive because it is seen as an avenue to Ivy League colleges and high-paying careers, so thousands of families pay astronomical sums for the tutoring every year. Prices range widely. Based on online advertising, New York Academics offers one-on-one instruction at fees ranging from $100 to $120 per hour. The Kaplan company offers individual SHSAT Premier Tutoring starting at $2,599 and classes at $849. The Princeton Review also has multiple levels of preparation. Its Premier Level cost $6,300, its Master Level cost $3,879, and its low-cost online offering is a bargain at only $1,500. The Kuei Luck Enrichment Center in Fresh Meadows, Queens, targets Chinese-American students and offers tutoring for only $2,200.

Why is it cheating to copy homework or send your friends a text of the test, but not cheating to review the test questions over and over again with a paid tutor in advance?

Of course Stuyvesant students are not the only ones who are cheating on tests and homework. In fact, it seems almost everyone is. In 2009, the *Atlanta Constitution* discovered that teachers and principals at forty-four out of fifty-six schools had changed student answers on state standardized exams.[30]

In 2004, twenty-three Houston, Texas, schools were investigated for possible cheating on the Texas Assessment of Knowledge and Skills. The *Dallas Morning News* found "unusual test score patterns" in nearly four hundred schools statewide.[31]

The *San Francisco Chronicle* revealed actions that compromised the validity of California's high-stakes achievement tests in at least 123 public schools between 2004 and 2006.[32]

In the affluent Great Neck school district in suburban New York City, students from well-off families paid as much as $3,600 for other students to take their college admissions exams. As many as forty students were implicated in the scam.

Alfie Kohn, who writes and speaks widely on education issues, offers interesting insights into the phenomenon of cheating in schools. In an article published in the October 2007 issue of *Phi Delta Kappan*, "Who's Cheating Whom?,"[33] Kohn identifies the conditions that promote a culture of cheating:

1. Teachers in the school have no real connection to students and do not seem to take it seriously when they cheat on exams.
2. Cheating is more common when students experience academic tasks as "boring, irrelevant, or overwhelming."
3. Students cheat when the ultimate goal of education is presented to them as getting good grades rather than learning.
4. Students feel pressured to improve their performance on standardized tests by any means necessary, even if they regard the methods as unethical.
5. Students are forced to compete with each other for school rewards and admission to prestigious colleges.

Kohn believes "Competition is perhaps the single most toxic ingredient to be found in a classroom, and it is also a reliable predictor of cheating . . . a competitive school is to cheating as a warm, moist environment is to mold." I believe Kohn is right. As long as schools promote competition between students, they are establishing the conditions, promoting, and even requiring that students cheat.

Melky did not want to take a chance on returning to poverty in the Dominican Republic when with a little bit of illicit help he could be on top of the baseball world and very rich. The students at Stuyvesant did not want to go to second-tier colleges when with a little bit of illicit help they could go to Ivy League schools and be on the road to wealth, power, and success. In a competitive society where some people amass great wealth and others are forced to struggle with very little, where the gap between rich and poor is increasing, everybody is looking for an edge. Melky and the Stuyvesant students felt like they would be fools not to get their edge by any means necessary.

I am not sure I want baseball players to stop competing. I love the game. But clearly money has undermined everything that is taking place in the national pastime. But even if baseball players and teams must compete against each other, schools do not have to be this way—unless our goal is to promote cheating as a positive value unless you are dumb enough to get caught.

For the record, I always copied homework as a high school student, most of which was busywork that was not worth doing. I also discussed test questions with friends who had taken exams earlier in the day. We considered this "research," not cheating, because teachers, if they cared, could always just give us different versions of the test. And last, I checked my answers on a neighboring student's exam during the French regents in June 1966. I was worried because I was weak in French and had a summer job so I could not afford go to summer school.

But to borrow a phrase from Bill Clinton when he was asked if he had ever smoked marijuana, I didn't "inhale."

G. Cheating on the Test—I May Be Guilty Also!

Based on an essay published on the *Huffington Post*, April 15, 2013
   www.huffingtonpost.com/alan-singer/new-york-standardized-tests_b_3080548.html

Questions to Consider

1.   What actually constitutes cheating?
2.   Do parents cheat when they help children with homework?
3.   Do teachers cheat when they review old tests with their classes?
4.   Do students cheat when they cram or go to private tutors?

I confess, I may be guilty of helping students improve their scores on standardized tests. Just last week I was helping my eight-year-old grandchildren, third-graders scheduled to take the new Common Core-based tests, with their math homework. When they were finished, I asked Gideon and Sadia if they had checked their work. Now Sadia values accuracy, so when she said she had checked her work I just initialed it. But Gideon values speed over accuracy and even though he said he had checked his work, I thought it advisable to take a closer look at it. Of course I found a couple of careless errors. I gave it back to him and told him he had to check his work again—which he knew meant he had made mistakes.

If these homework assignments are factored into their grades for the school year, Gideon, who ultimately got the questions right on his own, will get "inflated" grades because of the help he received at home. I guess in the new world of high-stakes testing even for the youngest children that makes me a cheater, but I thought as a grandparent, I was supposed to help them with their homework.

I wrote this blog because justified accusations about changing student answers on standardized tests in Atlanta, Georgia, became a witch hunt and all teachers were considered suspect of cheating. In Glen Cove, New York, a dozen teachers from two elementary schools were investigated for such nebulous infractions as "violating test protocol and not following the proscribed guidance in the testing manuals" during the spring 2012 elementary school reading and math tests.

I want to see hard evidence of cheating before teachers are charged with unprofessional conduct or criminal behavior. What happens during witch hunts, in Salem Village at the end of the seventeenth century and in the McCarthy Red Scare of the 1950s is that innocent people end up confessing to things they did not do and naming others, either because they begin to doubt themselves under pressure or because they want to strike a deal that will save their lives and careers. We do not need this to happen again.

I have proctored tests for forty years and I have no idea what the test protocol is nor have I ever checked a manual for guidance. Personally, I think I violate the "protocol" and the "manual" every time I check a box saying I read and agree to the conditions on some online application—because I never really read the pages of fine print. I doubt if anybody does.

I have another confession to make as well. As a high school social studies teacher for thirteen years starting in 1978 I taught what I estimate as two thousand students who took the New York State United States history regents examination and maybe an equal number who took the alternative regents competency tests. Before they took these tests we looked at old exams in class and I showed them how to systematically evaluate multiple-choice options and how to write an essay and receive partial credit even if you do not really know the answer.

But worse, at the end of every test, including the regents and the regents competency tests, when students came up to the front of the room to hand in their papers, I repeated the mantra:

- Did you answer all the multiple-choice questions?
- Did you check your multiple-choice answers?
- Did you write all the essays?
- Did you complete all the parts?
- Did you proofread and edit?

If a student answered no to any of these questions, I told them to sit back down and finish the test. The best teachers that I know did similar things because we wanted the tests to show what students had actually learned and understood. There were no financial bonuses involved and we were not being evaluated for tenure based on the test scores of our students. This practice was not considered cheating. It was just considered good teaching practice and having concern for students. My teachers did the same thing when I was in high school in New York City in the 1960s.

As I wrote earlier, I started teaching high school in 1978. Those students are now in their early fifties. In the name of absolute fairness and test integrity, the New York State Education Department may want to consider suspending their high school diplomas until they retake the exams. After all, their test results might have been tainted by caring teachers.

In fact, teaching itself skews test results. Maybe American schools should just give the tests without any pretense of teaching students at all.

Notes

1. Claude Steele and Joshua Aronson, "Stereotype Threat and the Intellectual Test Performance of African Americans," *Journal of Personality and Social Psychology,* 69, no. 5, (1995), pp. 797–811, http://mrnas.pbworks.com/f/claude+steele+stereotype+threat+1995.pdf.
2. Sean Reardon, "No Rich Child Left Behind," *New York Times* (April 28, 2013), http://opinionator.blogs.nytimes.com/2013/04/27/no-rich-child-left-behind/.
3. www.naacpldf.org/case-issue/new-york-city-specialized-high-school-complaint.
4. Philissa Cramer, "Fewer Black and Hispanic Students Admitted to Top High Schools," *Chalkbeat New York* (March 15, 2013), http://ny.chalkbeat.org/2013/03/15/fewer-black-and-hispanic-students-admitted-to-top-high-schools/.
5. Al Baker, "Girls Excel in the Classroom but Lag in Entry to 8 Elite Schools in the City," *New York Times* (March 23, 2013), www.nytimes.com/2013/03/23/nyregion/girls-outnumbered-in-new-yorks-elite-public-schools.html?hpw.
6. Ibid.
7. www.scribd.com/doc/158766611/Education-Commissioner-John-King's-letter-to-parents.

8. Javier Hernandez and Robert Gebeloff, "Test Scores Sink as New York Adopts Tougher Benchmarks," *New York Times* (August 8, 2013), www.nytimes.com/2013/08/08/nyregion/under-new-standards-students-see-sharp-decline-in-test-scores.html?hpw&_r=0.

9. Ibid.

10. Editorial, "New York's Common Core Test Scores," *New York Times* (August 8, 2013), www.nytimes.com/2013/08/08/opinion/new-yorks-common-core-test-scores.html?ref=nyregion.

11. www.fairtest.org/get-involved/opting-out.

12. Joie Tyrrell and Colleen Jaskot, "State Test Score Drop Could Strengthen Parents' Opt-Out Efforts," *Newsday* (August 8, 2013), www.newsday.com/long-island/education/state-test-score-drop-could-strengthen-parents-opt-out-efforts-1.5859428.

13. www.comsewogue.k12.ny.us/files/news/letter%20to%20sen.%20lavalle%20and%20attachment.pdf.

14. www.washingtonpost.com/blogs/answer-sheet/wp/2013/08/07/what-big-drop-in-new-standardized-test-scores-really-means/.

15. Javier Hernandez and Robert Gebeloff, "Test Scores Sink as New York Adopts Tougher Benchmarks," *New York Times* (August 8, 2013), www.nytimes.com/2013/08/08/nyregion/under-new-standards-students-see-sharp-decline-in-test-scores.html?hpw&_r=0.

16. Michael Winerip, "Despite Focus on Data, Standards for Diploma May Still Lack Rigor," *New York Times* (February 6, 2012), www.nytimes.com/2012/02/06/education/despite-focus-on-data-standards-for-diploma-may-still-lack-rigor.html.

17. www.nysedregents.org/comprehensiveenglish/.

18. Anemona Hartcollis, "Under Fire, Test Maker Says Its Work Is Reliable," *New York Times* (May 5, 2012), http://query.nytimes.com/gst/fullpage.html?res=9504EEDE1F3BF936A35756C0A9649D8B63.

19. Anna Phillips, "State Officials Throw Out Another Pearson Test Question," *SchoolBook* (May 2, 2012), www.wnyc.org/story/302903-state-officials-throw-out-another-pearson-test-question/.

20. Mortimer Adler, ed., *The Great Ideas, A Syntopicon of Great Books of the Western World* (Chicago, IL: Encyclopaedia Britannica, 1952). Wisdom is discussed in volume 3.

21. Ibid., pp. 1102–03.

22. Ibid., p. 1104.

23. Ibid., p. 1104.

24. Ibid., p. 1105.

25. Alan Judd and Heather Vogell, "A System-Wide Scandal," *Atlanta Journal-Constitution* (July 5, 2011), http://alt.coxnewsweb.com/ajc/_projects_and_planning_group/APS_investigations/APS.html.

26. Search online for "http://media.cmgdigital.com/shared/news/documents/2013/09/12/Pearson_Georgia_audit.pdf" for a PowerPoint report.

27. www.edweek.org/media/pas%20atlanta_case_study%2012–20–06%20edweek%20wp.doc.pdf.

28. Alan Judd and Heather Vogell, "A System-Wide Scandal," *Atlanta Journal-Constitution* (July 5, 2011), http://alt.coxnewsweb.com/ajc/_projects_and_planning_group/APS_investigations/APS.html.

29. Anne Barnard and Eric Newcomer, "At Stuyvesant, Allegations of Widespread Cheating," *New York Times* (June 27, 2012), www.nytimes.com/2012/06/27/nyregion/looking-into-mass-cheating-via-text-message-at-stuyvesant.html.

30. John Perry and Heather Vogell, "Are Drastic Swings in CRCT Scores Valid?," *Atlanta Journal-Constitution* (October 19, 2009), www.ajc.com/news/news/local/are-drastic-swings-in-crct-scores-valid/nQYQm/.

31. "Cheating Scandal Rocks Texas," FairTest, http://fairtest.org/cheating-scandal-rocks-texas.

32. "Cheating Cases Continue to Proliferate," *FairTest Examiner* (July 2007), http://fairtest.org/cheating-cases-continue-proliferate.

33. Alfie Kohn, "Who's Cheating Whom?," *Phi Delta Kappan* (October 2007), www.alfiekohn.org/teaching/cheating.htm.

10
CURRICULUM AND INSTRUCTION

What gets taught (curriculum), how it is taught (pedagogy), and how we measure what students learned (assessment), are constantly debated in the United States. The longer I teach, the more I realize that these debates are constantly reoccurring. In California in the 1990s, the social studies curriculum shifted into a chronological study of history. In New York, a multicultural focus on history was replaced by attention to human rights issues. But I am not sure whether in either case very much actually changed.

Periodically, there seems to be national outrage at student ignorance of United States history. At the same time history, or social studies as it is known in most K–12 schools, is one of the subject areas that gets squeezed when school officials feel pressure to boost student reading and math scores on standardized tests. Unfortunately, what does not get tested does not get taught. Additionally, what gets tested seems to determine how things are taught. This chapter examines debates over curriculum, pedagogy, and assessment in New York, Massachusetts, Texas, and California. Once again I was lucky enough to have my grandchildren help me figure out what was actually going on.

A. Don't Know Much About—History, Geography, or Civics
B. "Texas Conservatives Seek Deeper Stamp on Texts"
C. If Massachusetts Was a Country
D. Math in the People's Republic of Massachusetts (and in the Country of California)
E. Gideon's Math Homework

A. Don't Know Much About—History, Geography, or Civics

Based on an essay published on the *Huffington Post*, May 18, 2011

www.huffingtonpost.com/alan-singer/dont-know-much-about-hist_b_861711.html

Questions to Consider

1. How important is the study of history?
2. Will national standards actually drive down educational standards?
3. Should the most important part of civics education be promoting uncertainty?

In April 1943, as the United States prepared to invade Nazi dominated Europe and hopefully rebuild the continent on democratic foundations, the nation was shook, at least mildly, by a study that showed a tremendous "ignorance of U.S. History" by college freshman. A survey of seven thousand incoming students at thirty-six colleges and universities across the country exposed a "vast fund of misinformation on many basic facts."[1] Adding to the national concern was that most of these students had studied either American history, government, or social studies while in high school. Meanwhile, 80% of the colleges and universities did not require a United States history class to earn an undergraduate degree. For a week, the issue made the front page of the *New York Times* and was even debated in the United States Senate. Then it quietly faded from public attention, until it reappeared in 1976, 1987, and 2002 when new test scores were released. People somehow thought that saying the Pledge of Allegiance in school and singing the National Anthem at baseball games were enough to promote patriotism and respect for democracy; that is until the next Cold War or War on Terror scare.

Ignorance of United States history and the functioning of the United States government made the front pages again in 2011 when a National Assessment of Educational Progress (NAEP) civics exam showed that among other academic weaknesses, "Fewer than half of American eighth graders knew the purpose of the Bill of Rights" and "only one in 10 demonstrated acceptable knowledge of the checks and balances among the legislative, executive and judicial branches."[2] Former Supreme Court Justice Sandra Day O'Connor, who heads a group that promotes civics education, declared "Today's NAEP results confirm that we have a crisis on our hands when it comes to civics education."[3]

In many ways today's crisis is of the government's making, both on the national and state levels. It is also a crisis precipitated by the actions of both political parties: the Bush Republican "No Child Left Behind" and the Obama Democrat "Race to the Top." Both mis-education strategies stress continuous testing in reading and math at the expense of all other subjects, including history, social studies, and civics. Students, teachers, and schools are all evaluated solely on these tests. NO CHILD ON TOP/RACE TO THE BEHIND has transformed many of our schools, especially in inner-city communities, into cold, dry, boring test-prep academies rather than places where children learn how to learn and prepare to become active citizens in a democratic society. According to a report by my colleague Andrea Libresco, after five years of No Child Left Behind 36% of the nation's school districts had cut class time for social studies to focus on math and reading test preparation.

These so-called reforms make learning civics education, history, and geography at best haphazard in our schools. According to Amy Gutmann, president of the University of Pennsylvania,[4] civic education is the most important subject taught in American schools and should have "moral primacy over other purposes of public education in a democratic society." But in New York State, civics education was undermined by the virtual abandonment of social studies below the high school level. Standardized state social studies and history assessments were canceled for the fifth and eighth grades and may become optional in high school.

In the 1980s, Ry Cooder and the Moula Banda Rhythm Aces had a less-than-hit song called "Down in Mississippi." It celebrated a state with some of the lowest economic and social indices in the country. My fear is that current national and state educational policies that stress reading and math test prep at the expense of everything else will not only undermine civic understanding, but leave us all "Down in Mississippi."

Another disturbing thought is that people in power in this country may not want a truly educated population. When Osama Bin Laden was killed, both President Obama and former President Bush called it an act of "justice." I asked an eleventh-grade high school class if they agreed and every student who spoke, and there were many, said "Yes." I then asked how we define "justice" in the United States. There was general agreement that the key component is due process of law with the right to a trial.

My final question was, whether you agreed with the killing of Bin Laden or not, do you think it can correctly be described as justice? Students were now not so sure. For me as a social studies teacher, the most important part of civics education is promoting this kind of uncertainty.

B. "Texas Conservatives Seek Deeper Stamp on Texts"

Based on an essay published on the *Huffington Post*, March 23, 2010
www.huffingtonpost.com/alan-singer/testing-companies-corpora_b_506476.html

Questions to Consider

1. How does politics influence social studies curricula?
2. What role does social studies play in a democratic society?

On March 11, 2010, the *New York Times* ran an article "Texas Conservatives Seek Deeper Stamp on Texts." What worries me most about the Texas battle over curriculum is that Texas has unusual influence with textbook publishers. In most states individual school districts decide which books to use. In Texas, decisions are made statewide. That makes Texas an extraordinarily large market, a market publishers do not want to risk getting closed out of. That means anything stupid decided by the Texas State Board of Education can likely appear in textbooks across the country.

According to the article, the Texas State Board of Education wants conservatives portrayed in a more positive light, to emphasize the role played by Christianity in American history, and to include more Republican ideas and politicians in the history curriculum. The problem of course is always in the details. I certainly would favor focusing more on Dwight Eisenhower, a conservative, Christian Republican who warned the American people about the dangers of the military-industrial complex and used federal troops to enforce the desegregation of Little Rock, Arkansas, schools because it is the job of the president to enforce the law whether they agree with it or not.

I would also like students to know how Christianity was used to justify slavery, witch trials, the Ku Klux Klan, and nativism; how conservative groups opposed United States entry into World War II, the right of women to vote, and civil rights for minorities; and how Republican economic policies and leaders precipitated the Great Depression of 1929 to 1941 and the current Great Recession. However, I suspect these are not the things that the Texas School Board wants to emphasize.

The idea of developing national educational standards in social studies and other subject areas was fueled during the 1980s by concern that American secondary school students trailed their foreign contemporaries in academic performance. Clearly these concerns have not abated. National standards were endorsed by the Republican administration of George H. W. Bush at a national governors' conference in 1989, and in 1994 they were included in GOALS 2000 legislation signed by Democratic President Bill Clinton.

At first glance, the creation of broad, voluntary national content standards sounds like an activity appropriate for classroom teachers familiar with what is taught about different secondary school subjects on a daily basis. However, the development of national standards for social studies quickly became a contested battleground involving academics, public and private funding agencies, politicians, and competing professional organizations.

When the United States and world history standards were released by the National Center for History in Schools, they included suggested approaches to the study of history, statements outlining broad historical themes, lists of topics to analyze, and suggestions for how some of the themes and topics could be examined in social studies classes. Although the broader themes and topics were generally ignored by critics, the classroom suggestions quickly became a lightning rod for conservative discontent with public education, multiculturalism, immigration, ethnic identity movements, a declining United States economy, and "eroding family values." The standards were widely denounced in the popular media;

a columnist for *U.S. News and World Report* charged that they placed "Western civilization . . . on a par with the Kush and the Carthagians,"[5] and they were overwhelmingly rejected by the United States Senate.

Initially, the historians and educational groups who developed the history standards vigorously defended them at professional conferences and in social studies publications. The Organization of American Historians dedicated an entire theme issue of its magazine for secondary school teachers to a discussion of the standards. Spokespeople for the National Center for History in Schools stressed that the standards were voluntary, and accused critics of a "disinformation campaign."

In April 1996, the National Center for History in Schools issued a new single volume of revised national history standards. The *New York Times* noted that, based on recommendations by two review panels, the revised standards eliminated "their most criticized feature: the examples of classroom activities."[6] The review panels wanted the teaching examples dropped because of concern that they invited students "to make facile moral judgments." The new standards, minus the teaching suggestions, were almost as widely acclaimed as the original draft was condemned.

If I read the initial criticisms and the later praise correctly, the first versions of the national history standards were rejected because they moved beyond broad generalities and discussed the ideas and information that teachers would present in social studies classes. The teaching suggestions were unacceptable because they involved students in examining fundamental assumptions about history, American society, and world civilizations, exactly what I believe social studies is supposed to be about in a democratic society.

Post-It Note: I think the Dixie Chicks got it right when they said they were ashamed that George W. Bush came from Texas and I think Texans have a lot more to be ashamed of now.

C. If Massachusetts Was a Country

Based on an essay published on the *Huffington Post*, September 6, 2013
www.huffingtonpost.com/alan-singer/if-massachusetts-was-a-co_b_3880884.html

Questions to Consider

1. What are the benefits of the Massachusetts model for teaching math and science?
2. Why do children learn best by "doing"?

The self-proclaimed educational "reform" movement is busy packaging Common Core standards with high-stakes assessment, scripted curriculum, packaged test prep, the de-professionalization of teachers, and the privatization of school support services. A big part of their argument is that United States students perform poorly on international exams when compared to children from other countries. In a much cited book by Amanda Ripley, *The Smartest Kids in the World*,[7] she claimed that she found true educational excellence in Finland, South Korea, and Poland.

But wait a minute!

According to a Trends in International Mathematics and Science study (TIMSS) report on the math and science knowledge and skills of fourth- and eighth-graders around the world,[8] if the state of Massachusetts were a country, its eighth-graders would rank second in the world in science, behind only Singapore, and sixth in mathematics. Not only that, but according to the TIMSS report North Carolina was a top scorer on the fourth-grade math exam; Massachusetts, Minnesota, North Carolina, and Indiana were top scorers on the eighth-grade math exam; Massachusetts and Colorado were high scorers on the eighth-grade science exam; and the United States as a whole scored above the international average, tenth in science and ninth in math. In Massachusetts eighth-graders made significant gains in math and science performance on TIMSS between 1999 and 2007, starting before the Bush-era No Child Left Behind, the Obama/Duncan Race to the Top, the national Common Core standards, and before the high-states testing craze.

What makes science education in Massachusetts exceptional is its commitment, not to test prep, but to intensive hands-on instruction. Fifth-graders at Donald E. Ross Elementary School learn about fulcrums by using a ruler set up like a seesaw and balancing weights at both ends. Seventh-graders work in small groups "to brainstorm how a box of items—a plastic jar, beaker, water, and a mix of sand, soil, clay and pebbles—could help answer a question posed by the teacher: How do sediments carried in water get deposited? They devised small experiments and wrote down their observations, and at the end of class each group presented its findings."[9] These classes had no computer-generated instructions, no test prep booklets, and no scripted lectures or videos; just good, old-fashioned science experiments that encourage students to think about their world and test their ideas.

In Massachusetts, educational reform does not mean vouchers for private schools, closing poorly performing schools, eliminating tenure or merit pay for teachers, and replacing public schools with privately operated charters, although students are expected to pass competency tests to graduate from high school. In math, teachers are treated like professional educators and given the freedom to devise and improvise instruction.

I like the Massachusetts way of teaching math and science!

For my family's Rosh Hashanah dinner, my eight-year-old grandchildren Sadia and Gideon helped me bake the ceremonial bread known as challah. They were entering fourth grade this September so we did some math and science reviews while we baked. Our recipe was for two loaves, but we only wanted to make one, so they had to halve all the ingredients. Eight cups of flour easily became four cups, but figuring out half of the fraction 1/2 a cup of sugar took a little work.

The other fun thing about baking is change of states. The solid stick of margarine became a liquid in the microwave when we added energy. The powdery flour became a clay-like mass when we added water. But most impressively, once the yeast was revived with the addition of sugar and warm water it released a gas and our dough rose to double in size. We also worked in some family culture and social studies. Following traditional Jewish dietary rules, we used margarine instead of butter in the challah because margarine can be used with either meat or dairy while butter can only be used with dairy meals. Instead of using a loaf pan or braiding the dough, for Rosh Hashanah we baked a circular bread that represents the coming around of the new year and the circle of life and seasons, which I guess is a little bit of science as well.

My point is that this is what teaching should look like in elementary schools instead of constant test prep, answering questions about reading passages divorced from context or life, and mechanically calculating meaningless fractions.

Post-It Note: Amanda Ripley, author of The Smartest Kids in the World, *who promotes education in Finland, Poland, and South Korea is an Emerson fellow at the New America Foundation. According to its website,[10] major funders of the New America Foundation include the Bill and Melinda Gates Foundation, the Ford Foundation, and a foundation started by the CEO of Google, all major promoters of self-proclaimed "school reform." Other funders include the Peterson Foundation, the Bradley Foundation, and Walmart, who promote what they call free market solutions to education, which really means privatization and running schools to profit business interests.*

D. Math in the People's Republic of Massachusetts (and in the Country of California)

Based on an essay published on the *Huffington Post*, September 11, 2013
    www.huffingtonpost.com/alan-singer/math-in-the-peoples-repub_b_3908811. html

Questions to Consider

1. Why is the *Algebra Project* such a powerful idea?
2. How do we explain the disparity in test scores?

There is a scene in the movie *Stand and Deliver* where math teacher Jaime Escalante pleads with one of his Mexican-American students at Garfield High School in East Los Angeles, California, to "fill the hole," to balance the equation, to recognize that the positive and the negative of a number together must always equal zero. It is a very powerful scene.

I had a similar "ah-ha" moment when I was helping my son study for a chemistry test. He was trying to memorize chemical formulas without success and I was not much help because I had the same problem with chemistry when I was in high school. Suddenly we both realized that we were looking at algebraic equations and that the key to every chemical formula was balancing both sides of the equation. The only difference was that energy was a new unknown; it had to either be added to one side to make the equation work or released on the other side after the chemicals bonded into a new compound. If you add energy in the form of heat to a block of ice, you get water. If you mix carbon (C) from wood and oxygen (O_2) from air in a fire (heat energy), you get the gas carbon dioxide (CO_2).

I found an ally in my campaign to morph content, skills, and understanding in online videos by Dan Meyer, a former high school math teacher based in the San Francisco Bay Area. Meyer argues in "Math Class Needs a Makeover" that math classes need to focus on conceptualizing and solving problems rather than memorizing what are for students meaningless formulas.[11]

I believe Meyer's ideas fit in nicely with *The Algebra Project*,[12] an approached developed by Cambridge, Massachusetts-based Bob Moses, a Civil Rights activist from the 1960s, who promotes the idea that all children can master math. Because of its Civil Rights connection, *The Algebra Project* teachers and staff are now involved in a number of schools and school districts, including the Recovery School District of Louisiana in New Orleans; Halifax County, North Carolina; Jackson, Mississippi; Petersburg, Virginia; Clarendon County, South Carolina; and Edison High School in Miami Florida.

In *The Algebra Project*, Bob Moses lays out a five-step approach to teaching and understanding algebra that I discussed in Chapter 8. If it were up to me, I would write Moses's approach to pedagogy directly into the Common Core and mandate it, not only for mathematics instruction, but in every subject area. The five steps are:

1. Students participate in a physical experience, like a trip, where they see examples of what they are studying (e.g., arches, geometric shapes, suspension bridges).
2. Following the trip, students draw pictorial representations or construct models of what they have observed.
3. Next, they discuss and write about the event in their everyday dialect or intuitive language. Moses calls this stage "People Talk."
4. Their oral and written reports are then translated into the standard dialect or structured language as part of "Feature Talk."
5. In the last step, students develop symbolic or algebraic representations that describe what they have learned. They present these representations in class and explore how they can be used to describe other phenomena.

I use a similar approach in middle-school social studies classes. I take students on a walking tour that includes the Brooklyn Bridge that connects the New York City boroughs of Manhattan and Brooklyn. From an overlook on the Brooklyn side of the bridge they "see" how the completion of the bridge in the late nineteenth century made possible one integrated city. They sketch the bridge, take photographs, and walk across it. When we return to class they construct and present model suspension bridges using their images. Expert groups prepare reports on the history of the bridge, the geography of New York City, the people who constructed it, and the technology involved in creating a suspension bridge. They work in teams to assist each other in formalizing their reports and translating them into "Feature Talk." In the last step, students transform their reports into interactive electronic presentations.

The Algebra Project and the Meyers video reminded me of "math" experiences I had at a summer work camp for neighborhood teenagers from Brooklyn in the 1970s and 1980s. It illustrates the importance of real world problem-solving as part of mathematics. I was working with teams of six teenagers and our goal was to re-roof a cabin in the woods about fifty feet from the nearest road. We had to load ninety-pound rolls of three-foot-by–fifty-foot tar paper on a flatbed truck, drive as close to the cabin as possible, carry the ninety-pound rolls of tar paper to the cabin, and then carry the ninety-pound rolls of tar paper up the ladder to the roof. I think you get my point. These were heavy rolls of tar paper.

I asked my work team how many rolls of tar paper they thought we needed for the roofing job and suggested we could calculate the amount we needed using geometry. They did not want to be bothered. It would be easier to carry the tar paper from the road to the cabin and up the ladder to the roof than it would be to solve the problem, or so they thought.

By the time we got the rolls of tar paper to the work site they were rethinking their decision. It was hot and the tar paper was heavy. The first teen struggled getting up a few rungs of the ladder, but finally made it. He called down "this is too hard. We better learn the math." We measured the roof and then calculated exactly how many three-foot-wide by fifty-foot-long rolls of tar paper we needed for the job. It was still hard getting them up the ladder, but we only took as many as we actually needed. Real world math had triumphed over student resistance.

A close look at the Trends in International Mathematics and Science Study (TIMSS) report on eighth-grade mathematics reveals some interesting data that would be useful to American policy makers if they were actually interested in scientifically based conclusions instead of just finding ways to support preconceived beliefs.

In the People's Republic of Massachusetts every ethnic group scored above the international average of 500 on the eighth-grade mathematics test. The United States student average on the test was 509 and every group but one topped this score, and the other group almost matched it. Asian students in Massachusetts were the highest scores (599), followed by Whites (572), Multiracial (567), Blacks (516), and Hispanics (507). While there clearly is a racial/ethnic divide, at least students in every group are learning math.

But what was even more interesting were the class divisions measured by the percentage of public school students in a school eligible for free or reduced-price lunch, which is an indicator of poverty. In schools where fewer than 10% of the students were from low-income families, the average score was 584, but in schools where over 75% of the students came from low-income families the average score was only 491.

While student scores tended to be lower across the board in the Country of California, they followed a similar pattern. In schools where fewer than 10% of the students were from low-income families, the average score was 524, but in schools where over 75% of the students came from low-income families, the average score was only 455.

We need to have more teachers like Jaime Escalante teaching children how to balance equations by "filling the hole," but the best way to improve math performance is to address poverty in the United States.

Post-It Note: In an op-ed piece in the New York Times Sunday Review,[13] *a professor of social sciences at Northwestern University argued that the "great stagnation of American education" and poor quality of United States schools places the nation's future at risk because it "hurts our economy's capacity to grow." I think the author places the cart before the horse. Poor school performance is the result of economic stagnation and poverty, not the cause.*

E. Gideon's Math Homework

Based on an essay published on the *Huffington Post*, September 23, 2013
www.huffingtonpost.com/alan-singer/gideons-math-homework_b_3961495.html

Questions to Consider

1. What do the standardized math tests actually measure?
2. Would American students be better off with fewer standardized tests?

Gideon, my grandson, is almost nine years old and is starting fourth grade. He loves soccer, baseball, online videos, hip-hop, and school because that is where his friends are during the day. His attitude toward homework, and I suspect any school assignment, is to get it done fast so he can move on to more important and interesting things.

On the 2012 New York State third-grade Common Core-aligned math assessment Gideon scored in the proficient range, not the highest level, but not bad on a test where 70% of the students failed. While I was doing math homework with Gideon I noticed a couple of things that concerned me about how math was being taught to him. I am not blaming his teachers or the school. I am certainly not blaming Gideon. But I worry that the problems he was having in math reflect the push for test prep for standardized tests.

The first problem is that Gideon seems to be convinced that there is only one right way to solve a problem and if he does not solve it that way he will be marked wrong. This problem he will get over either as he learns more about how the world works or becomes less interested in pleasing his teachers.

The second problem is a bit more serious to me as a teacher and grandparent. Instead of trying to understand a math problem and being willing to play with the numbers, Gideon is committed to remembering a long, complicated sequence of steps to finding a solution. If he makes a mistake somewhere in the sequence he gets the answer incorrect, but he does not recognize it as incorrect, because his goal was following the prescribed steps, not coming up with a result that makes sense.

Kids are supposed to be learning to estimate from the start of elementary school so they can stop and say "This cannot possibly be the answer," but estimation requires both feeling comfortable with the relationships between numbers and a willingness to experiment and speculate, qualities that appear to be neglected in the test-prep math curriculum.

One night recently Gideon had to figure out how many tens are in 540. He set up number groups. There are 10 tens in one hundred so he had five groups of 10 tens each. There are 4 tens in forty. He then added $10 + 10 + 10 + 10 + 10 + 4 = 54$. I did not have a problem so far. But then he had to figure out how many tens were in 370 and he started to set up his number groups again instead of just saying if there are 54 tens in 540, there must be 37 tens in 370. He did not see or even look for the relationship between the two problems. They were separate entities.

The third question was how many twenties are in 640 and again he started by setting up his number groups. I asked him how many tens were in 640 and if there were more tens or twenties, but his response was "That's not the way we are supposed to do it."

Maybe that was what he was told, maybe he was misinterpreting instructions, but in either case, he would not play with the numbers and try to figure out a solution on his own. He was memorizing rules, not learning math.

Initially I thought the problem here might just be Gideon's stubbornness and anxiousness to be finished, after all there were other more rewarding things to be done. But email exchanges on the Long Island "Middle School Principals" listserv point toward much more serious problems with the way math is being taught and assessed in the new world of Common Core and high-stakes assessments.

A principal at one affluent Nassau County middle school reported that in his school 235 eighth-grade students took accelerated ninth-grade math and 190 of them, 78.6% of the students, earned a grade of 80% or better. But inexplicably, 82 out of the 190 high scorers, 43%, scored less than proficient on the eighth-grade common math assessment. Three other middle school principals from similar districts reported the same phenomenon.

A fifth principal from another affluent, high-performing Nassau County school district described the state math assessments as a "Kafkaesque system" that "does not make sense," as a "fake testing system" that "hurts kids" and their teachers. He has middle-school students who passed high school math exams with mastery level scores but who failed the Common Core standardized test and now must be assigned to remedial classes. He also cannot figure out how, when his school had the highest seventh-grade English and math assessment results in the state on the Common Core test, only one out of six of his seventh-grade ELA and math teachers was rated highly effective.

He charged that the current instructional and testing system "only enriched consultants, textbook companies and service corporations." He called it a "fiasco" that "only ensures further unfunded mandates, pushes schools to become test-prep centers, further institutionalizes an over-testing system that terribly hurts kids, and enshrines an unfair evaluation system that actually makes it harder to terminate unsatisfactory teachers."

Actually, I do not find the lack of correlation between the ninth-grade algebra test scores and the eighth-grade Common Core assessments inexplicable. I think the same phenomenon is at work that I saw in Gideon's homework. Students are not learning math, they are being prepped for tests to maximize test scores.

When you put different types of questions on the math test they are stymied because the procedures they were taught to follow do not quite line up with the problems and they either do not know how to or are afraid to adjust. They do not estimate, they do not hypothesize, they do not "do the math," they just get lost in the steps and get the answers incorrect.

I remember learning math the old-fashioned way; my friends and I had fun figuring out things we actually wanted to know and were very competitive at it. Back in the days before calculators and computers, the newspapers only updated baseball batting averages on Sundays, except for the league leaders. My friends and I were big baseball fans, our elementary and middle schools were about a mile from Yankee Stadium, and we needed to know the latest batting averages for Mickey Mantle, Roger Maris, Yogi Berra, Elston Howard, and "The Moose" Bill Skowron, so we calculated them every day during lunch (and sometimes when we were not paying attention in classes). It was not that we liked math—we loved baseball. Math was just a tool.

I walked into my high school tenth-grade statewide geometry math test without having paid attention for most of the year (Bill Cosby used to tell the joke that when he was a kid his family was so poor he couldn't afford to pay attention). But I was comfortable with math, numbers, and problem solving and actually figured out geometry while taking the test itself.

I like finding patterns in math, I enjoy problem solving, and I appreciate the way it helps me to think systematically and provide evidence to support my conclusions. But I am convinced my comfort level is rooted in my love of baseball and the Yankees.

The other night I asked a group of college students if Robbie Cano is batting .310 and goes one for three with a sharp single, two fly outs, and a base on balls, what happens to his batting average. Some of the students had no idea, some of them started to calculate, but I knew his batting average went up, by just a little bit, because I know the relationships between numbers. That is what I am trying to teach Gideon.

Post-It Note: Two hopeful things. By the end of October, Gideon's class started a new math program and his homework started to make more sense. Also, in response to protests by parents and school districts, the New York State education commissioner recommended that students who passed the state's ninth-grade math exam while in eighth grade should be excused from taking the new eighth-grade math assessment.

Notes

1. Benjamin Fine, "Ignorance of U.S. History Shown by College Freshman," *New York Times* (April 4, 1943), p. 1.
2. http://nces.ed.gov/nationsreportcard/pubs/main2010/2011466.asp.
3. Sam Dillon, "Failing Grades on Civics Exam Called a 'Crisis,'" *New York Times* (May 5, 2011), www.nytimes.com/2011/05/05/education/05civics.html.
4. http://prelectur.stanford.edu/lecturers/gutmann/.
5. J. Natale, "Bone of Contention," *American School Board Journal* (January 18–23, 1995).
6. Jo Thomas, "Revised History Standards Disarm the Explosive Issues," *New York Times* (April 3 1996), www.nytimes.com/1996/04/03/us/revised-history-standards-disarm-the-explosive-issues.html.
7. Amanda Ripley, *The Smartest Kids in the World* (New York: Simon & Schuster, 2013); www.nytimes.com/2013/08/25/books/review/amanda-ripleys-smartest-kids-in-the-world.html?pagewanted=all&_r=0.
8. http://nces.ed.gov/pubs2013/2013009_1.pdf.
9. Kenneth Chang, "Expecting the Best Yields Results in Massachusetts," *New York Times* (September 3, 2013), www.nytimes.com/2013/09/03/science/expecting-the-best-yields-results-in-massachusetts.html?ref=science.
10. http://newamerica.net/about/funding.
11. www.ted.com/talks/dan_meyer_math_curriculum_makeover.html.
12. Robert Moses and Charles Cobb, *Radical Equations: Civil Rights from Mississippi to the Algebra Project* (Boston: Beacon Press, 2002), www.algebra.org.
13. Robert Gordon, "The Great Stagnation of American Education," *New York Times* (September 8, 2013), http://opinionator.blogs.nytimes.com/2013/09/07/the-great-stagnation-of-american-education/.

11

REFORM OR DEFORM?

Major issues throughout this book are what actually constitutes school reform and what should be the goals of self-proclaimed reformers. Any change somehow is called reform, so it makes no difference the direction the change takes us. The word has lost all meaning. At the start of the book I introduced readers to John Dewey, who described himself as a progressive at the beginning of the twentieth century because of his commitment to educational reform. At one point so many people he disagreed with appropriated the name progressive that he had to deny being a progressive himself. I feel the same way about school reform. I AM NOT A SCHOOL REFORMER.

The 1983 report A Nation at Risk *charged that the country was threatened by a "rising tide of mediocrity" in public schools that fundamentally were not doing their jobs.[1] But what if the premise of the 1983 report is wrong? What if American schools are working exactly the way they are intended to work? What if every student in a capitalist country is not supposed to learn and succeed? What if the purpose of schools is to sort people out and mark some of them for failure? What if those who claim to be reformers are actually deformers who are selling products with the goal of making a profit with little regard for what they do to students, teachers, schools, and American society.*

A   What If Our Schools Are Working?
B.   Do You Want to Buy the Brooklyn Bridge?
C.   Does the Ghost of George Steinbrenner Run the Schools?
D.   Bloomberg and Klein Fail
E.   Guest Essay: Following Finland's Example . . . Backward by Joel Shatzky

A. What If Our Schools Are Working?

Based on an essay published on the *Huffington Post*, January 27, 2010
   www.huffingtonpost.com/alan-singer/what-if-our-schools-are-w_b_438733.
html

Questions to Consider

1. Why are educational reformers (deformers) so committed to small schools?
2. Is there a conflict between democratic and capitalist values?
3. Is the problem that American schools are working the way they were designed
    to work?

Thousands of protesters showed up at New York City's Brooklyn Technical
High School on January 26, 2010, to protest against the closing and reorganization
of nineteen public schools. Three hundred parents, teachers, students, and local
politicians testified that the closings were arbitrary and ignored the struggles and
successes taking place in those buildings. The hearing went on until after 2:30 in
the morning, when the Panel for Educational Policy, whose majority is appointed
by New York City's mayor, did exactly what it planned to do at the start; it voted
to rubber stamp the closings.

The panel's decision meant phasing out six comprehensive high schools, including Jamaica and Beach Channel in Queens, Paul Robeson and William Maxwell
in Brooklyn, and Alfred Smith and Christopher Columbus in the Bronx. The
closings were part of Mayor Bloomberg's campaign to replace comprehensive high
schools with small mini-schools and charters. Between 2002 and 2010, Bloomberg
and his deputy School Chancellor Joel Klein closed over ninety schools. What
the mayor and chancellor were unable to explain was why, if smaller schools are
a panacea for educational problems, six of the schools being closed in this round
were small high schools created in previous rounds of school reorganization.

A study by the Center for New York City Affairs at the New School discovered that Bloomberg/Klein were stacking the deck so it looked like comprehensive high schools could not perform as well as smaller ones. In 2003, academic
honors programs were removed from Columbus High School, which was then
deemed to be failing, and assigned to mini-schools located in the same building
that were being offered as a model success story for small schools.

When new mini-schools are created they accept few special education and
non-English-speaking students, so their standardized scores look good. Meanwhile the remaining comprehensive schools are forced to accept larger numbers
of students having difficulty, lowering their scores and creating more problems.
Higher-achieving students avoid the comprehensive schools and the situation
grows worse until the comprehensive schools are targeted for closing.

Sometimes, when new mini-schools are placed in the old buildings little else
changes. There are a large number of troubled, poorly performing students in

New York City and they have to be sent to school somewhere—and those schools become new additions to the failing schools list.

When the New York State Legislature renewed mayoral control over New York City schools in 2009, a condition of approval was that provisions be made so that parents would participate in decision-making. The January 2010 meeting proved that this provision was a farce. Just because parents are allowed to speak does not mean that anyone with authority will listen.

If the New York State Legislature had any courage, it would rescind mayoral control of the schools. Unfortunately there is too much Bloomberg money floating around for many of the legislators to risk taking a stand. Part of the problem with American schools is that no one wants to confront the real problems—not Bloomberg, not President Obama, and not Education Secretary Arne Duncan.

Since the 1983 report *A Nation at Risk* charged that the country was threatened by a "rising tide of mediocrity" in public schools that would cripple its ability to compete in international markets,[2] there have been five "education presidents" and innumerable education governors and mayors in the United States. George W. Bush campaigned on the slogan, "Leave No Child Behind." Barack Obama used the promise of federal grant money to get school districts to sign up for his "Race to the Top." But what if the fundamental premise of the 1983 report is wrong? What if American schools are working exactly the way they are intended to work? What if every student is not supposed to learn and succeed?

A big part of the problem with American schools is that there is a conflict between the goals of democracy and of capitalism. While "democrats" feel an obligation to teach everyone, capitalists are more concerned with the "bottom line" of profitability. In their world, there is a competitive marketplace that sorts out winners from losers, and there will always be losers.

In a society where education is organized to achieve capitalist goals, mass public education has two primary purposes. It sorts people out, determining who will be recruited to the elite, learn, and succeed; who will receive enough basic training to make an acceptable living; and who will be pushed to the margins of society. It does this through an elaborate system that includes racially and economically segregated school districts that receive different levels of funding; magnet, private, and charter schools that sift off the highest performing or most cooperative students; and rigorous testing and tracking within schools.

In order to do this type of sorting successfully, American society and its schools must convince parents and students to accept the legitimacy of a system where social and economic rewards are so unequally divided and many people are considered superfluous. Even though a sizable percentage of the population is predestined to fail, young people are repeatedly taught in school, and generally come to believe, that failure is their own fault.

Blaming schools, students, and teachers, while exempting our social system from scrutiny, allows those who support the status quo to propose relatively inexpensive, but ultimately ineffective, solutions to the problems affecting education.

Instead of spending money to lower class size; building new, safe, and welcoming schools for all children; enhancing the development of teachers throughout their careers; and supporting research on promoting learning, they vote to raise standards, reshuffle curriculum content, create new tests, and demand fool-proof teacher certification criteria. Few people ask what will happen in communities where 80% of the students who complete required high school classes are still unable to earn a diploma.

Can anything be done to change our schools and society and eliminate some of the gross inequalities? I am not sure. But a first step is to admit that the problem is not that schools are failing. Unfortunately, they are working exactly the way they are designed to work.

Post-It Note: Through his foundation, Bill Gates gave $2 billion over a nine-year period to influence localities to open smaller mini-high schools, a plan that became a major part of the Bloomberg educational reform plan in New York City. Then in 2009, Gates confessed that to his chagrin, "Many of the small schools that we invested in did not improve students' achievement in any significant way. . . . We had less success trying to change an existing school than helping to create a new school . . . we are trying to raise college-ready graduation rates, and in most cases, we fell short." Gates admitted, "Unlike scientists developing a vaccine, it is hard to test with scientific certainty what works in schools."[3] However, Gates' admission did not stop him or his political allies (Bloomberg, Duncan, and Obama) from using the rest of us as their guinea pigs. Gates' new idea was to have the people he designated as the best teachers put their "lectures online as a model for other teachers."[4] Unfortunately, the failure of his small schools initiative did not stop Gates from continuing to tell everybody else what they should do to improve the schools.

B. Do You Want to Buy the Brooklyn Bridge?

Based on an essay published on the *Huffington Post*, November 3, 2011
www.huffingtonpost.com/alan-singer/evaluating-bloomberg-school-reform_b_1066009.html

Question to Consider

1. Why are politicians and business leaders pressing for "reforms" that show no appreciable positive results?
2. Why are students graduating from high school without being able to do college-level work?

Sometimes I feel the current wave of educational reform promoting charter schools is little more than a scam perpetuated by entrepreneurs and politicians to privatize the public school system. In 2011, the New York City Department of Education released school report cards that included a college readiness measurement for the first time. Thirteen high schools had graduation rates of over 80%

with less than 10% of the graduates prepared to do college-level work. According to an article in the *Daily News*,[5] at the 135 new smaller high schools created by Mayor Bloomberg as the leading edge of his school reform initiative, on the average, roughly 70% of the students graduated in the regular four years. However, only 12% of their students graduated prepared to do college-level work. Similar schools founded before Bloomberg became mayor and started to reorganize the entire school system had on the average a 64% graduation rate and a slightly higher percentage of their students considered college ready.

The most egregious case was the New Heights Academy Charter School on Amsterdam Avenue in Manhattan, whose high school received a progress report grade of "A" for 2010–2011. It serves students from Harlem, Inwood, and Washington Heights. According to information on its website,[6] the New Heights Academy opened in 2006 as the first charter school in community school district six. It opened with 192 students in grades five and nine, but by fall 2011 it had expanded to include a high school and with 760 students was the largest charter school in New York City.

The student body at New Heights Academy Charter School was 100% Black and Hispanic and 95% of its students were eligible for free or reduced-priced lunch. The school, which was chartered by New York State, prided itself on small class sizes capped at twenty-four and its mandatory Saturday Academy, which provides struggling students with extra academic support. The school website claims that 90% of its first senior class graduated,[7] although the Department of Education website lists the graduation rate as 81%,[8] which is still very high given the student population.

One reason for the charter school's apparent success is the extra resources provided by its high-powered, influential, and affluent Board of Trustees. It includes representatives from the law firm Bingham McCutchen, Goldman Sachs, PricewaterhouseCoopers, Time Warner, and NRG Energy.

According to the charter school's mission statement,[9] "All young people deserve access to an excellent education; however, not all students are afforded this opportunity due to inequities in the public school system. New Heights Academy Charter School was founded in 2006 to address this disparity by providing a college preparatory education in a safe and nurturing environment to students in grades 5–12 living in Washington Heights and Inwood. Our students participate in a rigorous academic program and take pride in learning how our core values of perseverance, responsibility, integrity, discipline, and enthusiasm will support them in their pursuit of challenging post-secondary education and career goals. New Heights Academy Charter School is where success happens every day!"

These are certainly laudatory goals. But what is the reality? Only 21% of the school's students read at or above grade level, which was especially troubling because its incoming class actually performed better than students already in the program. Only 42% performed at grade level in mathematics.

But the worst figure was the school's performance on the college readiness assessment. According to CUNY college tests,[10] only 1.1% of its graduates were actually prepared to do college-level work without remediation. This was for a charter school that received a grade of "A" from New York City Department of Education assessors.

How long are the people of the United States supposed to put up with what appears to be a charter school scam? Does anybody at the Department of Education want to buy the Brooklyn Bridge?

Post-It Note: A crucial part of Common Core literacy standards is requiring students to show evidence from the text to support their interpretation and point of view. In the name of Common Core standards, charter school proponents need to show the evidence that they will make a difference in student performance.

C. Does the Ghost of George Steinbrenner Run the Schools?

Based on an essay published on the *Huffington Post*, September 12, 2011
www.huffingtonpost.com/alan-singer/does-the-ghost-of-george-_b_949681.html

Questions to Consider

1. Were students and schools being set up to fail to justify claims made by education reformers/deformers?
2. Are business management models directly transferable to public institutions and schools?

Between 1982 and 1995, George "Boss Bluster" Steinbrenner completely mismanaged the New York Yankees. The team won no pennants, churned through thirteen managers (although some were repeats), and signed countless expensive free agents, including Steve Kemp, Ed Whitson, and Danny Tartabull, who failed to perform in pinstripes. Meanwhile Steinbrenner insulted his players and even hired a private detective to spy on one of the team's stars. It was not until 1995, when Steinbrenner withdrew from active involvement in the management of the team, that stability in the form of homegrown young players (Jorge Posada, Derek Jeter, Mariano Rivera, Bernie Williams, and Andy Pettitte) and a long-term manager (Joe Torre) brought another round of success. It seems that Boss Bluster's disastrous management style, tossing money at problems and blaming other people for his failures, is alive and well in Mayor Michael Bloomberg's New York City Department of Education. Maybe Steinbrenner's ghost is running the New York City school system.

As schools reopened in September 2011, students and teachers returned to twenty-two public schools that were originally slated to be closed because of poor student performance on standardized tests. The schools, teachers, and students were granted a reprieve in May 2011 and were supposed to be reorganized under the RESTART program. The reality is that the New York City Department of Education, with support from the Obama administration and federal Race to the Top money, set the schools up to fail again.

The RESTART schools were slated to receive up to $6 million in federal money over three years to improve lower-than-average graduation rates. However, little of that money actually went to the schools to directly aid students. Most of the money went into the Department of Education general fund or to pay private management companies like New Visions for Public Schools, Urban Assembly, and Generation Schools to provide consultants to advise principals and magically turn the schools around. These organizations made recommendations about the hiring and dismissal of principals and teachers and trained surviving principals to "write up" teachers so they could more easily be dismissed. One principal, interviewed in the *New York* Times but speaking on the condition of anonymity because he did not want to criticize a program that would be evaluating his performance, said, "Restart is the wrong word, because they are not changing anything."[11]

Most of the schools on the RESTART list were there because the Bloomberg administration changed the student populations attending the schools to channel better performing students into new smaller high schools or because of changing community demographics. John Dewey High School in Brooklyn, which was based on the ideas of educational philosopher John Dewey, was once the pride of the public school system. When it opened in 1969 its student population was largely White, overwhelmingly middle class, and college directed. However in 2011, those students attended Leon M. Goldstein High School for the Sciences at Kingsborough Community College and a majority of Dewey's students were Black and Latino, many from the low-income housing projects that ring south Brooklyn.

There are no short cuts and miracle cures when it comes to educational improvement. Schools improve when conditions for students and their families improve and when the United States invests in teachers rather than simplistic solutions. A *New York Times* article reported that students in high-tech schools did not perform better on standardized assessments than students in regular schools.[12] Studies continually show that students in charter schools do not perform better than similar students in public schools. In Atlanta, Georgia, and Washington, DC, as well as in Texas, Indiana, Pennsylvania, and Florida, miraculous improvements on standardized tests turned out to be the result of changing student answers and other forms of cheating.

"Trickle down" does not work in economics and it does not work in education. If states and the federal government want instruction to improve in public schools, they need to put the money directly into the schools. One place to start would be to rehire aides, parent coordinators, assistant teachers, and teachers let go in recent round of budget cuts.

Another thought: maybe we do need to resurrect Boss Bluster. Once he calmed down in 1995 and the Yankees had some stability, the team went on a major winning-streak with thirteen straight playoff appearances and four World Championships.

Post-It Note: An aging Yankees team did not make the playoffs in 2013. Even worse, the organization was embarrassed by a drug scandal that implicated former All-Star and home run champion Alex Rodriguez. A-Rod and other aging Yankees were on the tail end of bloated long-term contracts negotiated by Yankee executives pressured by their boss George Steinbrenner.

D. Bloomberg and Klein Fail

Based on an essay published on the *Huffington Post*, August 16, 2010
www.huffingtonpost.com/alan-singer/bloomberg-and-klein-fail-_b_683375.html

Questions to Consider

1. What did Mayor Bloomberg and School Chancellor Klein claim to have achieved?
2. What happened to their claims?
3. How were their false claims exposed?

In 2008, brimming with pride and boasting of success, New York City Mayor Michael "Moneybags" Bloomberg and School Chancellor Joel "Clueless" Klein testified at a Congressional hearing that they had found the magic bullet that would improve the academic performance of inner-city minority youth. They claimed, "Over the past six years, we've done everything possible to narrow the achievement gap" between White and Asian students and Black and Latino students and "in some cases, we've reduced it by half."[13]

In 2009, while running for reelection on his record of supposed success in improving education in the city, Bloomberg trumpeted, "We are closing the shameful achievement gap faster than ever." As proof, Bloomberg presented test scores that showed 70% of the city's students were meeting state standards. For this supposed miracle, Moneybags and Clueless were praised by President Bush as champions of his No Child Left Behind initiative and the city received a prestigious award in urban education from the Eli Broad Foundation.

Unfortunately, the old maxim, "If it appears too good to be true, it's because it is too good to be true," once again proved to be accurate. When New York State reconfigured scoring guidelines to make standardized tests better predictors of student academic performance, passing rates plummeted, especially for Black and Latino students. On some tests passing rates dropped by 25% and the performance gap between Blacks and Latinos and Whites and Asians climbed significantly higher than previously had been reported. The racial achievement gap in 2010 was at the same level as it was when the Bloomberg/Klein team took control over the city's school system in 2002.

In the elementary and middle schools, only 40% of the Black and 46% of the Hispanic students met state math standards. Meanwhile 75% of the White and 82% of the Asian students passed. In English, roughly a third of the Black and Latino students are proficient readers, compared to 64% of the White and Asian students.

The new, larger racial performance gap actually mirrored what the National Assessment of Educational Progress had been telling us for more than a decade. The performance gap never decreased on the eighth-grade math test or the high school math SAT. Student improvement on state tests was either illusory or fraudulent.

What the new test scores showed is that the entire Bloomberg/Klein reform plan was fraudulent. They closed "failing" schools, blamed teachers and the unions, created designer theme and charter schools, and moved children around the city in the name of school choice. While middle-class, largely Asian and White students may have benefited, for working-class and poor minority families the only choice was between one inadequate test prep academy and another.

Test scores went up incrementally for Black and Latino children because students in the test-prep academies were constantly prepared for the exams instead of really being educated. Scores went up modestly, but enough students did better so the city could claim that the percentage of Black and Latino students passing the tests—not doing well, just passing the tests—had risen significantly and the racial gap had disappeared. But once the state reconfigured the scoring guidelines, and borderline scores became failures, it became clear that the miraculous improvement was all smoke and mirrors. It was really just a pretense to justify moving children from middle-class families into designer schools while segregating lower-performing working-class and poor Black and Latino youth into the test-prep academies.

In an interview with the *New York Times*,[14] Joel "Clueless" Klein remained "unbowed." He still felt "awfully good" about the Department of Education's performance under his tenure and denied having claimed in the past that the city had performed miracles. Klein promised to continue the same strategy Bloomberg and he had been following for the past decade with such "outstanding" results.

This meant that Moneybags and Clueless would continue to send middle-class kids from all racial and ethnic groups to designer high-performing small theme or charter schools while squeezing working-class and poor minority youth into test-prep academies where administrators beat on and blame teachers until test scores rise incrementally. After all, Moneybags and Clueless had fooled a president, prestigious foundations, and voters in two reelection campaigns, so there was no reason to change anything.

Unfortunately the Obama/Duncan "Race to the Top" is premised on the same assumptions and strategies as the New York City "miracle," and they are just as unlikely as Bloomberg and Klein to admit that student academic performance will not significantly improve until conditions in inner-city neighborhoods and for inner-city families get much better. Maybe they need a simple spelling test. The answer to improving education is spelling J-O-B-S.

Post-It Note: In November 2010, New York City School Chancellor Joel Klein left to take a much higher-paying position with Rupert Murdoch's News Corporation. Klein claimed he had "long admired News Corporation's entrepreneurial spirit and Rupert Murdoch's fearless commitment to innovation." He wanted "to bring the same spirit of innovation to the burgeoning education marketplace."[15] Murdoch, whose company is committed to privatizing public education in the name of innovation and invests in Teach For America and charter schools, returned Klein's effusive praise by describing him as "a man who works day and night for one goal: that every child who enters a New York City public school will leave with a solid education—and a fair shot at the American Dream."[16] Klein's new job was developing business strategies for selling technology to the schools across the United States.

E. Guest Essay: Following Finland's Example . . . Backward by Joel Shatzky

Based on an essay published on the *Huffington Post*, June 24, 2011
www.huffingtonpost.com/joel-shatzky/educating-for-democracy-f_b_883132.html

Post-It Note: Joel Shatzky was a Professor of English at SUNY-Cortland. He currently teaches English and writing at Kingsborough Community College in Brooklyn, New York. He is an author and playwright and writes regularly for Huffington Post and other online blogs. http://joellshatzky.com

Questions to Consider

1. Why do American reformers keep pointing at Finland?
2. What lessons should the United States learn from Finland?
3. Is if fair to compare student performance in Finland and the United States?

In an article in *The American Educator*, "Lessons from Finland," Pasi Sahlberg, a distinguished Finnish education specialist,[17] outlined Finnish educational policies that have led to the success of his country's school system, which is rated amongst the best in the world. Professor Sahlberg's main points are mirrored in policies being increasingly adopted by cities and states around the United States, encouraged by the federal Department of Education in the last decade with the No Child Left Behind and Race to the Top programs. Unfortunately American educational reformers are mirroring Finnish accomplishments in the true sense of the word because they are doing what the Finns are doing but in the opposite direction.

1. In Finland teacher-candidate selection and teacher preparation is very rigorous and demanding. Annually only one in ten applicants will be accepted to study to become a primary school teacher. They are required to receive a degree in a major area that is not centered on education courses. Rigorous mentoring and training is an additional part of the teacher-candidates' educational preparation.
2. In Finland, "high social prestige, professional autonomy in schools and an ethos of teaching as a service to society, and the public good" are powerful inducements for excellent students to pursue a teaching career.[18]
3. In Finland, "the teaching force . . . is highly unionized; almost all teachers are members of the Trade Union of Education."[19]
4. In Finland there is no formal teacher evaluation; teachers receive feedback from school principals and the staff itself. Because Finland does not have a standardized assessment for evaluating students, there are no formal outcomes in the evaluation. A good teacher is one who is able to help all children progress and grow in a holistic way.
5. A typical middle-school teacher in Finland teaches just under 600 hours annually. In the United States a teacher at the same level typically devotes 1,080 hours to teaching annually.
6. In Finland, part of the teachers' work day is devoted to "work with the community." For them "some of the most important aspects of their work are conducted outside the classroom."[20]
7. In contrast to teachers in this country, Finnish teachers have a high degree of autonomy. They are not micromanaged.
8. Unlike the high turnover rate of American teachers—50% in the first five years—only 10 to 15% of Finnish teachers leave the profession before retirement.

There are many other reasons besides good schooling that lead to academic success in Finland: an almost homogeneous ethnic population, a much smaller disparity in wealth between rich and poor, a more equitable system of school funding, and an excellent health and social welfare system for all. But certainly relying on the qualifications of its teachers is an important element in achieving excellence in education in Finland.

Generally, when someone admires another person or country for outstanding achievement, they try to emulate its practices. With the United States emphasis on teacher evaluation through standardized tests, it is moving in the very opposite direction from Finland. As far as Finland is concerned, we show our admiration by following the opposite of its example.

Notes

1. National Commission on Excellence in Education, *A Nation at Risk: The Imperative For Educational Reform* (1983), www2.ed.gov/pubs/NatAtRisk/risk.html.
2. Ibid.
3. Alan Singer, "Bill Gates Admits He Was Wrong (Bloomberg Doesn't)," *Huffington Post* (December 11, 2009), www.gatesfoundation.org/who-we-are/resources-and-media/ annual-letters-list/annual-letter-2009; www.huffingtonpost.com/alan-singer/bill-gates-admits-he-was_b_389289.html.
4. www.gatesfoundation.org/who-we-are/resources-and-media/annual-letters-list/ annual-letter-2009.
5. Rachel Monahan, "Mayor Bloomberg's Schools Set Students Up for Failure When It Comes to College Preparation, but More Graduate," *Daily News* (October 27, 2011), www.nydailynews.com/new-york/education/mayor-bloomberg-schools-set-students-failure-college-preparation-graduate-article-1.966263.
6. www.newheightsacademy.org.
7. Ibid.
8. "Graduating Students, but Then What?" *New York Times* (October 30, 2011), http:// query.nytimes.com/gst/fullpage.html?res=9C04EEDA153DF933A05753C1A9679 D8B63.
9. www.newheightsacademy.org/apps/pages/index.jsp?uREC_ID=103463&type= d&pREC_ID=202149.
10. Anna Phillips, "At Most High Schools, Fewer Than Half of Graduates Are Ready for College," *SchoolBook* (October 25, 2011), www.wnyc.org/story/303098-at-most-high-schools-fewer-than-half-of-graduates-are-ready-for-college/.
11. Sharon Otterman, "Nine City High Schools to Stay Open, With Private Management," *New York Times* (May 13, 2011), www.nytimes.com/2011/05/13/nyregion/9-low-scoring-new-york-high-schools-to-stay-open.html?_r=0.
12. Matt Richtel, "In Classroom of Future, Stagnant Scores," *New York Times* (September 4, 2011), www.nytimes.com/2011/09/04/technology/technology-in-schools-faces-ques tions-on-value.html?hp.
13. Sharon Otterman and Robert Gebeloff, "Triumph Fades on Racial Gap in City Schools," *New York Times* August 16, 2010), www.nytimes.com/2010/08/16/nyregion/16gap. html.
14. Ibid.
15. Brian Stelter and Tim Arango, "News Corp. Reels In a Top Educator," *New York Times* (November 9, 2010), http://mediadecoder.blogs.nytimes.com/2010/11/09/news-corp-reels-in-a-top-educator/.
16. Ibid.
17. www.aft.org/pdfs/americaneducator/summer2011/Sahlberg.pdf.
18. Ibid.
19. Ibid.
20. Ibid.

12
RESISTANCE!

I am proud to be what right-wing author Roger Kimball dismissed in 1990 as a "tenured radical."[1] *Kimball, who at the time was managing editor of* The New Criterion, *declared "My aim is to expose . . . ideologically motivated assaults on the intellectual and moral substance of our culture." For Kimball, tenured radicals were "indefatigable proselytizers, bent on winning converts in their war against the traditional moral and intellectual values" and they had to be stopped.*

I have been a left-leaning tenured radical for a long time, first as a high school teacher and then as a university professor. Tenure has not prevented me from being attacked by right-wing and pro-business forces that want to silence me, but I suspect they would prefer to have me fired.

In 1988, after students in my high school social studies class organized a forum where a spokesperson from the African National Congress's delegation to the United Nations spoke about the campaign to end apartheid, I was accused by a colleague at a department meeting of trying to brainwash students in my classes. Two years later, similar charges were made after I brought student members of the school's political action club to a pro-choice rally in Washington, DC. In 2008 my university was flooded with emails demanding that I be fired after I appeared on "The O'Reilly Factor" in a broadcast leading up to the presidential election debate at Hofstra.

When you stand up, when you stand out, you are exposed, but I cannot stop fighting for what I believe in. That is why I blog on the Huffington Post. *The* Huffington Post *has always supported me as long as I can document my information and support my views with evidence, even when they were pressured to drop some of my blogs by someone who claimed to represent Pearson. Hofstra University has also always been supportive. By the way, as anyone who has read this far knows, supporting views with evidence is a Common Core standard.*

Once my friend Pablo Muriel was called into his principal's office because the principal wanted to know what he was teaching that stirred students up to protest against what they perceived as injustices in the school. Pablo denied stirring up the students but "confessed" that students in his government class had been studying the Bill of Rights and Supreme Court decisions on due process and individual freedom.

One of my goals in these Huffington Post *essays has been to support teachers, students, and parents who challenge injustice, especially students who demand the right to define education and hopefully to improve society. This last chapter celebrates them.*

A. To Students Who Are Fighting Back
B. The Cupcake Resistance Movement
C. In Seattle Opposition Grows to School Deform
D. The Mayor's Powerful New Enemies
E. In New Jersey the Children Shall Lead
F. Teachers as Crap Detectors

A. To Students Who Are Fighting Back

Based on an essay published on the *Huffington Post*, February 1, 2010
www.huffingtonpost.com/alan-singer/to-students-who-are-fight_b_444214.
html

Questions to Consider

1. Should teachers encourage students to become active citizens and engage in
   political action?
2. Can high school students impact government policy?

   This essay began as an open letter to the students of University Heights High
School who were threatened with being thrown off the Bronx Community College campus; the students of Beach Channel, Christopher Columbus, Paul Robeson, Alfred E. Smith, and William Maxwell high schools who faced having their schools closed; and all the students who were fighting back against the unjust and ill-conceived education reform/deform policies in New York City.
   My friend Pablo Muriel, a teacher at University Heights High School, asked me what he should say to students who had been working responsibly to influence public policy but who found their reasoned and evidence-based arguments ignored by government officials who made arbitrary and arrogant judgments and the political toadies appointed to carry out their decisions. Pablo, and teachers in the other schools, these are my thoughts and I hope you share them with your students:

1. Yogi Berra, Hall of Fame catcher and former manager of both the New York Yankees and the New York Mets summed it up very nicely during the 1973 National League pennant race when he told reporters, "It ain't over till it's over." Students, parents, and teachers: you lost a few rounds, but the struggle to save your schools is not over yet. It is just moving to a new level. The teachers union threatened a lawsuit to block the school closings, but even more promising are the contacts you made with other elected officials. The New York State Legislature gave Mayor Bloomberg control over the New York City schools because he promised to listen to the input of the public, including parents, students, and teachers, and the legislature can take it away. By ignoring what students, parents, and teachers have to say he violated the agreement that led to the passage of the law. The campaign to save our schools needs to demand that mayoral control over the public schools be rescinded.
2. Freedom struggles take a long time. Social change is not for the faint of heart or shortsighted. In 1776 the Declaration of Independence declared that all men are created equal, but there was slavery in the United States and it did not end until 1865 with the ratification of the Thirteenth Amendment to the Constitution. Even with the end of slavery, African Americans had to struggle for another one hundred years to win equality before the law and the right

to vote in many states. In 1848 women issued the "Seneca Falls Manifesto" demanding rights promised in the Declaration of Independence, but Susan B. Anthony was arrested for trying to vote in 1872, women's suffrage did not become the law until 1920, and this country still does not have an equal rights amendment. These struggles took decades, but people did not give up and they created a more just society.

3. Social struggle is not just about winning. It is also about preparing yourselves for the next struggle. Students learned to organize their peers, to marshal evidence, to present ideas clearly orally and in writing, to influence the public, to attract media attention, and to present themselves in responsible and mature ways. Students may not succeed in keeping their schools open, but nobody can take away from them what they learned. These students will be a force to reckon with in the future.

4. This struggle by students puts them within the same tradition as other young people who organized to change the world. A student strike in Soweto, South Africa, in 1976 helped to bring down apartheid. In this country, student protesters played a major role in the African American Civil Rights movement of the 1950s and 1960s and in the anti-Vietnam War movement. Students have learned that young people can be activists and that there is power and exhilaration in group solidarity.

5. The current educational decision-makers will not listen, but they will not be in office forever. Eventually they will be consigned to the dustbin of history while you will continue to shape public policy for decades.

6. The struggle for schools that are really better and meet the needs of students is just beginning. In order to qualify for federal funds, New York State placed fifty-seven schools on a list of low-achieving schools that should be improved, reorganized, or closed. Students need to become part of the discussion about the future of these schools. State officials, unless pressured by the public, will likely reshuffle the deck without significantly improving anything. The campaign for real school reform must expand to the national level as well.

In 1915, just before he died, a labor union organizer named Joe Hill declared: "Don't mourn for me, organize!" In the spirit of Joe Hill, don't mourn for your schools, but continue to organize for justice.

Post-It Note: I was a speaker at the June 2010 graduation ceremonies at University Heights High School. In very bad Spanish, I paraphrased a quote from Isidora Dolores Ibárruri Gómez, "La Pasionaria," a leader of pro-republic forces during the Spanish Civil War. She is best remembered for the slogan "¡No Pasarán!" "They Shall Not Pass."

¡Ponte de pie! ¡Defender los derechos de los niños! Aguante el sacrificio antes que conceder la victoria de las fuerzas que representan la opresión y la tiranía. ¡Los maestros! ¡Los padres! ¡Los estudiantes! ¡Todos lugar de defender la educación pública! El irrita a toda la ciudad con furia a los salvajes que quieren hundir la educación pública en un infierno de terror y destrucción. ¡Sin embargo, no pasarán!

Stand up! Defend the rights of children! Endure sacrifice rather than grant victory to forces that represent oppression and tyranny. Teachers! Parents! Students! Everyone rise to defend public education! The whole city roils with fury at those savages who want to plunge public education into a hell of terror and destruction. But they shall not pass! ¡Sin embargo, no pasarán!

¡Venceremos! We will win!

B. The Cupcake Resistance Movement

Based on an essay published on the *Huffington Post*, October 9, 2009
www.huffingtonpost.com/alan-singer/resistance-has-begun_b_315521.html

Questions to Consider

1. Should cutting back on bake fairs be an important part of the education agenda?
2. What is the impact of budget cuts on schools and children?

In October 2009, Sadia and Gideon, five-year-old twins from Brooklyn, joined the Cupcake Resistance Movement. They baked forty cupcakes and brownies, smothered them with chocolate frosting, and covered them with sprinkles and gummy bears. The next day they smuggled the contraband into their school to celebrate their birthdays with their kindergarten friends in defiance of the New York City mayor's latest edict.

This is a true story. "Bizarro" Bloomberg was at it again. In an autocratic regime, the monarch's preferences are the law of the land and woe to anyone who questions them. Bloomberg's Department of Education apparently did not like cookies and cupcakes because they are fattening. They banned bake sales that are used by parent groups, student teams, and clubs to fund activities at a time when the mayor was cutting school budgets and demanding that families tighten their belts—which is probably why he wanted to eliminate cookies and cupcakes. The option of better funding for student teams, expanding gym classes, and running more afterschool programs had apparently been rejected.

Parent groups were granted one exception a month to sell cookies and cakes as long as it was after lunch. Department of Education officials were carefully monitoring school principals to make sure that the regulations were enforced. If a principal was unwilling to enforce the new rules, they were informed that "Noncompliance may result in adverse impact on the principal's compliance performance rating."[2]

I do not think we should over-stuff our kids with sweets. But I would like to be able to bring cupcakes to school so my grandchildren (the rebels mentioned earlier) can celebrate their birthdays with friends. I also suspect that denied the ability to purchase sweets in school, students will simply purchase more at the local grocery store on their way in and out of the building.

As a high school teacher I was the faculty advisor to a number of student clubs. In order to fund our programs we ran the school's bagel concession for a number of weeks a semester. This made it possible for the school's political action club to invite speakers, publish a newsletter, and travel to Washington, DC, to lobby politicians on different issues. It is not clear whether bagels are on the list.

Maybe the real reason for this policy was that as part of his reelection campaign Bloomberg was trying to win the shopkeepers' votes. Or else maybe the mayor will establish cake-free zones around the schools. Anyone selling cookies to underage customers between seven in the morning and five in the afternoon will face heavy fines and jail time.

C. In Seattle Opposition Grows to School Deform

Based on an essay published on the *Huffington Post*, January 24, 2013
www.huffingtonpost.com/alan-singer/opposition-grows-to-schoo_b_2533623.html

Questions to Consider

1. What does it mean to be a "country that leads the world in educating its people"?
2. Should other teachers follow the Seattle example and organize boycotts of standardized tests?
3. Are school closings in urban minority communities a violation of civil rights?

In his 2013 State of the Union address, President Barack Obama promised "a country that leads the world in educating its people." In his second inaugural address he promised to "reform our schools" as part of his administration's effort to promote "equality" and defend this country's "most ancient values and enduring ideals." But despite these promises, a growing number of parents and teachers are unhappy with his showcase program, Race to the Top. They argue it is the antithesis of the education, justice, and equality he claims is central to his ideas and American values.

A major battleground in the debate over whether Obama-initiated school reforms actually deform education in the United States was Garfield High School in Seattle, Washington. At Garfield, teachers organized a boycott of standardized tests, the Measures of Academic Progress (MAP), used to evaluate students and teachers. The governing board of the Seattle Public School system has also decided to review MAP and other tools used for assessing students and teachers.

The school district used MAP tests to track student progress and as part of its evaluation of teacher performance. Garfield High School teachers call the MAP testing regime useless at best and even harmful to many students. At the time of the rebellion, MAP tests were used by six thousand school districts across the country. Garfield teachers argued the tests were not aligned with school curriculum so they did not measure what was actually taught in classes. In addition, the tests, designed and marketed by the Northwest Evaluation Association, were never intended for use in evaluating teachers.

The test boycott was endorsed by the National Center for Fair & Open Testing (FairTest) and the American Federation of Teachers. An online petition signed by leading educators in the United States also supported the boycott.

Pressure was also growing to oppose what was considered the arbitrary and discriminatory closing of public schools because of Race to the Top mandates. Students, parents, and advocacy representatives from eighteen major United States cities testified at a hearing before the United States Department of Education in Washington, DC, on January 29, 2013, and rallied in front of the building and at the Martin Luther King Memorial. They demanded that the Department of Education declare a moratorium on school closings and design a plan to support community school improvement. Organizers requested a meeting with President Obama, but he was unavailable. According to organizers, at least ten cities have filed or are in the process of filing Title VI Civil Rights complaints with the United States Department of Education Office of Civil Rights arguing that school closings discriminate against low-income, minority communities.

D. The Mayor's Powerful New Enemies

Based on an essay published on the *Huffington Post*, March 25, 2010
www.huffingtonpost.com/alan-singer/bloomberg-and-kleins-powe_b_512501.html

Questions to Consider

1. What lessons did University Heights students learn from this campaign?
2. Based on what they learned, is it fair to say that these students actually won?

New York City Mayor Michael Bloomberg did succeed at something positive. He succeeded in turning students from University Heights High School in the Bronx into social activists and powerful enemies. These teenagers could not prevent him from moving their school off of the Bronx Community College campus and exiling it to the South Bronx, but in their struggle to save the school, they learned how to be organizers and agents for change. Bloomberg and his wealthy friends had better watch out. The attack on this school provided these students with the best education they could possibly receive and has helped to create a new generation committed to the struggle for social justice.

People like Bloomberg think the fight is over every time they win a round, but to paraphrase the immortal words of American naval hero John Paul Jones, the students of University Heights High School "have just begun to fight." Over 240 University Heights High School students and about twenty parents attended a Department of Education meeting in Staten Island, which was held there to make it difficult for the students to mobilize for and to attend. The teachers union and a community organization supplied them with buses to transport people. The rest of the students traveled to the hearing with their teacher Pablo Muriel by subway and by ferry, followed by a long walk. Many of the students spoke eloquently and the school chancellor was forced to acknowledge their presence.

As expected, the vote not to renew the school's lease was a sham. The decision to move the school off of the Bronx Community College campus had been made a long time before and behind closed doors.

Pablo said his students were disappointed and angry but that they now know how to fight for themselves and how to become more active citizens. Focused anger is more productive than apathy. He feels his educational mission was accomplished. Their messages to him and to me are definitely worth reading. Two of them are reprinted here.

> Tyrek Greene: At the beginning of this school year, Pablo warned us many times that something big was going to happen to us; I don't think we were completely comprehensive of what he meant. Little did we know, BCC was working behind our backs to throw us off of this campus. This is extremely unjust, being that my mom specifically put me in this school to shield me from the factory-like schools and prison-like learning institutes. In the middle of January, we rushed into Councilman Cabrera's office and made him promise to see that we would be allowed to stay on this campus. We worked with the Northwest Coalition and Sista's and Brotha's United to help us with rallying, lobbying, protesting, and basic organizing skills. We started protesting outside of BCC to get our point across. It seemed as though they didn't want to confront us and to tell us the real reason why they wanted us off campus. A couple of the core leaders and I almost forced the president of BCC to have a meeting with us. She curved all of our questions, saying she has our best interest at heart but she needs our building back. But what about us? Why should we have to suffer for BCC's mistake? They should not have enrolled more students than they can handle. We end up suffering because of money hungry BCC. Our two P.E.P. [Panel for Educational Policy] meetings before the last vote, we won the hearts of those four people. But yesterday, there were 12 new panel members. Why weren't we appealing to them in the first place? Why wasn't Joel Klein at the first two meetings? I personally witnessed this atrocity with my own eyes and it kills me because many of my peers learned that democracy is a lie.

> Christina Gomez: Before coming here the only type of protesting I've ever heard of was the Black Panthers. A couple of weeks ago, I found myself

doing the same thing. The feeling of being able to bring together a community of teenagers living in a world where "it is what it is" is used as an excuse for doing nothing is powerful. Instead of having a mind full of memories of just having a good time, I have a memory to last me a lifetime based on my experience at University Heights at BCC. I had the opportunity to stand side by side with people who you once thought couldn't care less. But now that stepped up to the plate and became the type of people you are proud to know. I fought, I listened, and I've changed for the better. I learned that anger could be turned into something so beautiful. Our voices actually can be heard.

E. In New Jersey the Children Shall Lead

Based on an essay published on the *Huffington Post*, April 28, 2010
    www.huffingtonpost.com/alan-singer/and-the-children-shall-le_b_554903.html

Questions to Consider

1. Why have school children been at the forefront of many political protest movements in the United States and around the world?
2. Should school children be involved in political action as part of their real world education?
3. When the children lead, will you follow?

In 2010, New Jersey high school students were at the forefront of the battle to oppose budget cuts and to save education in the United States. They understand—what adults, politicians, and government officials don't get—that if you vote down school budgets, lower taxes, and cut school funding you undermine both the economy today and the future viability of the nation. In April 2010, 58% of New Jersey school district budgets were rejected by voters and Governor Christie called for reductions in state aid to schools, funding freezes, and teacher layoffs.[3]

On a Facebook site promoting the protests, eighteen thousand students signed up to walk out of school. The largest rally was in Newark, New Jersey, where approximately two thousand high school students from seven schools marched on the city hall. They held signs and chanted "Save our schools!"

Student protesters were everywhere. At Columbia High School in Maplewood two hundred students marched around the building with signs declaring "We are the future" and "We love our teachers." In West Orange High School students rallied in the football stands. At Montclair High School half of the school's 1,900 students gathered outside the school chanting, "No more budget cuts." About fifty students at Gateway Regional High School in Deptford held up hand-made protest signs or wore white shirts with protest slogans written in black marker.

At Old Bridge High School, about two hundred students marched around the building chanting, "no more budget cuts." About eighty Parsippany High students walked out of class. At High Tech High School in North Bergen County over one hundred students protested in the school's parking lot, while dozens of students walked out of Ocean Township High School after a larger group staged a sit-in protesting cuts in state aid.

Johanna Pagan, 16, a sophomore at West Side High School in Newark,[4] told the crowd there, "It feels like he is taking money from us, and we're already poor. The schools here have bad reputations, and we need aid and we need programs to develop."

"This is not our mistake and we will not suffer for it," senior Robert Wilson shouted at West Orange High School as he led a chant: "Enough cuts! Enough is enough!"[5] At Montclair High School, Carolina Noguer said she was willing to serve detention for the cause. "I want to be a teacher when I grow up, but the way things are going it looks impossible," she said. "There are barely even any books here anymore."[6]

Michael Drewniak, press secretary for Governor Christie,[7] released a statement denouncing the demonstrations and saying that students belonged in the class-room and dismissed the protests as "youthful rebellion or spring fever." Bret D. Schundler, the state education commissioner, urged schools to enforce attendance policies and not let students walk out of class. Even the New Jersey Education Association urged students to return to class.

What education officials failed to realize was that the real education was tak-ing place in the streets and parking lots. These students were organizing, speaking, thinking, protesting, and learning. They were showing adults the way. If these pro-tests had taken place in China, Russia, or Iran, government officials in the United States would be celebrating them as an advance for democracy. What they fail to realize is that the struggle for democracy is going on right here.

And the children shall lead.

F. Teachers as Crap Detectors

Based on an essay published on the *Huffington Post*, May 23, 2012
    www.huffingtonpost.com/alan-singer/teachers-as-crap-detector_b_1530275. html

Questions to Consider

1. Are "crap detectors" just pains in the ass or do they perform a vital function for schools and democratic societies?
2. Are you a "crap detector" and should you be one?

In May 2012 I was invited to participate in the third annual conference on *Courageous Schools: Honoring Teaching as a Calling* at Bank Street College in New York City. The conference was sponsored by the Morningside Center for Teaching Social Responsibility and drew hundreds of enthusiastic classroom teachers.

The Morningside Center for Teaching Social Responsibility works in public schools in New York City promoting creative ways to resolve conflict and intercultural understanding, teaching bias awareness, developing the social and emotional intelligence of students, and championing respect and resolution as crucial components of holistic learning. It maintains a website, TeachableMoment.org,[8] which is a valuable curriculum resource for teachers.

At the conference Lauren Fardig, an English teacher from Banana Kelly High School in the South Bronx, received the Courageous Educator Award for her work teaching about problems faced by refugees from war. Lauren and her students were featured in a PBS NewsHour documentary, "Empathy 101."

I received the first annual "Crap Detector Award" for my work as a teacher, teacher educator, and *Huffington Post* blogger. Ernest Hemingway is reported to have advised writers that the most important thing they need is "A built-in shockproof crap detector." Crap detector sounds like a modern term for muckraker, the late nineteenth and early twentieth century journalists who stirred up the "muck" about corrupt politicians and exploitative business monopolies, and I am proud to be within that tradition.

In my acceptance speech, I told the audience that unfortunately there still is no working digital crap detector that you can buy or rent, so you have to depend on the internal GPS built into your brain. Its functioning, however, is often clouded by personal ambition and political ambivalence. If you want to get ahead, particularly in a world where Michael Bloomberg can purchase New York City Hall, where Rupert Murdoch decides what gets broadcast on television news, and where Bill Gates and the Pearson publishing empire determine what gets taught in public schools, a crap detector is going to interfere with your career path.

Crap detectors have to be prepared to never be rich and always be suspect. A conservative website once called me a "social predator,"[9] a label I proudly embrace. I have been attacked by colleagues for brainwashing students and people have written my supervisors demanding I be silenced, reprimanded, or fired because of my ideas.

A crap detector has to have the strength of Mary "Mother" Jones who defied authority and declared: "I am not afraid of the pen, or the scaffold, or the sword. I will tell the truth wherever I please." There will be a cost. You will be targeted and will probably eat lunch alone if you go to the teacher's cafeteria, but you can always eat with your students, who will appreciate that you are "for real."

Tom Roderick, executive director of Morningside Center, asked me to share my thoughts on teaching and crap detection. These are some of the things I learned from forty years as a teacher.

First, everybody's crap stinks. If you drop it, you should clean it up. Second, if something, like the latest educational magic bullet sounds too good to be true, that is because it is too good to be true, or as Huck Finn said: "It's too good for true, honey, it's too good for true." I also believe you should always be suspicious when rich people tell you how much they are doing or going to do for poor people or when White men tell you how much they are doing or are going to do for Black people.

I am not a big fan of the Obama presidency. I believe his signature "Race to the Top" program with its insistence on high-stakes testing and assessment-driven instruction is destructive to education in the United States. But President Obama is good at turning a phrase and he can be inspirational. His memoir *The Audacity of Hope* sold millions of copies. I like the title. We, as teachers, have to believe in the audacity of teaching.

Mary Lease's advice to Americans, which she shouted out during stump speeches in the 1890s, still remains terrific, especially since it was offered over one hundred years ago. According to Lease,[10] "Wall Street owns the country. It is no longer a government of the people, by the people, and for the people, but a government of Wall Street, by Wall Street, and for Wall Street. The great common people of this country are slaves, and monopoly is the master. . . . Our laws are the output of a system which clothes rascals in robes and honesty in rags."

Upton Sinclair had a great insight and a great quote worth remembering. The next time you try to convince an obstinate supervisor that you really know something about teaching, remember "It is difficult to get a man to understand something when his job depends on not understanding it."[11]

So did Margaret Mead: "Never doubt that a small group of thoughtful, committed citizens can change the world. Indeed, it is the only thing that ever has."[12]

I also like Frederick Douglass' "If there is no struggle, there is no progress," Black abolitionist and former slave Henry Highland Garnet's call for "Resistance! Resistance! Resistance!" and Italian anti-fascist Antonio Gramsci's endorsement for political activists of "pessimism of the intellect, optimism of the will."[13]

Lastly, my motto as a teacher, muckraker, social predator, and "crap detector," which kind of summarizes what I learned from these other people and from my students and colleagues during four decades as a teacher, is, "You only walk this way once, so you might as well kick ass."

Notes

1. Roger Kimball, *Tenured Radicals, How Politics Has Corrupted Our Higher Education* (New York: Harper & Row, 1990); www.nytimes.com/books/98/10/04/nnp/kimball-radicals. html; www.newcriterion.com/articles.cfm/-Tenured-Radicals—a-postscript-5386.
2. Jennifer Medina, "A Crackdown on Bake sales in City Schools," *New York Times* (October 3, 2009), www.nytimes.com/2009/10/03/nyregion/03bakesale.html.
3. Winnie Hu, "Schools in New Jersey Plan Heavy Cuts After Voters Reject Most Budgets," *New York Times* (April 22, 2010), www.nytimes.com/2010/04/22/education/22schools. html.

4. Winnie Hu, "In New Jersey, a Civics Lesson in the Internet Age," *New York Times* (April 28, 2010), www.nytimes.com/2010/04/28/nyregion/28jersey.html.
5. Ibid.
6. Ibid.
7. Ibid.
8. www.morningsidecenter.org/teachable-moment.
9. www.epi-us.com/social_predation.pdf.
10. http://en.wikipedia.org/wiki/Mary_Elizabeth_Lease
11. www.quotationspage.com/quote/34069.html.
12. http://en.wikiquote.org/wiki/Margaret_Mead.
13. Frederick Douglass, www.blackpast.org/1857-frederick-douglass-if-there-no-struggle-there-no-progress; Henry Highland Garnet, www.pbs.org/wgbh/aia/part4/4h2937t.html; Antonio Gramsci, www.alternet.org/story/151018/10_steps_to_defeat_the_corporatocracy.